RELIGION AND SOCIETY IN ENGLAND AND WALES, 1689–1800

D1484510

Documents in Early Modern Social History
Series Editor: William Gibson

This series provides students and researchers with accessible
collections of manuscript and primary source material for the study
of a variety of topics in early modern social history, thus enabling an
understanding of the issues and events regarding particular themes in
the past, through the perspectives of contemporaries. The sources
presented cover a wide variety of materials, and include items central
to the study of the topic; each item is briefly introduced by the
editor. Every volume includes an introductory essay by the editor,
which places the material in the context of current historical debates,
and explains the significance of the sources to the study of the topic.

RELIGION AND SOCIETY IN ENGLAND AND WALES, 1689–1800

Edited by William Gibson

Leicester University Press

London and Washington

Leicester University Press
A Cassell Imprint
Wellington House, 125 Strand, London WC2R 0BB, England
PO Box 605, Herndon, Virginia 20172-0605, USA

First published 1998

British Library Cataloguing in Publication Data
A catalogue record for this book is available from the British Library.

ISBN   0-7185-0162-4 Hardback
         0-7185-0163-2 Paperback

Library of Congress Cataloging-in-Publication Data
Religion and society in England and Wales, 1689–1800
edited by William Gibson
         p. cm.—(Documents in early modern social history)
         Includes bibliographical references and index
         ISBN 0-7185-0162-4 (hardcover). —ISBN 0-7185-0163-2 (pbk.)
         1. England—Church history—17th century—Sources. 2. Wales—Church history–18th century—Sources. 3. England—Church history–18th century—Sources. 4. Wales—Church history–18th century—Sources. I. Gibson, William, 1959– . II. Series.
         BR758.R38 1998
         274.2' 07—dc21   97-47392
                                                                                                                        CIP

Designed and typeset by Ben Cracknell Studios
Printed and bound in Great Britain by Creative Print and Design Wales, Ebbw Vale

CONTENTS

Five: Popular religion

Six: The Established Church

Seven: Catholicism

Eight: Religious continuity and change

Nine: Politics and religion

Ten: Foreign views of English religion

PREFACE

This book was first suggested to me by the publication of *Religion and Society in Early Modern England,* a sourcebook edited by David Cressy and Lori Anne Ferrell in 1996, which I was asked to review for *History.* In the course of reviewing the book it occurred to me that there was no comparable collection of source material for the study of eighteenth-century religion and society, other than a few isolated examples of primary sources, like those in E. N. Williams's *The Eighteenth Century Constitution* and in *English Historical Documents,* neither of which focuses primarily on religion in the eighteenth century.

The problem for an editor of such sources is the bewildering wealth of material that *could* be included, particularly that on personal piety, which perhaps justifies a volume of its own. During the preparation for this volume, referees were asked to comment on the idea of such a volume; all were positive, but most had long lists of material that they felt must be included. One commented that not to include an extract from Dr Johnson was rather like 'Hamlet without the Prince'. If I had incorporated all such suggestions this work would have been more than three times its present size. However from the outset I constrained myself with a number of disciplines to attempt to determine what would and would not be included. First, I have not attempted to produce a comprehensive sourcebook, which collects together *every* significant document on religion in the period. I have also tried to avoid simply editing a collection of sources which are readily (and recently) available elsewhere, though inevitably some of the sources, particularly the statutes, appear in other collections. Parson Woodforde, in spite of, and because of, his ubiquity, has been jettisoned in favour of a lesser-known ancestor, Mary Woodforde. I have, however, tried to give a broad view of religion and society in the period, rather than focusing just on the Church of England. I have deliberately included Methodism in the chapter on 'Religion Outside the Establishment' in part because the ultimate destination of Methodism was schism from the Church, but also because – as other documents contained in this collection show –

the Anglican Methodists were regarded by the church hierarchy as beyond the pale.

I have arranged the documents in chronological order within each chapter. I have also sought to include texts that are in themselves regarded as important 'events' in the period, but which are often overlooked (for example, extracts from Locke's *A Letter Concerning Toleration*; *Essay Concerning Human Understanding* and Hoadly's Bangorian sermon of 1717). Unlike Cressy and Ferrell I have also included a number of sources which are also narrative accounts of significant events in the period, the Sacheverell trial for example, as well as formal documents which stimulated or effected change. Naturally I have included the obscure and the idiosyncratic as well as some materials which support the growing revisionist interpretation of religion in the era as flourishing and pervasive. I have avoided the (all too great) temptation to make this a 'revisionist' collection, with a full-blown revisionist introductory essay. Instead, again like Cressy and Ferrell, I have written an introduction which places the sources in context and suggests connections between them.

I have a number of debts of thanks to discharge. To Canon William Price and Professor Jeremy Black for their encouragement. Ganey Bond undertook the herculean task of word processing the extracts. Alan Worth of Cassell advised on permissions and copyright. Janet Joyce of Cassell supported the project and numerous suggestions were made by friends and referees, some of whom, I fear, will be disappointed that their favourite source has not found its way into the volume.

William Gibson
Chandlers Ford, 1997

ACKNOWLEDGEMENTS

I am grateful to acknowledge the permission of the following publishers and organizations to reproduce extracts in this book: Cassell plc; the SPCK; the University of Wales Press; Oxford University Press; Epworth Press; J. M. Dent; the Presbyterian Church of Wales Historical Society; the Controller of Her Majesty's Stationery Office; the University of Illinois Press; the Guildhall Library; the British Library; the Surtees Society; Alan Sutton Ltd; Cheshire County Council; Routledge and Kegan Paul; Wiltshire Record Society; Burns & Oates; Bedfordshire County Records Office; Yale University Press; Random House UK Limited and Cambridge University Press.

While every effort has been made to trace all copyright holders, it has not been possible to do so in every instance. The publishers would be pleased to hear from any unacknowledged copyright holder so that the appropriate information may be included in any future editions.

INTRODUCTION*

The Glorious Revolution of 1689 did not end the religious and political tensions which had dominated seventeenth-century English society, it polarized attitudes towards them and intensified the concerns of clergy and laity alike. During the reign of Charles II the issues of toleration of dissent and the comprehension of broader religious views within the Church of England had been furiously debated. Moreover, before James II's departure from England in 1689, there were concerns about the nature of royal authority evident in the use of the dispensing power and the trial of the seven bishops. However, it would be simplistic to assume that reactions to the events of 1688–89 were other than mixed. Loyal Anglicans, like Mary Woodforde,* supported the seven bishops, but were against the prospect of bloodshed between the forces of William of Orange and James II; were in favour of the assumption of the throne by William and Mary but concerned for the soul of James. The politicians and generals who invited William to invade, and who gradually abandoned James and supported the Revolution, may have come to see the issues in stark terms, but many of their fellow countrymen could not detach themselves from James as easily. Gilbert Burnet's account* of the debates over which ideas should determine the resolutions and actions of the Convention of 1689 also indicated the fragmented nature of reactions to the flight of James II. The solution adopted by the Convention Parliament,* to declare the throne 'vacated' by James and to offer the crown to William and Mary jointly, permitted an element of confusion in the origins of royal authority, the contract between monarch and people, and the nature of the succession of 1689. Staunch Whigs, like Henry Compton,* Bishop of London, urged acceptance of the Revolution upon the clergy; and the Bill of Rights* sought to establish a parliamentary monarchy with sanctions of allegiance enforced by parliament. But the High Church clergy found these uncomplicated solutions to the complex issues unsatisfactory, and for the most part unacceptable. The eight bishops, headed by Archbishop William Sancroft of Canterbury, who led the non-jurors from the Church did so more in sorrow than anger. Their departure, and the

* An asterisk indicates a document in the sources.

antagonism of the Tory clergy who remained in the Church and took the oath to William and Mary, were encouraged by the passage of the Toleration Act of 1689* which granted a measure of recognition to Protestant dissenters. Humphrey Prideaux,* Archdeacon of Suffolk, found that the issues of allegiance to William and Mary and of acceptance of the Toleration Act were still the cause of ecclesiastical disruption in East Anglia three years after the Revolution.

The consequence of the Revolution for the Anglican clergy was to reconcile themselves to the idea of a civil authority ordained by parliament or to lose their livings. However, this choice connected with profound changes in the intellectual world of the late seventeenth century. John Locke's views* that the Church was a voluntary association, which involved a free choice to accept or reject faith and ecclesiastical authority, effected a dramatic change in how people viewed an institution which had previously required obedience and religious observance. Locke also promoted a rationalist and 'reasonable' model of Christianity. He embraced faith as an intellectual conviction, drawn from rational consideration of the Bible rather than from revelation and ecclesiastical dogma. For churchmen who agreed with Locke, the supposed authority of the Church was less important than the rational nature of a Protestant regime established by the Revolution which tolerated other denominations. But this view acknowledged that parliament had authority over the Church and the right to evict a tyrannical ruler. High Churchmen, in particular non-jurors like Bishops John Lake and Thomas Ken and Charles Leslie, could not accept such a view. Leslie* clung to a model of the civil power comparable to the natural authority of a parent in a family. He also denied the Church could be subject to any authority other than God's. For Leslie, civil jurisdiction over the Church had produced ruin and degradation: only an ecclesiastical establishment separate from the State and ruled by priests would restore the Church to its ancient integrity.

The consequences of the Revolution were not just seen in the way thinkers and clergy viewed the world. They were felt in the field of foreign affairs. Religious zeal against Catholicism was not the source of the wars with France ushered in by William III's Grand Alliance,* but it intensified the popular support for the war, and gave politicians a piquant motive in avoiding the restoration of James and his line. As William indicated in his Address to Parliament in 1701,* Protestantism was not simply a state policy, it was part of emerging ideas of British identity in a war with a foreign tyrant. The division between those who embraced a staunchly Protestant religion established by the Revolution, and those whose consciences prevented them from recognizing parliament's right to determine Church matters as easily as foreign policy, lasted for generations. Bishop Hough's letter from non-jurors★ in the 1740s and the existence of a non-juring episcopal line into the twentieth century indicates the longevity of the breach.

The Church of England at the end of the seventeenth century underwent a moral renewal stimulated by the creation of societies for the reformation of manners.★ The societies were instituted by William and Mary in 1691, following the plan of societies in Charles II's reign, in an attempt to prevent the growth of vice on the streets of London. The principal work of the societies was to enforce existing legislation against blasphemy, immorality and vice; dissenters often joined with Anglicans in this endeavour. Between 1691 and 1736, by which date the societies were largely defunct, over 100,000 people had been prosecuted. But the enforcement of morality from without was inevitably less effective than a self-discipline born of inner virtue and faith. The societies which were spawned in the wake of the movement for the reformation of manners, the Society for Promoting Christian Knowledge and the Society for the Propagation of the Gospel, increasingly turned to publication of works of devotion and missionary activities to encourage inner faith. As the account of a tour of Kent by John Skeat and Thomas Morrison in 1701★ shows, the activities of the societies were not without opposition and setbacks, but the aspirations for the eradication of blasphemy, vice and immoral behaviour remained an important standard of morality at the start of the eighteenth century. The same impetus, for a more moral society with greater regard for religion and respect for the priesthood, is evident in Robert Nelson's book on the fasts and festivals of the Church.★ The book contained a series of collects, prayers and homilies that could be used by the clergy to observe the various saints' and feast days of the Church.

In some areas, however, the eighteenth-century Church had a meagre inheritance. Erasmus Saunders's account of the Church in Wales★ was written at the request of Bishop George Bull of St David's in 1707 (though it was not published until 1721). The picture Saunders paints is one of a Church drastically denuded of endowments, whose temporalities were allowed to fall into disrepair. Worship was falling away in the wake of absentee clergy whose incomes were derisory. Clergy lacked knowledge and learning and struggled across an inhospitable countryside to discharge their duties. The Church appeared to have reached its lowest point.

The relationship between the Church and State was wracked with controversies during the eighteenth century. The first of these, the Convocation Controversy,* arose largely from William III's determination that the Convocation of the Church of England, divided between High and Low Churchmen, should not meet between 1689 and 1700 because its repeated divisions threatened the stability of the establishment of 1689. The suppression of Convocation fuelled the more extreme claims of the Lower House, dominated by Tory High Churchmen. The Lower House bemoaned the erosion of the Church's position following the Toleration Act, it claimed the right to meet independently of the House of Bishops, it advanced claims to clerical privileges and it tried to silence and censure Whig and Low Church writings. The meeting of Convocation in 1705* was especially violent and riven with factionalism. The furious battle between Whig and Tory divines continued through much of the reign of Queen Anne, reaching its climax with the Sacheverell trial of 1710.*

Dr Henry Sacheverell had preached a virulently anti-Whig sermon in St Paul's Cathedral in 1709. The sermon portrayed the Whig Low Church clergy as 'false brethren' and, worse still, Sacheverell asserted the Tory doctrine of non-resistance to rulers, which implicitly condemned the Glorious Revolution. It was a sermon which advanced popular Tory prejudices and attracted much support. The government impeached Sacheverell and throughout the trial Whig and Tory factions resorted to violence in their support or opposition. Parliament found Sacheverell guilty, but his sentence was so modest as to appear to sanction his sermon. The effect was to spur on the movement of popular opinion towards the Tories and played a crucial role in determining a Tory victory at the election of 1710. The new Tory government of 1710–14 demonstrated its commitment to the claims of the Tory High Church clergy by passing two pieces of legislation, the Occasional Conformity Act, 1711* and the Schism Act, 1714.* The first of these sought to stamp out the practice of dissenters qualifying for public and political office by conforming to the Church of England on an occasional basis; in effect it bolstered the Test Act, which granted a political monopoly to Anglicans. The Schism Act tried to reverse some of the effects of the Toleration Act, by penalizing teaching by dissenters. Both laws were passed against strong Whig opposition, and were reversed following the Hanoverian succession.

Just as the Tory victory of 1710 brought rewards for their clerical supporters, the succession of George I in 1714 on the death of Anne brought recompense for those Whigs who had suffered during the Tory heyday and who had continued to work for the Protestant succession. Foremost among these was Benjamin Hoadly, the Low Church rector of St Peter Poor. A royal chaplaincy and the bishopric of Bangor were recognition for his stout support for the Whigs in the pulpit and with his pen as an election pamphleteer. In 1717 Hoadly, who had long argued for comprehension of dissenters within the Church of England, preached a sermon which questioned whether the Church as an earthly institution had any biblical foundation. 'My Kingdom is not of this world', the text and title of Hoadly's sermon,* suggested that there was no visible authority for Christianity on earth. The impact of Hoadly's sermon was to ignite the glowing embers of Low and High Church fury, and a fierce war of tracts and sermons ensued. The intensity of the controversy was such that Convocation had to be silenced rather than openly attack Hoadly, on whose side the full weight of the government's support fell. Of the numerous opponents of Hoadly, William Law, a non-juror, was one of the most effective. Law's defence of the legitimate authority of the Church and of revelation was a re-statement of the High Church Anglican view of the Church's rights as a temporal institution.*

The importance of the Bangorian Controversy was the debate it raised on the nature of the Church, for without a clear definition of the Church as a temporal institution, its relations with the State would also remain indistinct. If there was no biblical authority for a Church with the privileges and rights claimed by the High Churchmen, the State could reasonably legislate to change the Church's status, powers and the allegiance due it. If, as Locke and Bishop William Warburton* claimed, the Church was simply a voluntary association with no claims to compulsion over people and their consciences, it could not assert a monopoly in spiritual matters which the State claimed in the civil sphere. Its right to exercise discipline over the morals and behaviour of people in parishes up and down the country would be equally invalid. Unlike many High Church divines, Warburton claimed the Church was quite separate from the State, but allied to it for reasons of mutual political and social expediency. It was a view taken up and developed later in the century by William Paley,* whose proto-utilitarian views argued that a Church established by law was justified by the spiritual and secular advantages it accrued. A more explicitly political view of the relationship between Church and State, though for similarly expedient ends, was advanced by Edmund Burke. For Burke the idea of the State, sanctioned and legitimized by the Church, suggested a settled social order, with divine backing at a time of great social upheaval in Europe, and particularly in France.

The nature of the Church's relationship with the State was also affected by the existence of dissenting religious groups. They had been a source of concern to clergy of the Church of England since the Reformation; but after the Glorious Revolution the toleration afforded to dissenters fuelled fears that Anglicanism would lose ground to the nonconformist churches. The level of dissent was estimated in 1715. Dr John Evans's list* – though not always regarded as accurate – suggested that Presbyterians, Independents, Particular and General Baptists and Quakers made up between 6 and 7 per cent of the population of England, with about a third of a million adherents, in about 1800 congregations. Locally the strength of the dissenters varied enormously. The calculation of the level of support among dissenters is problematic, but there is no doubt that it fluctuated during the century, falling until the middle of the century and then rising again.

One of the greatest areas of religious growth, initially within the Church of England, was Methodism. John Wesley's work at Oxford attracted the scorn of students and fellow dons alike.* Wesley, much influenced by William Law, was travelling to London to deliver his late father's manuscript, *Dissertations on Job*, to the publisher when he met the founders of the Georgia colony and was persuaded to take a post as a preacher with the colony. The experience was a depressing one for Wesley, though it introduced him to the Moravian brothers who also influenced his religious development. Wesley returned to London in 1737 and the following May, as he related in his journal,* he experienced a conversion which was the motive for his later work field preaching and travelling the country, visiting the many congregations which sprang up in the wake of his efforts. Unlike the rationalist-deist Anglicans, Wesley's religious thinking embraced enthusiasm in worship, though he also denounced false enthusiasm; his sermons also attracted the poor by emphasizing that justification by faith was an integral element in Christianity.* Not all preachers were as talented and able as Wesley. John Gambold's experiences in Wales in 1743* confirmed that many preachers lacked the skill and imagination of the founder of Methodism. 'Methodism' as a name for Wesley's followers was initially a term of derision, and the group attracted much animosity from the established powers in the Church. Bishops Lavington of Exeter and Gibson of London* were strong opponents of the Methodists. But Methodists also attracted opposition from local people which spilled over into violence.*

Until 1784, when Wesley effectively broke away from the Church by ordaining his own presbyters,* Methodists were officially a part of the Church of England. Outside the Church, Presbyterianism flourished in many centres. Dissenting academies like those in Northampton, where Phillip Doddridge presided, kept Presbyterian doctrine alive.★ However, the relationships between dissent and the Church were, by the mid-eighteenth century, closer and warmer than historians often concede.★ The essential problem for many nonconformist groups was that they were often dependent on local factors: the ability of a minister or the strength of the congregation to remain united. As the young Samuel Davies★ from New Jersey discovered, congregations were often disunited and in confusion. One of the principal factors which increasingly affected nonconformity and its growth was the growth of industrialization. In Wales, where mining expanded to fuel the industrial revolution, towns like Merthyr Tydfil★ saw three-quarters of the industrial population turn to nonconformity from the Church of England. The social diversification of England into industrial classes undoubtedly affected religion. When in 1768 six students were expelled from St Edmund's Hall, Oxford★ for their Methodist views and practices, the deed of expulsion made clear that their lowly social background was an ingredient in the judgement against them.

Traditional dissent, represented by the Protestant Dissenting Deputies, however, attracted growing sympathy as the century progressed. Bishops, like Shute Barrington of Llandaff, found that the Church's response to dissent could be heartless, as in the case of the burial of a minor in 1770, though it was one which was corrected.★ A measure of relief removed penalties from dissenting ministers and teachers by Act of Parliament in 1779 and reflected growing toleration towards them. Churchmen, like Bishop Porteus of Chester, recognized that as long as dissenters were prepared to swear an oath of allegiance they should be permitted to hold services and teach in Sunday schools. However, as his account of the passage of the Dissenters' Relief Act shows, there remained strong opposition among dissenters to an equal measure of Catholic relief.★

The changes that nonconformity worked in the lives of individuals is sometimes hard to define and quantify. However, Silas Told's life,★ published in 1786, was an example of the transformation religious conversion could effect. Told had been hardened to life in the most vicious stratum of English life by experiences on slave ships and with pirates. However, his conversion by Wesley, though opposed by his wife, led him to spend twenty years preaching redemption to those on their way to execution. In their congregations too, as Hazlitt recounted in 1805, dissenting ministers could be pillars of Christian virtue for their hearers.

Beyond Christianity, religion in England was severely limited; there were only about 8000 Jews in England in the eighteenth century. Judaism, like Catholicism, was not covered by the Toleration Act; however, in a burst of reforming zeal – which included the 1753 Marriage Act – Henry Pelham's ministry passed the Jewish Natural-isation Act of 1754.* The latter permitted Jews to become naturalized British citizens, though it was widely seen as an erosion of British citizens' rights and an assault on Church authority and was repealed within a year.

The popular experience of religion in the eighteenth century was strongly influenced by liturgical practice such as the separation of the sexes during worship.* But as religious observance took on an element of public display, irreligion and immodest behaviour became an occasional feature of worship. As music entered religious observance more fully, it provided opportunities for unedifying as well as hallowing experiences.* Naturally, the quality of worship was in a large measure dependent on the quality of the clergy. Although the clergy in the eighteenth century underwent an increase in social status, and greater numbers were graduates, there remained clergy who were poorly educated* or inadequate to the demands of their duties. In some areas superstition and ancient religious practices survived. Those practices related to rites of passage were often most deeply ingrained in the minds and experiences of the people, and funeral practices in particular often harked back to ancient customs.*

The growth of ideas of sociability and politeness affected the Church as much as the rest of eighteenth-century society. Some aristocratic clergy, like Dean Cowper,* were resentful of the demands of the public nature of their duties; but in many churches the opportunity for social superiors to condescend to their inferiors and to provide a spectacle was grasped as firmly as it was at the Magdalen Chapel charity sermon of 1760.* The letters of John Penrose from Bath in 1766* also show how much the social life of a fashionable spa town revolved around worship and religious activities. For men and women of fashion, religion provided many opportunities for display and social interaction and satisfied the need for performance and entertainment. The growth of Sunday entertainments, even enjoyed by the court of George III, attracted some disapproval.

The Church's role in the lives of the people of eighteenth-century England was underscored by the status of the vestry as a principal institution of local government. As the parishioners of Winchcombe discovered, the church rate was put to a wide range of ecclesiastical and secular uses.★ Yet its status as the official religion of the nation did not secure universal respect for the Church, as the Vicar of Warton testified in 1778.★ The spread of contempt for religion and of immorality, so much abhorred by the religious societies at the start of the century, was also the motive for Robert Raikes's establishment of Sunday schools in Gloucester in 1783.★ It was in the gradually declining population of rural England that a rosy view of the Church's work can be fully sustained. The Vicar of Hampsthwaite's notice to his parishioners in 1786★ suggests such a settled rural existence, content and comfortable with the ebbs and flows of the Church's liturgical seasons. Nevertheless, historians should not be too quick to condemn the state of urban religion. The churches in London and other cities underwent a revival of daily religious observance,★ with more and more churches offering daily services and more frequent communions than the canonical minimum of four a year. The Church's influence in matters of personal behaviour is also regarded by historians as declining in this period. However, the archdeacon's courts, the 'bawdy courts' so much enjoyed by social historians, still received and heard cases of irreligion and immorality★ late into the century, and they imposed penalties and required and achieved reform.

The Church of England in the eighteenth century has been portrayed by historians as a ruined and slumbering Church. This view has been encouraged by accounts like that of William Cowper,★ though this interpretation has been revised in the last few decades as a result of a number of studies which suggest it was more effective and vibrant than traditionally believed. The episcopate had extraordinarily high professional standards. Perhaps the foremost bishop of the century was Thomas Wilson of Sodor and Man. The account of his work as bishop★ shows a high view of the episcopal function, which many of his brethren shared, though their ability to effect it was limited in their larger and less easily traversed dioceses. Wilson's diocese undoubtedly benefited from his long tenure of the see, and from the fact that, as a member of the Manx parliament, he did not possess a vote in the House of Lords and therefore played only a minor role in English politics. By the 1720s there was concern that Church appointments were made by ministers on political grounds rather than on clerical qualities. The concern lay behind Bishop Edmund Gibson's proposal for Church reform in 1724.★ Gibson, a respected canonist, made his proposals in the hope that the creation of Whitehall preacherships would draw closer the Church and State through the appointment of distinguished academics from the two universities to state preacherships. He also hoped that the removal of

Church appointments from the hands of ministers, and the appointment of Church dignities from within the dioceses, would create greater confidence in the ability of clergy to be preferred for other than political qualities. The first proposal was taken up by the government, but though King George endorsed the second, his ministers found it too great a temptation to reward clergy for their political support.

In their parishes, the clergy of the eighteenth-century Church of England underwent a growth in income and, as a result, in social status. The tithe, the basic income for beneficed clergy, brought higher yields of increasing value. But tithes were not without difficulty, not least in collection. The accounts of tithe payments to Parsons Rogers, Jones and Darwell★ indicate some of the problems caused by the conflict of interest of a clergyman who has to extract a living from the people to whom he must also minister. For many less fortunate than Rogers, Jones and Darwell, there were protracted legal suits and the last resort of tithe agents who distressed goods by force to pay the parson. The esteem in which the clergy were held was doubtless affected in some areas, but recent work also suggests that for many of the laity there was a belief that the parson was worthy of his hire. A clergyman's income often had to stretch a long way. Mr Wymondesold,★ a Wiltshire clergyman in 1756, spent a considerable sum renovating his church near East Hendred. A parson's income also had to permit him to develop a relationship with the local landowners. In the seventeenth century the relationship between squire and parson was one of social superior and inferior, for the parson's income and status were frequently low. But with higher levels of learning and greater incomes the eighteenth-century parson was often regarded as the squire's peer. The eulogy of Parson Richard Bulkeley by his squire★ suggests that their relationship was one of some regard. Clergy were also increasingly marked by their professionalization, both as a social group and in their professional practices. Among those for whom the professionalization of the clergy was important were the evangelicals. For Henry Venn, the opportunity to move to Huddersfield★ to continue his work was one at which he jumped. Preaching was a major element in his work. Eighteenth-century evangelicals were often emotional and dramatic preachers. Conversely many, like Oliver Goldsmith, felt that the Church was also handicapped by the dry rationalism and logic of the clergy who eschewed evangelicalism.★

The diocesan duties of the episcopate were many and onerous. Attendance at parliament demanded increasing amounts of time, as parliamentary sessions grew. Travel to dioceses was long, slow and costly. Bishop Nicolson of Carlisle took weeks to get to London, and bishops of the Welsh dioceses often found ships the quickest means to get to their sees. Once in their dioceses, the opportunities of bishops to govern them well were often a reflection of the care with which records had been maintained. Some bishops, like Thomas Secker, were paragons of careful recording of the state of their dioceses, leaving voluminous materials on each parish in their care.* The biography of Bishop Thomas Newton,* one of Secker's successors in the diocese of Bristol, is a good example of the labours that even ageing bishops sometimes undertook. For bishops, visitation was the most onerous of their duties, requiring triennial tours of their dioceses. The eighteenth century saw the evolution of the practice, with enquiries sent out in advance of a visitation, and the episcopal functions of confirmation and ordination often combined with the tour. Visitation returns are a very useful window onto the eighteenth-century Church. Those for Wiltshire, in the diocese of Salisbury, in 1783* are a good example of how the apparent clerical abuses of non-residence and pluralism were in fact often realistic and sensible solutions to local problems. Non-residence did not only affect lower clergy: Bishop Richard Watson of Llandaff found himself in a diocese without a bishop's residence and lived for much of his time in Cumberland. Nevertheless, Watson argued for ways of reducing non-residence.*

For those clergy without parishes, the unbeneficed, life was difficult. They often survived on payments for temporary services as assistant curates or as schoolmasters and eked a living on a few pounds a year. For such clergy, like William Bickerstaffe,* the only path to advancement was by asking for help or preferment from a great patron, in this case the Lord Chancellor, who retained the right to appoint to livings in the King's gift of a certain income. Ecclesiastical patrons, like Lord Chancellor Thurlow, often kept books in which requests were recorded; and whilst this seems a curious way to appoint clergymen, without modern mechanisms of competitive recruitment it was a robust system, and one which was accorded moral legitimacy.

The Catholic church in the eighteenth century experienced both its nadir and its greatest opportunity for reform. The expulsion of James II spawned a determination to avert a Catholic succession, and the exclusion of Catholics from the throne was written into the Act of Succession. The Catholic population was also affected by the experience of the rebellions of 1715 and 1745, which sought to restore the Stuarts. Leading Catholic laity looked to the continent for their education, and the clergy and the poorer Catholics were largely dependent on the laity for support and for worship, since many priests were often sheltered in the homes of the gentry. The priests landed from France on deserted coasts and travelled the country incognito; the bishops, termed vicars-apostolic since England lacked an established Catholic hierarchy, also lived in poverty and as much obscurity as their offices permitted. The ability of laity and clergy to support the vicars-apostolic was severely limited, as Bishop Williams discovered in 1731.★ Nevertheless, there were those who abandoned Anglicanism for Catholicism, like Edward Gibbon.★ As the century progressed a sense of toleration grew, at least among the higher clergy of the Church of England. The indulgent response of Bishop Newton and the authorities to the activities of Catholics in Bristol in 1764★ was perhaps conditioned by the declining spectre of Catholic-supported attempts to overthrow the House of Hanover. By 1778, bi-partisan sympathy for the position of Catholics emerged in part because of the growing awareness that Catholicism did not exclude loyalty to the establishment of 1689, and the Catholic Relief Acts of that year★ and 1791 eased the position of Catholics. Nevertheless, the total Catholic population of the country declined in the years before 1780, and though industrialization and urbanization swelled the urban Catholic numbers after that date, rural Catholicism remained in decline.

The eighteenth century was a period of dramatic social as well as political change. Perhaps the greatest changes were those experienced in the growing industrial towns and cities. Although there were numerous churches, of various denominations, built in Leeds, Manchester, Liverpool, Birmingham and across Yorkshire and Lancashire, the visitation of Bishop Porteus in 1778 revealed a picture of irreligion in these industrial cities.★ The changes pressed on society by industrialization caused clergy like John Venn, Henry Venn's son, to seek new ways of reaching the labouring classes in his congregation.★ But manufacturing brought changes to how men and women viewed the world and the providential powers that religion advanced. As Benjamin La Trobe's letter in 1786 shows,★ dissent grew apace in these circumstances and wooed the industrial worker with some success. One element in the limitation of eighteenth-century Anglicanism was its inability rapidly to build churches to accommodate the new populations. Though galleries, side aisles and new seating could increase accommodation without affecting the figures for new church buildings, the construction of new churches could never have kept pace with demand. In Sheffield the effect of heightened demand for church seatings was a growing market for pews for rent or purchase.★ Rural changes also affected the

Church. For beneficed clergy, enclosure, like that at Blunham in 1792,★ could operate in their favour, increasing income from tithes and glebe; but it could of course transform the lives of the people to whom the parson ministered. Independent yeoman farmers with smallholdings were converted to wage labourers dependent on the market and the local landowners for work.

The eighteenth century was an era in which participation in politics was still associated with membership of the Church of England and property ownership – indeed the former was the effect of the Test Act. It was therefore no surprise that the clergy were active in politics. Bishop Compton's call to his clergy to support the Whig candidate in the election of 1701★ was morally legitimate according to the tenets of the time. In spite of Bishop Gibson's hopes in 1724, political principles and electoral advantage continued to be a factor in determining the distribution of livings. Power brokers, like the Duke of Newcastle, saw the ecclesiastical patronage at their disposal as a means to secure parliamentary support, as he did in the 1733 election.★ On a local level, the control of an archdeacon's court was also an opportunity to advance political ends, as Thomas Ball suggested in 1741.★

The problem that this created for the Whigs, who dominated government for forty years after the Hanoverian succession, was that they drew considerable support from the dissenters, and were inclined to seek access to power for them. The claim of the dissenters for access to power was expressed in 1735★ but Walpole, dependent on the episcopal votes in the House of Lords, was evasive.★ However, in the following year Walpole sought to introduce a measure of relief from tithe payments for Quakers, a major constituency for the Whigs. Quaker tithe reform brought down the fury of the bishops on the government, including that of Bishop Gibson,★ the chief architect of the alliance between the Whigs and the bishops. The role of the Church as a great pillar of State was called upon in 1745 during the Jacobite Uprising of that year. The Pretender, Charles Stuart, swept into northern England, at one point even capturing Derby. In such circumstances the Archbishop of York, Thomas Herring, swung into action as a military strategist and an agent of political intelligence. He saw no incongruity between his ecclesiastical office and his endeavours for the defence of the House of Hanover: on the contrary, his position required him to defend the State with all the weapons at his hands.★

Throughout the century there were countless examples of personal piety. The lives of many men and women were shot through with devotional activities, which punctuated their hours and days. Men like

Sir Thomas Warton★ spent as much, if not more, time in devotion as their predecessors. Moreover, the household remained the smallest unit of the Church, with chaplains still leading devotions in many great houses. Sir George Wheler's account★ of the nature of domestic worship in the year of the Glorious Revolution indicates that domestic worship was flourishing in the period. As in the seventeenth century, women played an important role in piety. Women like Lady Maynard and Mrs Godolphin were models of godliness and devotion, who made religious observance a central element in their lives, though they refrained from evangelicalism.★ Flavia, a fictional character from William Law's *Serious Call,*★ was equally a leader in her attitudes to religion, and like many women later in the century led the way from strict observance to a more liberal attitude to the Sabbath.

Throughout the century comparisons were made between English and continental religion and visitors from the continent wrote accounts of religion in England. César de Saussure's account★ described the lifestyle and clothing of Quakers, who were clearly less well known in France; but he also indicated that Catholicism and Judaism were able to survive in various, often fashionable, parts of London. In contrast, Carl Moritz visited a 'typical' English parish, Nettlebed, which he liked so much he found difficulty in leaving.★ It was perhaps an archetype of eighteenth-century rural Anglicanism. François de la Rochefoucauld's account is a far more sophisticated, and perhaps a more synthetic, view of English religion.★ De la Rochefoucauld claimed that every Englishman had his own beliefs, that English clergy were more hard working than French, and described many of the religious practices of the people. For the dilettante Frenchman, English religion was both more earnest than French, and therefore to be regarded with greater scepticism.

For eighteenth-century society religion was perhaps the most pervasive influence on the lives of people. It conditioned attitudes to the State; it determined or excluded political participation; it defined emerging ideas of national identity; it framed moral expectations and contributed to ideas of continuity and change and of urbanity and ruralism. Whether they conformed, dissented, worshipped in Catholic chapels or Jewish synagogues, the lives of eighteenth-century people were immersed in the practices, debates, controversies, culture, music, artefacts and comforts of religion. The 'long eighteenth century' was an era in which faith can be taken for granted, and is perhaps the last period in which this can be done. In effect, the disciplines and liberties offered by religion conditioned men and women's views of themselves and the world they inhabited.

Editorial note

In some places I have edited the text to make the documents more accessible to the modern reader. In particular I have excised many of the apparently random instances of capitalization and punctuation; I have also modernized spellings where there is a modern spelling, though I have left contractions. I have also left unchanged words which have not survived into modern English usage, and which therefore justify their eighteenth-century spelling. For consistency, I have altered numbers to words where they are below a hundred. I have also eradicated some ellipses where they would inhibit the clarity of the document; this is especially the case in some of the Acts of Parliament where formulaic language has been excised without repeated ellipses. In all cases original parentheses have been retained in brackets, editor's clarifications have been placed in square brackets.

RELIGION BEFORE AND AFTER
THE REVOLUTION OF 1689

1. Tension in the last days of James II's reign

Humphrey Prideaux, Prebendary of Norwich, wrote to John Ellis, the secretary to the Commission of the Revenue of Ireland, in July 1688. Prideaux was a staunch Whig who welcomed William III's invasion later in 1688 and his apprehensions for the future under James II are clear, as is the tension following the Declaration of Indulgence of May which suspended penal laws against Catholics. Prideaux's mention of 'ye matter of the Declaration' is a reference to the imprisonment of the seven bishops who had been arrested for refusal to read the Declaration in their dioceses. The acquittal of the bishops took place on the same day that leading Whigs asked William of Orange to invade. The tone of Prideaux's letter does not presage the disruption to the quiet to come.

Norwich, July 12th, 1688
It hath been so long since I have heard from you that I begin to fear I must lose your correspondence. I confess we are now at a great distance; however I should be loath our old friendship should be forgot. Your brother being now a great man at Court, I have been expecting that by his interest a translation might be procured for you to some place in the English Court as advantageous to you as that you have in ye Irish, and I hope some time or other it may be done, that I may have my good friend again where I may some times have ye happiness of enjoying his conversation. Things look cloudy upon us here, and ye matter of ye Declaration hath, I fear, put us much under the King's displeasure. However, I thank God we still live in quiet, and, if God continues that, we may be content patiently to bear all things else. At present we are only hurt in imagination, and our greatest torment is our fears of what may after happen; but I hope they will prove to be

only fears and nothing else. I hope when you come to England you may think Norwich worth your seeing, when you have a friend here that would so heartily make you welcome.

[From E. M. Thompson, *The Letters of Humphrey Prideaux to John Ellis 1674–1722* (Camden Society, 1875)]

2. The Revolution seen by Mary Woodforde, 1688–89

Mary Woodforde, the wife of Dr Samuel Woodforde, Canon of Chichester, was a staunch Anglican, yet references in her diary to the events of 1688–89 reflected the divided loyalties of many. She had been appalled by the Duke of Monmouth's rebellion against James II but there is no doubt that she felt growing concern at James's policy of indulgence to Catholics. Her attitude to the seven bishops and the perception of an unhappy land frequently rent by dispute are clear. But her attitude to James, even after his departure from England, and her wish that he might repent of his Catholicism are evidence of the painfully divided loyalties of his subjects.

June 8 [1688]. This day is a day of trial for our good bishops, they being brought up before the Council for not reading the King's Declaration for Liberty of Conscience contrary to their judgement. Now Lord make good thy promise to them, and give them a mouth which all their, and our, enemies may not be able to gainsay nor resist. And be forced to say of a truth the Lord is with us, and in us, to which end dear Lord give us all true repentance for all our sins. . .

November 5. Was the day, as we hear the Prince of Orange landed at a place in the west. Ever since we have the sound of wars and desolation in our land, and soldiers continually passing up and down which keeps us in continual expectations of a battle. But good God of all battles do thou bring good out of all our distractions and preserve our King, and establish the Church on a firm foundation. And put an end to all wars and differences between us and give us peace in our days O Lord. . .

February 14 [1689 n.s.]. This morning we heard the Princess of Orange came safe to London the 12th being the fast day, and that the Prince and Princess are to be proclaimed King and Queen of England this day at nine o'clock. God Almighty grant them to reign in righteousness and make them great instruments of his honour and glory, and a blessing to this unsettled land, and make us obedient to them in the Lord. . .

Ash Wednesday. The Prince and Princess of Orange were proclaimed at London, King and Queen of England. God grant they may reign in righteousness and establish it by a firm decree, and make them a blessing to this unhappy land. And grant us all to give to God his due, and to love him, and that true religion may flourish till the end of time. And good Lord bless our late King James (wheresoever he is) with all the grace of thy Holy Spirit. Open his eyes to the ways of truth, and embrace them before it is too late that tho' he has lost his earthly crown, he may obtain a Heavenly [one]. For Christ's sake. Amen. Amen. . .

March 12 [1690]. This day is kept as a fast to beg forgiveness of our sins, and God's blessing on King William and Queen Mary's forces by sea and land in their expedition to reduce Ireland to its former state. God hear our prayers, and accept our humiliations.

[From D. H. Woodforde, *Woodforde Diary and Papers*
(London: Peter Davies, 1932)]

3. Gilbert Burnet's account of the Glorious Revolution, 1689

Gilbert Burnet was a leading clergyman, who had converted from Presbyterianism to Anglicanism after the Restoration. His political talents were evident under Charles II, but he was exiled under James II. In 1686 he had been in Holland with William and Mary, and was engaged to warn the Electress Sophia of Hanover of the impending invasion of England. He travelled with William's army during the invasion of 1688–89 and was rewarded with the bishopric of Salisbury. His account of the Revolution shows how difficult the Settlement of 1689 was to achieve. A staunch Whig, he was active in politics during William's reign. His *History of His Own Time* was written during the last years of his life, and published in a series of volumes between 1723 and 1734.

The King [James] now sent for all the lords in town that were known to be firm Protestants. And, upon speaking to some of them in private, they advised him to call a general meeting of all the privy councillors and peers, to ask their advice what was fit to be done. All agreed in one opinion that it was fit to send commissioners to the Prince to treat with him. This went much against the King's own inclinations: yet the defection he was in, and the desperate state of his affairs, forced him to consent to it. So the Marquis of Halifax, the Earl of Nottingham, and the Lord Godolphin, were ordered to go to the Prince, and to ask him what it was that he demanded. The Earl of Clarendon reflected the most, on the King's former conduct, of any in that assembly, not without some indecent and insolent words, which were generally condemned. He expected, as was said, to be one of the commissioners, and upon his not being named he came and met the Prince near Salisbury. . . The King stayed long enough to get the Prince's answer, and when he had read it, he said he did not expect so good terms. He ordered the Lord Chancellor to come to him next morning. But he had called secretly for the Great Seal. And the next morning, being the tenth of December, about three in the morning, he went away in disguise with Sir Edward Hales, whose servant he seemed to be. They passed the river, and flung the Great Seal into it; which was some months after found by a fisherman, near Fox Hall. The King went down to a miserable fisher-boat that Hales had provided for carrying them over to France. Thus a great King, who had a good army and a strong fleet, did choose rather to abandon all, than either to expose himself to any danger with that part of the army that was still firm to him, or to stay and see the issue of a parliament. . .

With this his reign ended: for this was a plain deserting his people, and the exposing the nation to the pillage of an army, which he had ordered the Earl of Feversham to disband. And the doing this without paying them, was the letting so many armed men loose upon the nation; who might have done much mischief, if the execution of those orders that he left behind him had not been stopped.

He was not gone far, when some fishermen of Feversham, who were watching for some priests, and other delinquents, as they fancied were making their escape, came up to him. And they, knowing Sir Edward Hales, took both the King and him, and brought them to Feversham. The King told them who he was. . . Here was an accident that seemed of no great consequence; yet all the strugglings which that party have made ever since that time to this day, which from him were called afterwards the Jacobites, did rise out of this: for, if he had got clear away, by all that could be judged, he would not have had a party left: all would have agreed that here was a desertion, and that therefore the nation was free, and at liberty to secure itself. But what followed upon this gave them a colour to say, that he was forced away, and driven out. Till now, he scarce had a party, but among the papists: but from this incident a party grew up, that has been long very active for his interests. As soon as it was known at London that the King was gone, the apprentices and the rabble, who had been a little quieted when they saw a treaty on foot between the King and the Prince, now broke out again upon all suspected houses where they believed there were either priests, or papists. They made great havoc of many places, not sparing the houses of ambassadors: but none were killed, no houses burnt, nor were any robberies committed. Never was so much fury seen under so much management. . .

It was a tender point how to dispose of the King's person. Some proposed rougher methods: the keeping him a prisoner, at least till the nation was settled, and till Ireland was secured. It was thought his being kept in custody would be such a tie on all his party, as would oblige them to submit, and be quiet. Ireland was in great danger; and his restraint might oblige the Earl of Tyrconnel to deliver up the government, and to disarm the papists, which would preserve that kingdom, and the Protestants in it. But, because it might raise too much compassion, and perhaps some disorder, if the King should be kept in restraint within the kingdom. . . The revolution was thus brought about, with the universal applause of the whole nation. . .

The King continued a week at Rochester. And both he himself, and everybody else, saw that he was at full liberty, and that the guard about him put him under no sort of restraint. . . He declared, that though he was going to seek for foreign aid, to restore him to his throne, yet he would not make use of it to overthrow either the religion established, or the laws of the land. And so he left Rochester very secretly, on the last day of this memorable year, and got safe over to France. . .

The elections were managed fairly all England over. The Prince did in no sort interpose in any recommendation, directly or indirectly. Three parties were formed about the town: the one was for calling back the King, and treating with him for such securities to our religion and laws, as might put them out of the danger for the future of a dispensing or arbitrary power. These were all of the High Church party, who had carried the point of submission and non-resistance so far, that they thought nothing less than this could consist with their duty and their oaths. . .

When this notion was tossed and talked of about the town, so few went into it, that the party which support it went over to the scheme of a second party: which was, that King James had, by his ill administration of the government, brought himself into an incapacity of holding the exercise of the sovereign authority any more in his own hand; but, as in the case of lunatics, the right still remained in him: only the guardianship, or the exercise, of it was to be lodged with a prince regent: so that the right of sovereignty should be owned to remain still in the King, and that the exercise of it should be vested in the Prince of Orange as prince regent. A third party was for setting King James quite aside, and for setting the Prince on the throne.

The third party was made up on those who thought that there was an original contract between the kings and the people of England: by which the kings were bound to defend their people, and to govern them according to law; in lieu of which the people were bound to obey and serve the king. The proof of this appeared in the ancient forms of coronations still observed: by which the people were asked if they would have that person before them to be their king; and, upon their shouts of consent, the coronation was gone about. But, before the king was crowned, he was asked if he would not defend and protect his people, and govern them according to law: and, upon his promising and swearing this, he was crowned; and then homage was done him. And, though of late the coronation has been considered rather as a solemn instalment, than that which gave the king his authority, so that it was become a maxim in law that the king never died, and that the new king was crowned in the right of his succession, yet these forms, that were still continued, showed what the government was originally. Many things were brought to support this from the British and Saxon times. . .

If the oaths to King James were thought to be still binding, the subjects were by these not only bound to maintain his title to the Crown, but all his prerogatives and powers. And therefore it seemed absurd to continue a government in his name, and to take oaths still to him, when yet all the power was taken out of his hands. This would be an odious thing, both before God and the whole world, and would cast a reproach on us at present, and bring certain ruin for the future on any such mixed and unnatural sort of government. . .

There were also great disputes about the original contract: some denying there was any such thing, and asking where it was kept and how it could be come at. To this others answered that it was implied in a legal government: though in a long tract of time, and in dark ages, there was not such an explicit proof of it to be found. . . There were also many debates on the word 'abdicate'; for the Commons came soon to a resolution, that King James, by breaking the original contract, and by withdrawing himself, had abdicated the government; and that the throne was thereby become vacant. They sent this vote to the Lords, and prayed their concurrence. . .

There were other differences in the form of the settlement. The republican party were at first for deposing King James by a formal sentence, and for giving the crown to the Prince and Princess by as formal an election. But that was overruled in the beginning. . .

The party for a regency was for some time most prevailing; and then the protests were made by the lords that were for the new settlement. The House was very full; about a hundred and twenty were present; and things were so near an equality, that it was at last carried by a very small majority, of two or three, to agree with the Commons in voting the abdication, and the vacancy of the throne; against which a great protest was made; as also against the final vote, by which the Prince and Princess of Orange were desired to accept of the crown, and declared to be King and Queen. . .

But, before matters were brought to a full conclusion, an enumeration was made of the chief heads of King James's ill government. And in opposition to these, the rights and liberties of the people of England were stated. . .

The last debate was concerning the oaths that should be taken to the King and Queen. Many arguments were taken during the debate, from the oaths in the form in which the allegiance was sworn to the crown to show that in a new settlement these could not be taken. And to this it was always answered, that care should be taken, when other things were settled, to adjust these oaths, so that they should agree to the new settlement. In the oaths, as they were formerly conceived, a previous title seemed to be asserted, when the King was sworn to, 'as rightful and lawful King'. It was therefore said, that these words could not be said of a king who had not a precedent right, but was set up by the nation. So it was moved, that the oaths should be reduced to the ancient simplicity, of swearing to bear faith and true allegiance to the King and Queen. This was agreed to.

A notion was started, which by its agreement with their other principles had a great effect among them and brought off the greatest number of those who came in honestly to the new government. This was chiefly managed by Dr Lloyd, Bishop of St Asaph, now translated to Worcester. It was laid thus: the Prince had a just cause of making war on the King; in that most of them agreed. In a just war, in which an appeal is made to God, success is considered as the decision of Heaven. So the Prince's success against King James gave him the right of conquest over him; and by it all his rights were transferred to the Prince. His success was indeed no conquest of the nation, which had neither wronged him, nor resisted him. So that, with relation to the people of England, the Prince was no conqueror, but a preserver, and a deliverer, well received, and gratefully acknowledged. Yet with relation to King James, and all the right that was before vested in him, he was, as they thought, a conqueror. By this notion they explained those passages of scripture, that speak of God's disposing of kingdoms, and of pulling down and setting up another.

[From G. Burnet, *History of His Own Time* (London, 1724)]

4. Bishop Compton of London urges acceptance of the Revolution on his clergy

Henry Compton wrote to the Revd John Strype, incumbent of Leyton and lecturer at Hackney, in January 1689. Compton had been the tutor of Princesses Mary and Anne, and since 1675 Bishop of London. Under James II he had been suspended from his episcopal functions and was one of the leading men of the kingdom who invited William of Orange to England in 1688. During the Revolution, he escorted Princess Anne to safety and assumed colonelcy of a regiment. His enthusiastic support for the Settlement of the Crown on William and Mary can be see in his letter to Strype.

Good Brother,   Jan. 1689

It is to be feared, that, as the enemies to the present government have omitted no occasion hitherto of doing mischief to it, so, in all probability, they will likewise upon this late tax of two shillings per pound, endeavour to make the people as uneasy as they can by false and malicious Insinuations. You may therefore do a considerable service to the King, by disposing our brethren in your deanery, to take all opportunities at this time, to lay before the people the great blessings we enjoy by this wonderful Revolution, which has procured to us so full a deliverance from popery and arbitrary power, that, during our captivity, we would have purchased with the hazard of our lives and expense of our fortunes. And now pray use your discretion, and believe me,

Sir,

Your most assured Friend and Brother

H. LONDON

[From H. Ellis (ed.), *The Original Letters of Eminent Literary Men* (Camden Society, 1843), 191]

5. The Bill of Rights, 1689

The Convention Parliament, having declared the throne vacant, by virtue of

James's flight, agreed a Bill or Declaration of Rights, on 12 February 1689 [n.s.], which sought to make James's practices illegal and establish new rights for the kingdom. On the following day, the accession of William and Mary as joint monarchs was made in Whitehall and contained the Declaration of Rights. The effect was to indicate that the offer of the throne to William and Mary was that of a parliamentary monarchy limited by the rights contained in the Bill.

Bill of Rights (1689)

An Act Declaring the Rights and Liberties of the Subject and Settling the Succession of the Crown.

Whereas the Lords Spiritual and Temporal and Commons assembled at Westminster, lawfully, fully and freely representing all the estates of the people of this realm, did upon the thirteenth day of February in the year of our Lord one thousand six hundred eighty-eight (o.s.) present unto their Majesties, then called and known by the names and style of William and Mary, Prince and Princess of Orange, being present in their proper persons, a certain declaration in writing made by the said Lords and Commons in the words following, viz:

Whereas the late King James the Second, by the assistance of divers evil counsellors, judges and ministers employed by him, did endeavour to subvert and extirpate the Protestant religion and the laws and liberties of this kingdom;

By assuming and exercising a power of dispensing with and suspending of laws and the execution of laws without consent of Parliament;

By committing and prosecuting divers worthy prelates for humbly petitioning to be excused from concurring to the said assumed power;

By issuing and causing to be executed a commission under the great seal for erecting a court called the Court of Commissioners for Ecclesiastical Causes;

By levying money for and to the use of the Crown by pretence of prerogative for other time and in other manner than the same was granted by Parliament;

By raising and keeping a standing army within this kingdom in time of peace without consent of Parliament, and quartering soldiers contrary to the law;

By causing several good subjects being Protestants to be disarmed at the same time when papists were both armed and employed contrary to law;

By violating the freedom of election of members to serve in Parliament;

And thereupon the said Lords Spiritual and Temporal and Commons, pursuant to their respective letters and elections, being now assembled in a full and free representative of this nation, taking into their most serious consideration the best means for attaining the ends aforesaid, do in the first place (as their ancestors in like case have usually done) for the vindicating and asserting their ancient rights and liberties declare:

That the pretended power of suspending the laws or the execution of laws by regal authority without consent of Parliament is illegal;

That the pretended power of dispensing with laws or the execution of laws by regal authority, as it hath been assumed and exercised of late, is illegal;

That the commission for erecting the late Court of Commissioners for Ecclesiastical Causes, and all other commissions and courts of like nature, are illegal and pernicious;

That levying money for or to the use of the Crown by pretence of prerogative, without grant of Parliament, for longer time, or in other manner than the same is or shall be granted, is illegal;

That it is the right of the subject to petition the king, and all commitments and prosecutions for such petitioning are illegal;

That the raising or keeping a standing army within the kingdom in time of peace, unless it be with consent of Parliament, is against law;

That the subjects which are Protestants may have arms for their defence suitable to their conditions and as allowed by law. . .

Having therefore an entire confidence that his said Highness the Prince of Orange will perfect the deliverance so far advanced by him, and will still preserve them from the violation of their rights which they have here asserted, and from all other attempts upon their religion, rights and liberties, the said Lords Spiritual and Temporal and Commons assembled at Westminster do resolve that William and Mary, Prince and Princess of Orange, be and be declared King and Queen of England, France and Ireland and the dominions thereunto belonging, to hold the crown and royal dignity of the said kingdoms and dominions to them, the said Prince and Princess, during their lives and the life of the survivor to them, and that the sole and full exercise of the regal power be only in and executed by the said Prince of Orange in the names of the said Prince and Princess during their joint lives, and after their deceases the said crown and royal dignity of the same kingdoms and dominions to be to the heirs of the body of the said Princess, and for default of such issue to the Princess Anne of Denmark and the heirs of her body, and for default of such issue to the heirs of the body of the said Prince of Orange. And the Lords Spiritual and Temporal and Commons do pray the said Prince and Princess to accept the same accordingly.

And that the oaths hereafter mentioned be taken by all persons of whom the oaths have allegiance and supremacy might be required by law, instead of them. And that the said oaths of allegiance and supremacy be abrogated:

I, A.B., do sincerely promise and swear that I will be faithful and bear true allegiance to their Majesties King William and Queen Mary. So help me God.

And whereas it hath been found by experience that it is inconsistent with the safety and welfare of this Protestant kingdom to be governed by a popish prince, or by any king or queen marrying a papist, the said Lords Spiritual and Temporal and Commons do further pray that it may be enacted, that all and every person and persons that is, are or shall be reconciled to or shall hold communion with the see or Church of Rome, or shall profess the popish religion, or shall marry a papist, shall be excluded and be for ever incapable to inherit, possess or enjoy the crown and government of this realm and Ireland and the dominions thereunto belonging or any part of the same, or to have, use or exercise any regal power, authority or jurisdiction within the same; and in all and every such case or cases the people of these realms shall be and are hereby absolved of their allegiance; and the said crown and government shall from time to time descend to and be enjoyed by such person or persons being Protestants as should have inherited and enjoyed the same in case the said person or persons so reconciled, holding communion or professing or marrying as aforesaid were naturally dead. . .

[From 1 William & Mary, session 2, c. 2]

6. Gilbert Burnet recounts the cause of the non-jurors and the passage of the Toleration Act, 1689

During the early days of the new reign, Burnet was nominated to succeed Seth Ward as Bishop of Salisbury, and as a member of the House of Lords had a close view of the events that led to the non-juror bishops refusing oaths to William and Mary. He also witnessed the debates over toleration and comprehension that absorbed the energies of Parliament in 1689.

The first thing proposed to be done was to turn the Convention into a parliament, according to the precedent set in the year 1660. This was opposed by all the Tories. . . And though the like was done at the Restoration, yet it was said that the Convention was then called when there was no king nor great seal in England; and it was called by the consent of the lawful King, and was done upon a true and visible, and not on a pretended, necessity; and they added, that after all, even then the Convention was not looked on as a legal parliament: its acts were ratified in a subsequent parliament, and from thence they had their authority. So it was moved that the Convention should be dissolved, and a new parliament summoned; for in the joy which accompanied the Revolution, men well affected to it were generally chosen; and it was thought that the damp, which was now spread into many parts of the nation, would occasion great changes in the new election. . .

Eight bishops absented themselves; who were Sancroft of Canterbury, Thomas of Worcester, Lake of Chichester, Turner of Ely, Lloyd of Norwich, Ken of Bath and Wells, Frampton of Gloucester, and White of Peterborough. But, in the meanwhile, that they might recommend themselves by a show of moderation, some of them moved the House of Lords, before they withdrew from it, for a Bill of Toleration, and another of Comprehension; and these were drawn and offered by the Earl of Nottingham: and, as he said to me, they were the same that he had prepared for the House of Commons in King Charles's time, during the debates of the exclusion; but then things of that kind were looked on as artifices to lay the heat of that time, and to render the Church party more popular. After those motions were made, the bishops that were in the House withdrew; Sancroft, Thomas, and Lake, never came; the two last died soon after. Ken was a man of warm imagination; and, at the time of the king's first landing, he declared heartily for him, and advised all the gentlemen that he saw to go and join with him. But, during the debates in the Convention, he went with great heat into the notion of a prince regent. And now, upon the call of the House, he withdrew into his diocese. He changed his mind again, and wrote a paper, persuading the clergy to take the oaths, which he showed to Dr Whitby, who read it, as the doctor has told me often. His chaplain, Dr Eyre, did also tell me that he came with him to London, where at first he owned he was resolved to go to the House of Lords, and to take the oaths. But the first day after he came to town, he was prevailed on to change his mind; and he has continued ever since in a very warm opposition to the government. Sancroft went on in his inactive state, still refusing the oaths, but neither acting nor speaking, except in great confidence, to any against their taking them. . .

Upon the bishops refusing the oaths, a bill was brought into the House of Commons, requiring all persons to take them by a prefixed day under several forfeitures and penalties. The clergy that took them not were to fall under suspension for six months, and at the end of those they were to be deprived. This was followed with a particular eagerness by some, who were known enemies to the Church: and it was then generally believed, that a great part of the clergy would refuse the oaths. So they hoped to have an advantage against the Church by this means. . .

That which was long insisted on, in the House of Lords, was, that instead of the clause positively enacting that the clergy should be obliged to take the oaths, the King might be empowered to tender them, and then the refusal was to be punished according to the clause, as it stood in the act. It was thought such a power would oblige them to their good behaviour, and be an effectual restraint upon them; they would be kept quiet at least by it. Whereas, if they came under deprivation, or the apprehensions of it, that would make them desperate, and set them on to undermine the government. It was said, that the clergy, by the offices of the Church, did solemnly own their allegiance to God, in the sight of all their people; that no oath could lay deeper engagements on them than those acts of religious worship did; and if they should either pass over those offices, or perform them, otherwise than as the law required, there was a clear method, pursuant to the act of uniformity, to proceed severely against them. It was also said, that in many different changes of government, oaths had not proved so effectual a security as was imagined; distinctions were found out, and senses were put on words, by which they were interpreted so as to signify but little, when a government came to need strength from them; and it well became those who had formerly complained of these impositions, to urge this with so much vehemence. On the other hand, it was urged, that no man ought to be trusted by a government, chiefly in so sacred a concern, who would not give security to it; especially, since the oath was brought to such low and general terms. The expedient that was proposed would put a hardship upon the king, which was always to be carefully avoided. The day prefixed was at the distance of some months; so that men had time sufficient given them to study the point; and, if in that time they could not satisfy themselves, as to the lawfulness of acknowledging the government, it was not fit that they should continue in the highest posts of the Church. . .

The Bill of Toleration passed easily. It excused dissenters from all penalties for their not coming to church, and for going to their separate meetings. There was an exception of Socinians; but a provision was put in it, in favour of Quakers; and, though the rest were required to take the oaths to the government, they were excused upon making in lieu thereof a solemn declaration. They were to take out warrants for the houses they met in; and the justices of peace were required to grant them. Some proposed that the Act should only be temporary, as a necessary restraint upon the dissenters, that they might demean themselves so as to merit the continuance of it, when the term of years now offered should end. But this was rejected; there was now an universal inclination to pass the Act; but it could not be expected that the nation would be in the same good disposition towards them at another time. I showed so much zeal for this Act, as very much sunk my credit, which had arisen from the approbation I had gained for opposing that which enacted the taking the oaths. As for the Act of Comprehension, some progress was made in it. . .

When the Bill was sent down to the House of Commons, it was laid on the table; and, instead of proceeding in it, they made an address to the King, for summoning a convocation of the clergy to attend, according to custom, on the session of parliament. The party that was now beginning to be formed against the government, pretended great zeal for the Church, and declared their apprehensions that it was in danger, which was imputed by many to the Earl of Nottingham's management. These, as they went heavily into the toleration, so they were much offended with the Bill of Comprehension, as containing matters relating to the Church, in which the representative body of the clergy had not been so much as advised with.

Nor was this Bill supported by those who seemed most favourable to the dissenters; they set it up for a maxim, that it was fit to keep up a strong faction both in Church and State; and they thought it was not agreeable to that, to suffer so great a body as the Presbyterians to be made more easy, or more inclinable to unite to the Church; they also thought that the toleration would be best maintained when great numbers should need it, and be concerned to preserve it; so this good design being zealously opposed, and but faintly promoted, it fell to the ground.

The clergy began now to show an implacable hatred to the non-conformists, and seemed to wish for an occasion to renew old severities against them; but wise and good men did very much applaud the quieting the nation by the toleration. It seemed to be suitable, both to the spirit of the Christian religion, and to the interest of the nation. It was thought very unreasonable, that, while we were complaining of the cruelty of the church of Rome, we should fall into such practices among ourselves; chiefly, while we were engaging in a war, in the progress of which we would need the united strength of the whole nation.

This Bill gave the King great content. He in his own opinion always thought, that conscience was God's province, and that it ought not to be imposed on; and his experience in Holland made him look on toleration as one of the wisest measures of government: he was much troubled to see so much ill humour spreading among the clergy, and by their means over a great part of the nation.

[From G. Burnet, *History of His Own Time* (London, 1724)]

7. The Toleration Act, 1689

By a law of Elizabeth I's reign, public exercise of religion other than that of the Church of England was outlawed. Charles II had tried measures of toleration, but they were interpreted as relief for Catholics which few were prepared to countenance. The 1689 Act confirmed that situation, but made an exception in the case of all Trinitarian Protestant dissenting congregations whose public worship was no longer an offence. However, the Test Act of 1673 remained in force and denied dissenters the right to participate in public affairs.

An Act for exempting their Majesties Protestant subjects, dissenting from the Church of England, from the penalties of certain laws.

Forasmuch as some ease to scrupulous consciences in the exercise of religion may be an effectual means to unite their Majesties Protestant subjects in interest and affection:. . .

Be it enacted. . . That the statute made in the reign of the late Queen Elizabeth, entitled, An Act for the Uniformity of Common Prayer and service in the Church. . . whereby all persons, having no lawful or reasonable excuse to be absent, are required to resort to their parish church or chapel, or some usual place where the common prayer shall be used, upon pain of punishment by the censures of the Church, and also upon pain that every person so offending shall forfeit for every such offence twelve pence; shall be construed to extend to any person or persons dissenting from the Church of England, that shall take the oaths mentioned in a statute made by this present parliament (1 Will. and

Mary, c. 1, 29). . . which oaths and declaration the justices of peace at the general sessions of the peace. . . are hereby required to tender and administer to such persons as shall offer themselves to take, make, and subscribe the same, and thereof to keep a register.

And be it further enacted. . . that all persons that shall take the said oaths, and make and subscribe the declaration aforesaid, shall not be liable to any pains, penalties, or forfeitures, mentioned in an act made in the five and thirtieth year of the reign of the late Queen Elizabeth (35 Eliz. c. 1.). . . nor an act made in the two and twentieth year of the late King Charles the Second (22 Cha. II, c. 1.). . . nor shall any of the said persons be prosecuted in any ecclesiastical court, for or by reason of their non-conforming to the Church of England.

Provided always. . . That if any assembly of persons from the Church of England shall be had in any place for religious worship with the doors locked, barred, or bolted, during any time of such meeting together, all and every person or persons, which shall come to and be at such meeting, shall not receive any benefit from this law, but be liable to all the pains and penalties of all the aforesaid laws recited in this act, for such their meeting, notwithstanding his taking the oaths, and making and subscribing the declaration aforesaid.

Provided always, That nothing herein contained shall. . . exempt any of the persons aforesaid from paying of tithes or other parochial duties, or any other duties to the church or minister, nor from any prosecution in any ecclesiastical court, or elsewhere for the same.

And whereas there are certain other persons, dissenters from the Church of England, who scruple the taking of any oath; be it enacted. . . That every such person shall make and subscribe the aforesaid declaration, and the declaration of fidelity following, viz:

I, A.B. do sincerely promise and solemnly declare before God and the world, that I will be true and faithful to King William and Queen Mary; and I do solemnly profess and declare, That I do from my heart abhor, detest, and renounce as impious and heretical, that damnable doctrine and position, That princes excommunicated or deprived by the pope, or any authority of the see of Rome, may be deposed or murthered by their subjects, or any other whatsoever. And I do declare, that no foreign prince, person, prelate, state, or potentate hath, or ought to have, any power, jurisdiction, superiority, pre-eminence, or authority, ecclesiastical or spiritual, within this realm.

And shall subscribe a profession of their Christian belief in these words: I A.B. profess faith in God the father, and in Jesus Christ his eternal son, the true God, and in the holy spirit, one God blessed for evermore; and do acknowledge the holy scriptures of the Old and New Testament to be given by divine inspiration. . . And every such person that shall make and subscribe the two declarations and profession aforesaid. . . shall be exempted from all the penalties of all. . . the aforementioned statutes made against popish recusants, or Protestant nonconformists, and also from the penalties of an Act (s Eliz. c. 1.) and also from the penalties of an Act (13 & 14 Cha. II, c. 1.); and enjoy all other the benefits, privileges, and advantages. . . which other dissenters shall or ought to enjoy by virtue of this act.

Provided always, and it is the true intent and meaning of this act, That all the laws made and provided for the frequenting of divine service on the Lord' s day, commonly called Sunday shall be still in force, and executed against all persons that offend against the said laws, except such persons come to some congregation or assembly of religious worship, allowed or permitted by this Act.

Provided always. . . That neither this Act, nor any clause, article, or thing herein contained, shall. . . extend to give any ease, benefit, or advantage to any papist or popish recusant whatsoever, or any person that shall deny in his preaching or writing the doctrine of the blessed Trinity, as it is declared in the aforesaid articles of religion.

Provided always, That no congregation or assembly for religious worship shall be permitted or allowed by this Act, until the place of such meeting shall be certified to the bishop of the diocese, or to the archdeacon of that archdeaconry, or to the justices of the peace at the general or quarter sessions of the peace for that county, city, or place in which such meeting shall be held and registered in the said bishop's or archdeacon's court respectively, or recorded at the said general or quarter sessions; the register or clerk of the peace whereof is hereby required to register the same, and to give certificate thereof to such person as shall demand the same, for which there shall be no greater fee nor reward taken than the sum of sixpence.

[From 1 William & Mary, c. 18]

8. Humphrey Prideaux reports the impact of the Glorious Revolution, 1692

Humphrey Prideaux, now Archdeacon of Suffolk, again writing to John Ellis, gave an account of troubles with a Jacobite clergyman, Thomas Alexander, who stirred up anti-government feeling. Jacobites were in turn encouraged and disappointed by James II's military venture in Ireland in 1692. Prideaux, a Whig and supporter of the Revolution, also expressed his reservations of the Toleration Act which he felt diluted religion and was more recognized in its breach than its observance.

Norwich, June 13th, 1692

I do most heartily thank you for ye favour of yours, w'ch were more then ordinarily welcome for ye sake of ye good news they brought. Till this happy turn our Jacobites were come to that height of confidence to talk openly that now all was their own, and some of them suspended their payment of ye taxes; and at ye bishops visitation at Norwich, which was the three latter days of Whitsun week, the Jacobite clergy would not own his jurisdiction and refused to appear; but on Sunday night ye news coming to us of ye victory, they came all the next day and made their submission, and I hope now they will have ye wit to carry themselves better, and if they do not, that ye government will have ye courage to call all such to an account. For in the strength of such a victory the King may now begin to act according to his own measures. I remember, when last in London, I was with one of ye deprived Bishops, who seemed as confident of going home again, but I thank God he is like now to be disappointed. I perceive the French King and our Jacobites deceived each other; he made them believe wonders he would do for them, and they made him believe as much that they [would] do for him. I hope they will now be both undeceived, and an end be put to that great confidence w'ch was between them. I have for three years been exceedingly troubled at Ipswich with an untoward clergyman there, one Alexander. He was lecturer of the town, a place very considerable, but, being turned out for his misdemeanour in ye beginning of the revolution by the town on whom he depended, he got another church in ye town, although of little or no value, and there did nourish such a faction and division in ye place, and was so closely stuck to by ye Jacobites, as being looked on a martyr for that cause, that he had almost undone ye place in setting the people together by ye ears. I had authority enough of my side to have routed him, and will enough to do it, but found him backed by men of that power both in Church and State that I durst not meddle with him for fear of drawing them upon myself, but reserv'd the case for ye Bp., his authority better enabling him to encounter him. But the truth is, I found his Lordship as cautious in the matter as myself, and the mischief must have gone on to ye utter undoing of this place, but that this Jacobite design, God be thanked, hath delivered us from him. It seems he, being an agent employed to give ye party warning to be in readiness, put on a tinkers habit with a knapsack on his back, and so went on foot through all Essex; but in one place being discovered, where he had been too free of his talk as to ye design on foot, he was followed to Ipswich, and there ceased on and laid in jail for treason, w'ch puts an end to the whole controversy. . .

Saham near Watton, in Norfolk, June 27th, 1692

I have yours of the 16th, but it came not to my hands till last Friday, for I was absent at Ipswich on a visitation. I there had ye whole of Alexander's affair. . . I thought it best to let it alone, and so it hath stood ever since, and the town and he have been at law ever since. . . In the interim he makes it his endeavour to make his landlord a Jacobite; tells him King James was a coming; that if he would not declare for him now he would be glad to doe it two months hence, for he was a coming; that they were sure of ye major part of ye fleet; and a great deal more to this purpose; and that he had three horses ready to be employed in his service, whereof one was kept in London, and ye others elsewhere. However, it will be that advantage to ye town of Ipswich to get rid of him that, in case he will quit that place and create no more disturbances there, ye Bp. hath undertook to intercede for him; and I should be heartily glad ye cause would fall this way. He is a fellow of parts, but employs them mostly to do mischief. The Bp. hath finished his visitation and is again gone to London, but it was little more than pro forma, for ye truth is, in our present case of unsettlement the times will not bear doing more. The Act of Toleration hath almost undone us, not in increasing ye number of dissenters but of wicked and profane persons; for it is now difficult almost to get any to church, all pleading ye licence, although they make use of it only for ye alehouse. There must be a regulation in these matters, and yet it will be difficult to get a parliament sober enough to doe it. Fanaticism hath got ye prevalency in corporations, and ye gentlemen must humour them this way or else they will not be chosen.

[From E. M. Thompson, *The Letters of Humphrey Prideaux to John Ellis 1674–1722* (Camden Society, 1875)]

9. The intellectual consequences of the Revolution: John Locke

John Locke was brought up a puritan, and after Oxford was patronized by Lord Shaftesbury. During the 1670s he spent much time in France and during the 1680s lived in Holland after he came under suspicion because of Shaftesbury's violent intrigues. After the Revolution he came to England with Queen Mary in February 1689. In the years after the Revolution, Locke published an astonishing series of works of philosophy which were the foundation stones of modern rationalist philosophy. The works published here are: firstly *An Essay Concerning Human Understanding*, which was abridged by John Wynne and widely used at the universities within a few years. Secondly, *The Reasonableness of Christianity as delivered in the Scripture*. Thirdly, *A Letter Concerning Toleration*, a book which directly addressed the Bible without reliance on ecclesiastical doctrine and formed an example of biblical criticism for years to come. These works also give the lie to claims that Locke was an atheist.

From *An Essay Concerning Human Understanding*

Though GOD has given us no innate ideas of himself; though he has stamped no original characters on our minds, wherein we may read his being: yet having furnished us with those faculties our minds are endowed with, he hath not left himself without witness: since we have sense, perception, and reason, and cannot want a clearer proof of him, as long as we carry ourselves about us. Nor can we justly complain of our ignorance in this great point, since he has so plentifully provided us with the means to discover and know him, so far as is necessary to the end of our being, and the great concernment of our happiness; but though this be the most obvious truth that reason discovers and though its evidence be (if I mistake not) equal to mathematical certainty: yet it requires thought and attention; and the mind must apply itself to a regular deduction of it from some part of our intuitive knowledge, or else we shall be as uncertain, and ignorant of this, as of other propositions, which are in themselves capable of clear demonstration. To show therefore, that we are capable of knowing, i.e. being certain that there is a God, and how we may come by this certainty, I think we need to go farther than ourselves, and that undoubted knowledge we have of our own existence.

I think it is beyond question, that man has a clear perception of his own being; he knows certainly that he exists, and that he is something. He that can doubt whether he be anything, or no, I speak not to, no more than I would argue with pure nothing, or endeavour to convince non-entity, that it were something. If any one pretends to be so sceptical, as to deny his own existence, (for really to doubt of it, is manifestly impossible) let him for me enjoy his beloved happiness of being nothing, until hunger, or some other pain convince him of the contrary. This then, I think, I may take for a truth, which every ones certain knowledge assures him of, beyond the liberty of doubting, viz. that he is something that actually exists.

In the next place man knows by an intuitive certainty, nothing can no more produce any real being, than it can be equal to two right angles. If a man knows not that non-entity, or the absence of all being cannot be equal to two right angles, it is impossible he should know any demonstration in Euclid.

If therefore we know there is some real being, and that non-entity cannot produce any real being, it is an evident demonstration, that from eternity there has been something; since what was not from eternity, had a beginning; and what had a beginning, must be produced by something else. Next, it is evident, that what had its being and beginning from another, must also have all that which is in, and belongs to its being from another too. All the powers it has, must be owing to, and received from the same source. This eternal source then of all being must also be the source and original of all power; and so this eternal being must be also the most powerful.

Again, a man finds in himself perception, and knowledge. We have then got one step farther; and we are certain now, that there is not only some being, but some knowing intelligent being in the world.

There was a time then, when there was no knowing being, and when knowledge began to be; or else, there has been also a knowing being from eternity. If it be said, there was a time when no being had any knowledge, when that eternal being was void of all understanding, I reply, that then it was impossible there should ever have been any knowledge. It being as impossible that things wholly void of knowledge, and operating blindly and without any perception should produce a knowing being, as it is impossible that a triangle should make itself three angles bigger than two right ones. For it is as repugnant to the idea of senseless matter, that it should put into itself sense, perception, and knowledge, as it is repugnant to the idea of a triangle, that it should put into it self greater angles than two right ones.

Thus from the consideration of ourselves, and what we infallibly find in our own constitutions, our reason leads us to the knowledge of this certain and evident truth, that there is an eternal, most powerful, and most knowing being; which whether any one will please to call God, it matters not. The thing is evident, and from this idea duly considered, will easily be deduced all those other attributes, which we ought to ascribe to this eternal being. If nevertheless any one should be found so senselessly arrogant, as to suppose man alone knowing and wise, but yet the product of mere ignorance and chance; and that all the rest of the universe acted only by that blind hap-hazard: I shall leave with him that very rational and emphatical rebuke of Tully. . . to be considered at his leisure. 'What can be more sillily arrogant and mis-becoming, than for a man to think that he has a mind and understanding in him, but yet in all the universe beside, there is no such thing? Or that those things, which with the utmost stretch of his reason he can scarce comprehend, should be moved and managed without any reason at all?'

From what has been said, it is plain to me, we have a more certain knowledge of the existence of a God, than of anything our senses have not immediately discovered to us. Nay, I presume I may say, that we more certainly know that there is a God, than that there is anything else without us. When I say we know, I mean there is such a knowledge within our reach, which we cannot miss, if we will but apply our minds to that, as we do to several other enquiries.

From *The Reasonableness of Christianity as delivered by the Scriptures*

The faith and the obedience which God requires

This is the law of that kingdom, as well as of all mankind; and that law by which all men shall be judged at the last day: only those who have believed Jesus to be the Messiah, and have taken him to be their King, with a sincere endeavour after righteousness, in obeying his law, shall have their past sins not imputed to them; and shall have that faith taken instead of obedience; where frailty and weakness made them transgress, and sin prevailed after conversion in those who hunger and thirst after righteousness (or perfect obedience) and do not allow themselves in acts of disobedience and rebellion, against the laws of that kingdom they are entered into.

He did not expect, 'tis true, a perfect obedience void of all slips and falls: He knew our make, and the weakness of our constitutions too well, and was sent with a supply for that defect. Besides, perfect obedience was the righteousness of the law of works; and then the reward would be of debt, and not of grace; and to such there was no need of faith to be imputed to them for righteousnes. . . But whether Christ does not require obedience, sincere obedience is evident from the laws he himself pronounces (unless he can be supposed to give and inculcate laws only to have them disobeyed) and from the sentence he will pass when he comes to judge. The faith required was, to believe

Jesus to be the Messiah, the anointed; who had been promised by God to the world.

The Fundamental Articles of faith discovered in the Gospels and the Acts better than in the Epistles

The Epistles therefore being all written to those who were already believers and Christians, the occasion and end of writing them, could not be to instruct them in that which was necessary to make them Christians, this 'tis plain they knew and believed already; or else they could not have been Christians and believers. And they were writ upon particular occasions; and without those occasions had not been writ; and so cannot be thought necessary to salvation: though they resolving doubts, and reforming mistakes, are of great advantage to our knowledge and practice. I do not deny, but the great doctrines of the Christian faith are dropped here and there, and scattered up and down in most of them. But 'tis not in the Epistles we are to learn what are the fundamental articles of faith, where they are promiscuously, and without distinction mixed with other truths in discourses that were (though for edification indeed, yet) only occasional. We shall find and discern those great and necessary points best in the preaching of our Saviour and the Apostles, to those who were yet strangers, and ignorant of the faith, to bring them in, and convert them to it, and what that was, we have seen already out of the history of the evangelists, and the acts; where they are plainly laid down, so that nobody can mistake them.

Christianity suited to plain men

Though all divine revelation requires the obedience of faith; yet every truth of inspired Scriptures is not one of those that by the law of faith is required to be explicitly believed to justification. What those are, as we have seen by what our Saviour and his Apostles proposed to, and required in those whom they converted to the faith. Those are fundamentals; which 'tis not enough not to disbelieve: every one is required actually to assent to them. But any other proposition contained in the Scripture, which God has not thus made a necessary part of the law of faith, (without an actual assent to which he will not allow any one to be a believer) a man may be ignorant of, without hazarding his Salvation by a defect in his faith. He believes all that God has made necessary for him to believe, and assent to: and as for the rest of divine truths, there is nothing more required of him, but he receive all the parts of divine revelation, with a docility and disposition prepared to embrace, and assent to all truths coming from God; and submit his mind to whatsoever shall appear to him to bear that character. Where he, upon fair endeavours, understands it not; how can he avoid being ignorant? And where he cannot put several texts, and make them consist together; what remedy? He must either interpret one by the other, or suspend his opinion. He that thinks that more is, or can be required, of poor frail man in matters of faith, will do well to consider what absurdities he will run into. God out of the infiniteness of his mercy, has dealt with man as a compassionate and tender father, He gave him reason, and with it a law: that could not be otherwise than what reason should dictate; unless we should think, that a reasonable creature, should have an unreasonable law. But considering the frailty of man, apt to run into corruption and misery, He promised a deliverer, whom in his good time He sent; and then declared to all mankind, that whoever believe him to be the Saviour promised, and take him now raised from the dead, and constituted the Lord and judge of all men, to be their king and ruler, should be saved. This is a plain intelligible proposition; and the all-merciful God seems herein to have consulted the poor of this world and the bulk of mankind. These are articles that the labouring and illiterate man may comprehend. This is a religion suited to vulgar capacities; and the state of mankind in this world, destined to labour and travel.

The writers and wranglers in religion fill it with niceties, and dress it up with notions; which they make necessary and fundamental parts of it; as if there were no way into the Church, but through the academy or lyceum. The bulk of mankind have not leisure for learning and logic, and superfine distinctions of the schools. Where the hand is used to the plough, and the spade, the head is seldom elevated to sublime notions, or exercised in mysterious reasonings. 'Tis well if men of that rank (to say nothing of the other sex) can comprehend plain propositions, and a short reasoning about things familiar to their minds, and nearly allied to their daily experience. Go beyond this, and you amaze the greatest part of mankind: and may as well talk Arabic to a poor day labourer, as the notions and language that the books and disputes of religion are filled with; and as soon you will be understood. The dissenting congregations are supposed by teachers to be more accurately instructed in matters of faith, and better to understand the Christian religion, than the vulgar conformists, who are charged with great ignorance. How truly I will not here determine. But I ask them to tell me seriously, whether half their people have leisure to study? Nay, whether one in ten of those who come to their meetings in the country, if they had time to study them, do or can understand, the controversies at this time so warmly managed amongst them, about justification, the subject of this present treatise. I have talked with some of their teachers, who confess themselves not to understand the difference in debate between them. And yet the points they stand on, are reckoned of so great weight, so material, so fundamental in religion, that they divide communion and separate upon them.

Had God intended that none but the learned scribe, the disputer or wise of this world, should be Christians, or be saved, thus religion should have been prepared for them; filled with speculations and niceties, obscure terms, and abstract notions. But men of that expectation, men furnished with such acquisitions, the Apostle tells us. . . are rather shut out from the simplicity of the Gospel to make way for those poor, ignorant, illiterate, who heard and believed promises of a deliverer; and believed Jesus to be him; who could conceive a man dead and made alive again, and believe that he should at the end of the world, come again, and pass sentence on all men, according to their deeds. That the poor had the Gospel preached to them; Christ makes a mark as well as business of his mission, and if the poor had the Gospel preached to them, it was, without doubt, such a Gospel, as the poor could understand, plain and intelligible: and so it was, as we have seen, in the preachings of Christ and his Apostles. . .

From *A Letter Concerning Toleration*
The Toleration of those that differ from others in matters of religion, is so agreeable to the Gospel of Jesus Christ, and to the genuine reason of mankind that it seems monstrous for men to be so blind, as not to perceive the necessity and advantage of it, in so clear a light. I esteem it above all things necessary to distinguish exactly the business of civil government from that of religion, and to settle the just bounds that lie between the one and the other. If this be not done, there can be no end put to the controversies that will be always arising, between those that have, or at least pretend to have, on the one side, a concernment for the interest of men's souls, and on the other side, a care of the commonwealth.

The commonwealth seems to me to be a society of men constituted only for the procuring, preserving, and advancing of their own civil interests. Civil interests I call life, liberty, health, and indolency of body;

and the possession of outward things, such as money, lands, houses, furniture, and the like. It is the duty of the civil magistrate, by the impartial execution of equal laws, to secure unto all the people in general, and to every one of his subjects in particular, the just possession of these things belonging to this life. If any one presume to violate the laws of public justice and equity, established for the preservation of these things, his presumption is to be check'd by the fear of punishment, consisting in the deprivation or diminution of those civil interests, or goods, which otherwise he might and ought to enjoy. But seeing no man does willingly suffer himself to be punished by the deprivation of any part of his goods, and much less of his liberty or life, therefore is the magistrate armed with the force and strength of all his subjects, in order to the punishment of those that violate any other man's rights.

Now that the whole jurisdiction of the magistrate reaches only to these civil concernments; and that all civil power, right, and dominion, is bounded and confined to the only care of promoting these things; and that it neither can nor ought in any manner to be extended to the salvation of souls; these following considerations seem unto me abundantly to demonstrate.

First, because the care of souls is not committed to the civil magistrate any more than to other men. It is not committed unto him, I say, by God; because it appears not that God has ever given any such authority to one man over another, as to compel any one to his religion. Nor can any such power be vested in the magistrate by the consent of the people, because no man can so far abandon the care of his own salvation, as blindly to leave it to the choice of any other, whether prince or subject, to prescribe to him what faith or worship he shall embrace. For no man can, if he would, conform his faith to the dictates of another. All the life and power of true religion consists in the inward and full persuasion of the mind: and faith is not faith without believing. Whatever profession we make, to whatever outward worship we conform, if we are not fully satisfied in our mind that the one is true, and the other well pleasing unto God; such profession and such practice, far from being any furtherance, are indeed great obstacles to our salvation. For in this manner, instead of expiating other sins by the exercise of religion; I say, in offering thus unto God Almighty such a worship as we esteem to be displeasing unto him, we add unto the number of our other sins those also of hypocrisy, and contempt of his divine Majesty.

In the second place, the care of souls cannot belong to the civil magistrate, because his power consists only in outward force: but true and saving religion consists in the inward persuasion of the mind;

without which nothing can be acceptable to God. And such is the nature of the understanding, that it cannot be compell'd to the outward force, confiscation of estate, torments, nothing of that nature can have any efficacy as to make men change the inward judgement they have framed of things. . .

In the third place, the care of the salvation cannot belong to the magistrate; because, though the laws and the force of penalties were capable to change men's minds, yet would not that help at all salvation of their souls. For there being but one true way to heaven; what hopes is there that more men would be led into it, if they had no other rule to follow but the religion of the court; and were put under a necessity to quit the light of their own reason; to oppose the dictates of their own consciences; and blindly to resign up themselves to the will of their governors, and to the which either ignorance, ambition, or superstition had chanced to establish in the countries where they were born?

Let us now consider what a Church is. A Church then I take to be a voluntary society of men, joining themselves together of their own accord, in order to the public worshipping of God, in such a manner as they judge acceptable to him, and effectual to the salvation of their souls. I say it is a free and voluntary society. No body is born a member of any Church, otherwise the religion of parents would descend unto children, by the same right of inheritance as their temporal estates, and every one would hold his faith by the same tenure he does his lands; than which nothing can be imagined more absurd. Thus therefore that matter stands. No man by nature is bound unto any particular Church or sect, but every one joins himself voluntarily to that society in which he believes he has found that profession and worship which is truly acceptable unto God. The hopes of salvation, as it was the only cause of his entrance into that communion, so it can be the only reason of his stay there. For if afterwards he discover any thing either erroneous in the doctrine, or incongruous in the worship of that society to which he has joined himself. Why should it not be as free for him to go out, as it was to enter? No member of a religious society can be tied with any other bonds but what proceed from the certain expectation of eternal life. A Church then is a society of members voluntarily uniting to this end. It follows now that we consider what is the power of this Church, and unto what laws it is subject.

Forasmuch as no society, how free soever or upon whatsoever slight occasion instituted (whether of philosophers for learning, of merchants for commerce, or of men of leisure for mutual conversation and discourse,) no Church or company, I say, can in the least subsist and hold together, but will presently dissolve and break to pieces, unless it be regulated by some laws, and the members all consent to observe some order. Place and time of meeting must be agreed on, rules for admitting and excluding members must be established. Distinction of officers, and putting things into a regular course, and such like, cannot be omitted. But since the joining together of several members into this Church-society, as has already been demonstrated, is absolutely free and spontaneous, it necessarily follows, that the right of making its laws can belong to none but the society itself; or at least (which is the same thing) to those whom the society by common consent has authorised thereunto. Some perhaps may object, that no such society can be said to be a true Church, unless it have in it a bishop, or presbyter, with ruling authority derived from the very Apostles, and continued down unto the present times by an uninterrupted succession.

To these I answer, let them show me the edict by which Christ has imposed that law upon his Church. And let not any man think me impertinent, if in a thing of this consequence, I require that the terms of that edict be very express and positive. For the promise he has made us, that wheresoever two or three are gathered together in His Name, he will be in the midst of them, seems to imply the contrary. Whether such an assembly want any thing necessary to a true Church, pray do you consider. Certain I am, that nothing can be there wanting unto the salvation of souls; which is sufficient to our purpose.

But since men are so solicitous about the true Church, I would only ask them, here by the way, if it be not more agreeable to the Church of Christ, to make the conditions of her communion consist in such things, and such things only, as the Holy Spirit has in the Holy Scriptures declared, in express words, to be necessary to salvation; I ask, I say, whether this be not more agreeable to the Church of Christ, than for men to impose their own inventions and interpretations upon others, as if they were of divine authority; and to establish by ecclesiastical laws, as absolutely necessary to the profession of Christianity, such things as the Holy Scriptures do either not mention, or at least not expressly command. Whosoever requires those things in order to [obtain] ecclesiastical communion, which Christ does not require in order to life eternal; he may perhaps indeed constitute a society accommodated to his own opinion, and his own advantage; but how that can be called the Church of Christ which is established upon laws that are not his, and which excludes such persons from its communion as he will one day receive into the kingdom of Heaven, I understand not.

The end of a religious society (as has already been said) is the public worship of God, and by means thereof the acquisition of eternal life. All discipline ought therefore to tend to that end, and all ecclesiastical laws to be thereunto confined. Nothing ought, nor can be transacted in this society, relating to the possession of civil and worldly goods. No force is here to be made use of, upon any occasion whatsoever. For force belongs wholly to the civil magistrate, and the possession of all outward goods is subject to his jurisdiction.

But it may be asked, by what means then shall ecclesiastical laws be established, if they must be thus destitute of all compulsive power. I answer, they must be established by means suitable to the nature of such things, whereof the external profession and observation, if not proceeding from a thoro' conviction and approbation of the mind, is altogether useless and unprofitable. The arms by which the members of this society are to be kept within their duty, are exhortations, admonitions, and advices. If by these means the offenders will not be reclaimed, and the erroneous convinced, there remains nothing farther to be done, but that such stubborn and obstinate persons, who give no ground to hope for their reformation, should be cast out and separated from the society. This is the last and utmost force of ecclesiastical authority. No other punishment can thereby be inflicted, than that the relation ceasing between the body and the member which is cut off, the person so condemned ceases to be a part of that Church.

[From *The Collected Works of John Locke* (London, 1847)]

10. The intellectual consequences of the Revolution: Charles Leslie

Charles Leslie was Chancellor of Connor at the time of the Revolution, but refused the oaths to William and Mary. Deprivation by virtue of his non-jury led him to attack the Settlement of 1689 in a series of bitter tracts which flowed from his pen for nearly thirty years. In 1710, to escape arrest, he fled to France to live at the court of James the Old Pretender. His claims for the Church and for the clergy were the highest flown of all non-jurors. He denied the idea of a contract between ruler and people and asserted the patriarchal source of authority in the state, a view akin to the divine right of kings. In the work presented here, *The Case of the Regale*, published in 1700, he asserted that the Church was not subject to any temporal power, a view that made the oaths required by parliament to William and Mary quite unacceptable. Leslie's works were often cited by those Tory High Churchmen who denied that right of the State to interfere in the deliberations of the Church in Convocation.

We find by experience that the State, particularly in England, have been out in their politics, in reducing the Church to so low an ebb of credit and authority with the people; for we have seen that laws and constitutions have prov'd too weak to restrain the unruly passions and ambition of designing men. The State have no security so great as the principles of the people, when they are taught to obey for conscience sake, and to believe that rebellion is a damning sin; which the Church cannot inculcate into them, farther than her credit reaches with them. And when they see bishops made by the court, they are apt to imagine that they speak to them the court-language; and lay no farther stress upon it, than the charge of a judge at an assizes, who has receiv'd his instructions before-hand from the court. And, by this means, the State has lost the greatest security of their government.

Besides, this does insensibly draw men into a disesteem and suspicion of religion in the general; whose foundation they cannot think to be divine, while they see the Church deposable by the State. Hence they are inclin'd, and easily impos'd upon by deists and atheists, to resolve all into priest-craft, managed by a superior state-craft. This looses all bonds sacred and civil; dissolves all relations, as well natural as political; and gives full reins to all lewdness, immoralities, rebellion, and whatever wickedness, where there is prospect of success, or that can be acted impugn.

That the State can never find their security in such a frame of things: that if religion were a state-craft, it were not such, unless they can make the people believe it not to be so; which they cannot do, while they see the governors of the Church exercising almost no ecclesiastical power, but what is dependent upon the State: that the heathen governments understood this so well, as to preserve their religion most sacred; and the priests inviolable, and superior to all others, in what related to their function, that God himself did so ordain it among the Jews: that it were a greater security to the State, to have a false religion, so it were believ'd by the people, than to have no religion at all: that nothing can be believ'd to be religion by any people, but what they think to be divine, that is, sent immediately from God; and they think nothing to be so, that is in the power of man to alter, or transverse.

Then it was urg'd, that the Erastian principle has had two visible effects in England: that it had turn'd the gentry, deists; and the common people dissenters: for the dissenters, one and all, from Presbyterians down to Muggletonians, pretend to divine commission, independent of all the powers upon the earth; therefore the people run to them and look upon the Church of England, as a parliamentary religion, and establishment of the State: and the deists, when they find themselves in committees of religion, can never think that there is anything divine in that which they see stand and fall by their vote. That next to the obligation of conscience, before spoke of, there is no security so great to any government, as that mutual trust and confidence which ought to be betwixt a prince and his people. Where that is once broken, it is the hardest thing in the world to cement it again: the best actions are misconstru'd on both sides; no promises or oaths are longer believ'd or trusted.

Now this of the Regale is so far from promoting of these good ends, that it is almost unavoidable but it must dissolve them. It is a perpetual seed of jealousy and discontent on both sides: for a king may look upon those who are zealous for religion and the Church of Christ, as enemies to his Crown and dignity, and seeking to impair his prerogative: and on the other hand, the friends of the Church may be tempted to think his Regale an encroachment upon her original and inherent rights; and consequently that instead of being a defender of the faith, and nursing-father to her, he is her greatest invader and enemy.

This consequence is so natural, that in every place almost, where the Regale has obtain'd, the effects of it have been seen: not only in the great [rise] of dissenters, before-mentioned; but even in contexts betwixt the Church and the king, especially where he happens to be of a different communion from that of the establish'd Church; and yet must have the disposal of bishoprics, and other affairs of the Church in his power, can set up ecclesiastical commissions, in what hands he thinks fit; hinder convocations to sit, or act, etc. of this we have seen instances at home. . .

Now because it wou'd look so preposterous, and against the common sentiments of mankind, especially of Christians, not to give the Church the preference to the State: therefore kings have taken upon them to be heads of the Church within their own dominions: and because this look'd heterogeneous in the hands of a mere lay-man who might not be a member of that Church, therefore the king were made of an amphibious nature, and complemented with the title of *mixta persona*, an hermaphrodite, half lay and half clergy. And the nobility got in too under the new invention of lay-elders, as now in Scotland, and govern all the affairs of the Church.

And considering how they have (by these means) reduc'd her commission and authority, it can be attributed to nothing but the wonderful and over-ruling providence, that there is so much left, as that shadow of a Church that is left! Or any, tho' but outward and seeming reverence, paid to sacraments or other institutions of religion, that are administer'd by her hands! Or that the administration of them should be still left in her hands! Tho' that is not done by all. That our Churches should be frequented or kept in repair, where the major and more prevailing number would wish them under ground! But in such instances as these God is wont to show his power: as he placed the sand for a bound to the sea, that tho' it rage and swell, yet is limited by the decree, hitherto shalt thou come, and no farther, here shall thy proud waves be staid.

Nothing but this could have restrain'd that spirit of atheism, deism, fanaticism, and prophaneness, that rages without human control. And the Church is laid as low and fenceless as the sand under their storms.

[From C. Leslie, *The Case of the Regale* (London, 1700)]

11. The religious consequences of the Revolution in foreign policy: William III's Address to Parliament, 1701

One of the immediate consequences of the Revolution was the declaration of war by both Holland and England against France on 12 May 1689. The French support for James II's vain attempts to regain his throne by war in Ireland, and the haven they provided for papists and Jacobites thereafter, led to popular antagonism as well as military conflict. The discovery of invasion plans in 1692 spurred on the military campaign and in 1697 Louis XVI recognized William as King at the Treaty of Ryswick. But French ambitions were not quenched and Louis's hopes of a union between France and Spain led to more antagonism between France and England, expressed in part in William's address of 1701, which refers to the Grand Alliance signed earlier that year against France.

King William of England Addresses Parliament on the French Question, 31 December 1701

My Lords and Gentlemen; I promise myself you are met together full of that just sense of the common danger of Europe, and the resentment of the late proceedings of the French king, which has been so fully and universally expressed in the loyal and seasonable Addresses of my people. The owning and setting up the pretended Prince of Wales for king of England, is not only the highest indignity offered to me and the nation, but does so nearly concern every man, who has a regard for the Protestant Religion, or the present and future quiet and happiness of his country, that I need not press you to lay it seriously to heart, and to consider what further effectual means may be used, for securing the Succession of the Crown in the Protestant line, and extinguishing the hopes of all Pretenders, and their open and secret abettors. By the French king's placing his grandson on the throne of Spain, he is in a condition to oppress the rest of Europe, unless speedy and effectual measures be taken. Under this pretence, he is become the real master of the whole Spanish Monarchy; he has made it to be entirely depending on France, and disposes of it, as of his own dominions, and by that means he has surrounded his neighbours in such a manner, that, though the name of peace may be said to continue, yet they are put to the expense and inconveniencies of war. This must affect England in the nearest and most sensible manner, in respect to our trade, which will soon become precarious in all the variable branches of it; in respect to our peace and safety at home, which we cannot hope should long continue; and in respect to that part, which England ought to take in the preservation of the liberty of Europe.

In order to obviate the general calamity, with which the rest of Christendom is threatened by this exorbitant power of France, I have concluded several Alliances, according to the encouragement given me by both houses of Parliament, which I will direct shall be laid before you, and which, I doubt not, you will enable me to make good. There are some treaties still depending, that shall be likewise communicated to you as soon as they are perfected. It is fit I should tell you, the eyes of all Europe are upon this Parliament; all matters are at a stand, till your resolutions are known; and therefore no time ought to be lost. You have yet an opportunity, by God's blessing, to secure to you and your posterity the quiet enjoyment of your religion and liberties, if you are not wanting to yourselves, but will exert the ancient vigour of the English nation; but I tell you plainly, my opinion is, if you do not lay hold on this occasion, you have no reason to hope for another. . .

Let me conjure you to disappoint the only hopes of our enemies by your unanimity. I have shown, and will always show, how desirous I am to be the common father of all my people. Do you, in like manner, lay aside parties and divisions. Let there be no other distinction heard of amongst us for the future, but of those, who are for the Protestant Religion, and the present establishment, and of those, who mean a popish prince, and a French government. I will only add this; if you do in good earnest desire to see England hold the balance of Europe, and to be indeed at the head of the Protestant interest, it will appear by your right improving the present opportunity.

[From 12 William, c. 3]

12. The longevity of the consequences of the Revolution: non-jurors question Bishop Hough in the 1740s

The constitutional consequences of the Revolution continued to reverberate into the eighteenth century, though they were less controversial after the Hanoverian Succession in 1714, but the religious settlement remained a matter of controversy for many years. In the 1740s, Bishop Hough of Worcester received a letter from two non-jurors, successors of those who refused to take the oaths to William and Mary in 1689. The issues of civil deprivation of bishops, absolution from oaths and regular succession all date from the deprivation of the non-juring bishops who were removed from their sees after the Revolution. Hough treated their enquiries with courtesy, but refused a reply, inviting them instead to debate the issue with him.

My Lord

As we esteem it our misfortune that we are of sentiments different from those of your Lordship in some affairs that relate to civil governments, it would be of the last concern to us to find ourselves under a necessity to dissent from your Lordship in matter purely ecclesiastical.

In the first case, the arguments seem to us to be so plain and convincing that they leave no room for enquiries, nor had we (as we apprehended) that immediate obligation upon us to apply to your Lordship.

But we hold ourselves in duty bound to refer all difficulties of the other kind to our Diocesan; and my Lord we find them so numerous, and of that importance that we are not capable of extricating ourselves without your Lordship's assistance.

But that we might not give too great an interruption to your Lordship's more weighty affairs, we have drawn the substance of some of our difficulties into the following short queries, which we humbly beg leave to lay before your Lordship.

Qu. 1   Can orthodox bishops be deprived of their ecclesiastical jurisdiction by a civil magistrate?

Qu. 2   Have not bishops so deprived a right of communion with other Churches?

Qu. 3 Are the clergy and the people absolved from their canonical obedience by such kind of deprivation?

Qu. 4 Is not an unlawful ejection of regular and Catholic bishops and putting others uncanonically in their places a setting up altar against altar?

Qu. 5 Are not the clergy and people who join in communion with such succeeding bishops involv'd likewise in the schism?

Qu. 6 And have not the regular successors (if any such there are) to such deprived bishops a right to all the privileges of their predecessors?

And now we beg leave to assure you, my Lord, that as we have always regarded schism as a crime of the most provoking nature so our apprehensions of either continuing in, or falling into, one, must necessarily make us uneasy.

Shall we not, therefore, in the midst of our difficulties, have recourse to him, whom by the disposition of Providence 'tis our duty to consult, whose known abilities make it easy to him and whose duty must incline him to assist us?

We therefore hope 'twill be unnecessary to importune your Lordship to favour us with a resolution to the preceding queries, especially when we profess it to be of the utmost importance to,
My Lord.
Your Lordships most obedient and Most dutiful sons and servants,
Ellis Ffraneworth,
George Osborne
If your Lordship please to favour us with an answer, please to direct for me at Wirksworth, or to Mr Osborne in St Peter's parish, in Derby.

> [From M. Burrows (ed.), 'The table talk and
> papers of Bishop Hough 1703–1743' in *Collectanea*
> (Oxford Historical Society, 1890)]

RELIGION IN THE EARLY
EIGHTEENTH CENTURY

1. Josiah Woodward's account of the religious societies in London, 1697

Woodward was a Gloucestershire clergyman, who joined one of William Beveridge's religious societies in the years after the Restoration and moved to become minister of Poplar in London. It was a second wave of societies, established in 1691, that occupied his *Account* published in 1697 (which ran to four editions within a dozen years). The societies for the reformation of manners were set up in London to enforce the laws against vice. Some societies encompassed dissenters as well as Anglicans. The societies lasted for almost forty years. Their attentions were focused on profanity, blasphemy, immorality and sexual licence. Often they entrapped those committing immorality, they undertook prosecutions and presented evidence. The purpose of the book was to promote the formation of such societies in England and Wales by providing a model.

An Account of the progress of these societies: and of their real aim and design

The first design of those who join'd in this religious fellowship looked no further than the mutual assistance and consolation one of another in their Christian welfare. That by their interchanged counsels and exhortations, they might the better maintain their integrity in the midst of a crooked and perverse generation, but as their sense of the blessedness of religion, and the value of immortal souls increased, they could not but exercise. . . compassion towards such as discovered little concern about these important matters, this inclined them to endeavour, by discourse with their acquaintances in proper seasons, to press upon them those divine arguments whereby themselves had been roused out of a state of carnal insensibleness. And finding that the grace of God many times seconded these their Christian admonitions to good effect, they became more habituated to good discourse, especially where there was any probability of a civil acceptance of it. Insomuch, that at length they could not but stand amazed at the success which it pleased God to give them. One of them, to whom God had given a very deep sense of religious matters, and a very moving manner of expressing it, had such success, that he had, under God, induced most of his intimate acquaintances at least to an inward reformation. . .

By the blessing of Almighty God upon these endeavours, a very considerable sense of religion has been revived in many of this nation, and a very conspicuous check given to debauchery. Insomuch that the general odium, and the threatening dangers of informing against vice and profaneness are almost extinguished, and the blessed work of reformation set into such an excellent and successful method, that the outward part of it would soon be effected, would but some few in every street or parish, who are of place and power, engage heartily in this honourable and necessary work; or would others, who are of ability, but contribute as it becomes them, towards the expense of it. For the apprehending of lewd people, (as was before observed) and the prosecution of them in the course of our law, is very chargeable; insomuch, that near a thousand pounds have been expended in work, within the space of the last four years, by a society of worthy gentlemen, who seem to prosecute vice with as much pleasure as others commit it: to their immortal honour be it mentioned.

And that none may be discouraged on account of the general overflowing of vice, and the disproportionable fewness of the hands engaged to put a stop to it; let it be considered, that the chief part of this opposition to public immorality, has been occasioned by the meeting of four or five private persons together: who duly considering and bewailing the height and extent of the sins of this nation, came to a resolution of doing their utmost to oppose it, in the due course of our laws. . .

A Specimen of the Orders of the societies before mentioned, copied out of that at Poplar

That the sole design of this society being to promote real holiness of heart and life. It is absolutely necessary that the persons who enter into it; do seriously resolve, by the Grace of God, to apply themselves to all means proper to accomplish these blessed ends, trusting in the divine power and gracious conduct of the Holy Spirit, through our Lord Jesus Christ, to excite, advance, and perfect all good in us.

That in order to their being of one heart and one mind in this design, every member of this society shall own and manifest himself to be of the Church of England, and frequent the liturgy, and other public exercises of the same. And that they be careful withal to express due Christian charity, candour and moderation towards all such dissenters as are of good conversation,

That the members of this society shall meet together one evening in the week at a convenient place, in order to encourage each other in practical holiness, by discoursing on such subjects, as tend thereunto; observing the Holy Scriptures as their rule; and praying to God for his grace and blessing.

That at such meetings they decline all disputes about controversial points, and all unnecessary discourse about state-affairs, or the concerns of trade and worldly things: and that the whole bent of the discourse be to glorify God, and edify one another in love. . .

That any respective member may recommend any object of charity to the stewards, who shall (with the consent of the rest) give out of the common stock, according as the occasion requires, and in a case of extraordinary necessity, every particular person shall be desired to contribute farther, as he shall think fit.

That every one that absents himself four meetings together, (without giving a satisfactory account to the stewards) shall be look'd upon as disaffected to the society.

That none shall be admitted into this society without giving due notice thereof to the stewards, who shall acquaint the whole society therewith, and after due enquiry into their religious purposes and manner of life, the stewards may admit them, if the major part of the society allows of it, and not otherwise, and with the like joint consent, they may exclude any member proved guilty of any mis-behaviour, after due admonition, unless he gives sufficient testimony of his repentance and amendment, before the whole society.

It is hereby recommended to every person concerned in this society, to consider dangerous snares of gaming; and the open scandal of being concerned in those games which are used in public houses; and that it is the safest and most commendable way to decline them wholly; shunning all unnecessary resort to such houses and taverns, and wholly avoiding lewd play-houses.

That whereas the following duties have been too much neglected to the scandal and reproach of our holy religion, they do resolve, by the Grace of God, to make it their serious endeavour,

1. To be just in all their dealings, even to an exemplary strictness
2. To pray many times every day 'Remembering our continual Dependence upon God both for Spiritual and temporal things.'
3. To partake of the Lord's-supper at least once a month, if not prevented by a reasonable impediment.
4. To practise the profoundest meekness and humility.
5. To watch against censuring others.
6. To accustom themselves to holy thoughts in all places.
7. To be helpful one to another.
8. To exercise tenderness, patience, and compassion towards all men.
9. To make reflections on themselves when they read the Holy Bible, or other good books, and when they hear Sermons.
10. To shun all foreseen occasions of evil: as evil company, known temptations, &c.
11. To think often on the different estates of the glorified and the damned, in the unchangeable eternity, to which we are hastening.
12. To examine themselves every night, what good or evil they have done in the day past.
13. To keep a private fast once a month, (especially near their approach to the Lord's Table) if at their own disposal; or to fast from some meals when they may conveniently.
14. To mortify the flesh, with its affections and lusts.
15. To advance in heavenly mindedness, and in all grace.
16. To shun spiritual pride, and the effects of it; as railing, anger, peevishness, and impatience of contradiction, and the like.
17. To pray for the whole society in their private prayers.
18. To read pious books often for their edification, but especially the Holy Bible; and herein particularly.
19. To be continually mindful of the great obligation of this special profession of religion; and to walk so circumspectly, that none may be offended or discouraged from it by what they see in them; nor occasion given to any to speak reproachfully of it.
20. To shun all manner of affectation and moroseness, and be of a civil and obliging deportment to all men.

[From J. Woodward, *An Account of the Religious Societies in the City of London and their endeavours for The Reformation of Manners* (London, 1712)]

2. The work of the Society for the Reformation of Manners

The materials below are those produced by the Society to promote the prosecution of offenders. Blank warrants for the use of constables and magistrates were printed in books so that members of the society could issue them in reaction to cases of profanity and tippling. The Society also produced information on the numbers of prosecutions for these and other offences in its first fourteen years in *The Account of the Progress Made in Suppressing Profaneness and Debauchery*, published in 1708. This 'black list' was subsequently produced annually in the Society's report between 1715 and 1738 (see Table 2.1 overleaf).

Whereas [A. B.], being [above sixteen years of age] is convicted before me of profane swearing [five times], within the parish of [ ], this being the [second] time of his conviction, these . . . charge and command you to demand of the said [A. B.], [20s] for the use of the poor of the parish. If he refuse or neglect, you are to levy the same by distress, and in default of this, set him in the stocks for [two hours]. And this shall be your warrant, etc.

Whereas [A. B.] Innkeeper, is convicted before me of having allowed tippling on Sunday [date], these . . . charge and command you to demand of the said [A. B.] to forfeit twenty shillings for the use of the poor of the parish. If he refuse or neglect, you are to levy the same by distress, and in default of this to take him to gaol until such time as he shall make payment . . . And of the due execution of this you are to give an account when it shall be demanded of you. And hereof fail not at your peril.

[From G. Portus, *Caritas Anglicana* (London, 1912)
by permission of Mowbray, a Cassell imprint]

Table 2.1 Annual reports of prosecutions by the Society for the Reformation of Manners, 1715–38

Year (Dec to Dec)	1715	1716	1717	1718	1719	1720	1721	1722	1723	1724	1725	1726
Lewd and disorderly practices (includes sodomy in some years)	1152	1066	1927	1253	*	1189	1197	1223	1622	1951	*	*
Keeping bawdy and disorderly houses	36	9	33	31	*	14	15	35	36	21	*	*
Sabbath breaking	1066	621	524	492	*	615	709	653	648	600	*	*
Profanity and swearing	263	102	400	205	*	114	161	201	96	108	*	*
Drunkenness	46	14	25	17	*	11	13	8	5	12	*	*
Keeping common gaming houses and gaming	8	8		8	*	16	4	104	42	23	*	*
Total number of persons prosecuted by the SRM since its inception						75,270	77,469	84,720	86,944	89,393	91,899	92,959
No. of books, etc., distributed						400,000	400,000	400,000	400,000	400,000	410,000	412,000

Year (Dec to Dec)	1727	1728	1729	1730	1731	1732	1733	1734	1735	1736	1737	1738
Lewd and disorderly practices (includes sodomy in some years)	*	*	*	251	*	230	89	170	318	*	95	52
Keeping bawdy and disorderly houses	*	*	*	30	*	9	3	*	*	*	*	*
Sabbath breaking	*	*	*	424	*	275	395	240	268	*	393	493
Profanity and swearing	*	*	*	22	*	14	*	*	*	*	*	*
Drunkenness	*	*	*	*	*					*		
Keeping common gaming houses and gaming	*	*	*	15	*					*		
Total number of persons prosecuted by the SRM since its inception	94,322	95,100	96,326	97,060	*	98,483	98,970	99,380	99,970	*	101,138	101,683
No. of books, etc., distributed	415,000	417,000	418,000	420,000	*	423,000	440,000	442,000	443,400	*	444,750	

* = particulars not published

[From G. Portus, *Caritas Anglicana* (London, 1912)]

3. A tour of the religious groups of Kent, 1701

The account below was written by John Skeat, who with Thomas Morrison, as agents of the Society for the Propagation of Christian Knowledge, toured Kent in 1701 with the intent of making connections with religious societies and groups which could work with the SPCK. Their interest in distributing religious tracts, schools and raising funds for the 'plantations' (America) was characteristic of the SPCK and early eighteenth-century society. The SPCK sought to promote the formation of societies for the reformation of manners and to establish local correspondents with whom they could establish a national connection.

We set out Friday, Aug. 15th for Canterbury, and next morning we arrived there, and the same day we reached Dover, where we fixed up a chain book at the Ship Tavern (the place where passengers going and coming from France resort to), and left a *Help* and papers of all sorts there. The master of the house returned many thanks for the favour we had done him, and promised to use the books and papers to the best advantage, and seemed to be a very sober man. At the Lion, which is the first post house, we left a *Help*, and papers of all sorts, the like at Mr Young's, vintner, the Fountain, and at Mr Richard's Coffee House, and at the George Tavern, at all which places we are returned thanks for what we had done, and all promised to show them to their guests and to make a good use of them. We understood the Mayor of the place was a sober man, and that Mr MacQueen, the Church Minister, was a pious good man, who, we were assured, would encourage anything for the promoting reformation. We had not opportunity of waiting on him, or the Mayor, but have since sent them a packet. The same night we returned to Canterbury. The next day (being the Lord's day), in the evening we visited the Religious Society, which consists of about 30, who are men of religion, and meet in very good order, and we required of them what progress they had made in relation to the school, and they told us that they had raised a lecture-sermon in order to promote the same, and endeavoured at the same time to have a collection at the Church-doors, which as yet they could not effect by reason Mr Braddock was of a contrary opinion, which had hitherto hindered their progress in that matter. They told us that at Ipswich there was lately raised a school of forty boys which they clothed. Mr Lewis likewise acquainted us that he had made what progress he could in that matter, but hitherto had no success, by reason of many great obstructions he met with; but acquainted us that he had got several subscriptions towards propagating the Gospel in foreign plantations, and was in hopes of procuring many more (so desired he might have sent down twelve of the printed charters). Afterwards we took out two or three officers to the public houses, and found twelve with company in them, whereof one was a constable, and the next day convicted them before the Mayor, where were Mr Alderman Gibbs and Dr Taylor, a Justice of the Peace for the County, both Churchmen who were very well pleased with what we had done, and when we came away they told us we had done them a signal piece of service, for which they returned us hearty thanks, and assured us that nothing should hinder them from following so good an example as we have set them. . .

We presented to each of them one account of the progress in quarto gift, and several other papers. Several of the offenders paid the same day, we having warrants levying the money which amounted to [Blank] ourselves, and went with them to the execution of them. We gave to Mr Alderman Gibbs and Dr Taylor an account of those warrants which were not with the Constables' names, to whom they were delivered, who promised faithfully to have them put into execution. The whole city was alarmed at our proceedings, and the same night we met several of the constables, who were mightily encouraged by what we had done, and returned us thanks for the same, and promised to take some of the members belonging to the society out every Lord's day, to divide themselves over the whole city, and to do as we had done, which we understood, since by letter that they perform (and the two above-mentioned justices go with them). As to swearing, fruit being exposed for sale, and barbers shaving on the Lord's day, 'tis almost suppressed, we not hearing an oath all the while we were there, though we were in several public-houses; and, asking a barber if he could come and shave on the Lord's day, he told us he durst not do it, being strictly forbid by the Mayor.

[From Wanley Mss, SPCK, by permission]

4. The work of the SPCK, 1700

The Society for the Promoting of Christian Knowledge was founded in 1699 by Dr Thomas Bray with the aim of spreading religion to those areas in which irreligion and ignorance held greater sway than Christianity. The Society operated through a system of correspondents who kept in contact with the Society in London. The correspondents reported reactions to fund-raising activities, they pursued the introduction of schools and libraries, they circulated tracts and Bibles and formed committees and societies of clergy and laity locally. The three summaries of correspondence presented here indicate the positive and negative contemporary reactions of the clergy and laity to the initial proposals of the society.

1. Mr Robert Wynne from Carnarvon to Mr Chamberlayne, April 15th 1700, refers to a letter he sent to Dr Evans wherein he communicated ye state of religion and of ye societies of the clergy in ye diocese of Bangor. That ye clergy do highly approve ye good designs mentioned in Mr Chamberlayne's letter and resolve to pursue them. That the clergy of each deanery meet by themselves and make it their constant endeavour to stir up each other to strict and conscientious discharge of the ministerial functions. That divers of ye clergy have contributed towards schools and others disposed to do ye like and great numbers have been lately taught to read. That ye catechumens are much increased notwithstanding the miserable neglect of parents. That the vulgar understand not English books and the people are generally so poor yt little help can be expected of them. That ye Bishop and clergy have been at the sole charge of printing the Welsh books lately translated and are willing to subscribe to more, and will endeavour to obtain ye subscriptions from ye gentry. That the clergy never meet but they sent to the Bp. for his advice and instructions and also at every meeting, which he imparts to the A.bishops. That Dr Jones is leaving Anglesey and coming to settle at Bangor; so yt for the future his letter may serve Carnarvonshire, and upon a motion made him, he will recommend a successor to uphold ye correspondence in Anglesey.

2. Mr Lloyd of Alty Cadno, Carmarthenshire, South Wales, to Mr Chamberlayne, Aug. 1st 1700. That the clergy and members of his society are much encouraged by their correspondence with this society. Himself gratefully accepts the correspondence and promises his best assistance. That some of the prime clergy are cautious ab't associating, he supposes they delay it till the bishop is appointed. That some cavil at the word association and that has retarded several gentlemen. That they are so dispersed that they have few meetings unless accidentally and some promise to do their duty without entering into any society and those that have entered themselves to meet once a month or six weeks. That the proceedings at the quarter sessions hath had a visible effect on the gentry. That the design of schools is most likely to take effect, when the manners of the people are reformed, which they are

now endeavouring. That he will, from time to time, give account to the society of their success and difficulties.

3. Mr Marris of Lantrissent, Glamorganshire, to Mr Chamberlayne, 8 April 1701. Says that altho' he has communicated the society's letter and papers to some of the greatest of the county, it has been for the most part unsuccessful. That many of his brethren had promis'd to promote catechetical lectures according to the Bishop of Chichester's system translated into Welsh by Dr Evans. That there will be a meeting of the clergy in Easter week &c. That many of the Quaker's eyes have been open'd by the distributing Mr Keith's papers. That there are two schools in Llantrissent. That the poor are numerous, lazy and mutinous and so much addicted to sports even in divine service that he has been forced to become church-warden in order the better to restrain them. That about £200 per ann. is collected but doe's not suffice to put out all the poor and to maintain the aged. Lastly, that he shall be glad to receive farther directions and assistance.

[From M. Clement, *Correspondence and Minutes of the SPCK Relating to Wales, 1699–1740* (Cardiff, 1952), by permission of the University of Wales Press]

5. Robert Nelson on feasts and festivals, 1703

Robert Nelson was the son of a merchant and was a fellow of Trinity College, Cambridge. When he married, to the daughter of Lord Berkeley, he was forced to travel round Europe for the benefit of his wife's health, and he visited most of the courts of Europe. Gradually Nelson developed a reputation as a scholar and traveller. However in 1691, on his return to England, he became a non-juror, and befriended John Kettlewell, who encouraged him to become a member of the Society for the Reformation of Manners and to consider writing a book on fast days and festivals to revive their use. It is the introduction of the book that is extracted here. Nelson's separation from the Church of England was painful for him. He spent the rest of his life writing a biography of the elderly and saintly Bishop Bull of St David's and in promoting charities and parochial libraries.

I think myself so far obliged by that respect that is usually paid to the candid and charitable reader as to acquaint him. . . with what he may expect from the following treatise: the design whereof is an attempt to rescue the festivals and fasts of the Church of England not only from the prejudices of those who have not yet reconciled themselves to her constitution; but chiefly from the contempt and neglect of such as profess themselves her obedient members. . . It is the duty of all Christians to humble themselves before God with fasting and prayer, frequently to admire and adore the infinite wisdom and goodness of God in the mysteries of our redemption. . . But as to the certain seasons when these duties are publicly to be performed, and as to the way and manner of discharging them, that must be left to the determination of our lawful governors; for what we obliged to perform at some times cannot be less a duty when lawful authority enjoins a certain time for performing it. . . That the people might not neglect their duty in this particular every parson, vicar or curate is obliged to give notice every Sunday whether there be any holy day, or fasting days during the week following; and if he shall wittingly offend [the canon]. . . he is to be censured according to law. . . But thus we certainly owe, not only to the justice of our principles, but out of respect to those that are not friends to the constitution of the Church; for how can we suppose they will be prevailed upon to observe days, when we pay no regard to them ourselves; or if when we distinguish them from other days, it is only our vanities and follies, by our excess and intemperance, by dedicating them to pleasure and diversion, when piety and devotion, the great end of their design, is so much neglected. . .

Among those crying abominations, which like a torrent have overspread the nation, this age seems to distinguish itself by a great contempt of the clergy, than which, I think, nothing can be a greater evidence of the decayed state of religion among us. This barbarous and unchristian practice, setting all particular reasons aside, can be resolved into nothing so surely as into the great looseness of principles and corruption of morals, which have too much infected all ranks and orders of men; for though it may pass for a current maxim among some, that priests of all religions are the same; yet I am of the opinion it will appear a much truer observation by experience, that they of all religions that condemn the priesthood will be found the same, both as to their principles and practice; sceptical in one and dissolute in the other. To remedy, if possible, this great evil, I have endeavoured upon the Ember Fasts, to explain the nature of the several offices in the sacred function, to show the authority of their commission, the dignity of the priesthood, and those duties the laity owe to their spiritual superiors. . .

[From R. Nelson, *A Companion for the Festivals and Fasts of the Church of England* (London, 1703)]

6. Erasmus Saunders's bleak view of the Church in Wales, 1721

Erasmus Saunders began his account of the state of the Anglican Church in Wales in the first years of the eighteenth century, during the episcopate of Bishop George Bull of St David's. Although he held livings in England, Saunders was a canon of Brecon and had been brought up in Clydney, Pembrokeshire. The depressing view that Saunders presents here is of a Church riven by poverty and the ruination of decades of neglect and deterioration. Saunders's view is clearly that the temporal and spiritual inheritance of the eighteenth-century Church was a poor one.

The state of religion here is so very deplorable, as that it can scarce conflict with the prudence of any government, and much less with the care and wisdom of ours, that it should be still suffer'd to continue so.

But first, of the condition that our churches, chapels, and habitations of the clergy are in. Such is the melancholy and ruinous view that presents itself upon this head, that I know not well where to begin, for did you see the ruins of all things dedicated to pious and sacred uses throughout this country; did you see the pitiful condition of our once so celebrated and noble cathedral, and how great a part of it is demolish'd to prevent the charge of reparations; or did you see the stately ruins of the Bishop's Palace, of the College, the schools, the archdeacon's and the canons houses at St David's, and the like desolation of the collegiate church and houses belonging thereunto, and of the Bishop's Palace at Brecon? And also the desolate remains of the old collegiate church of Llandhewyfrefi in Cardiganshire; a Church once endow'd with a handsome provision for a dean and twelve prebendaries; but the endowment is now alienated to that degree that the poor incumbent there, tho' the tithes of his parish are said to be worth four hundred pounds per annum is oblig'd to content himself with about eight pounds salary. Again, did you see the havoc and desolation that has been made of all the Bishop's Palaces, the site and manors belonging to some of them, being quite alienated, of the rest there is nothing left but stately and magnificent ruins, excepting that of Abergwyly, which is the only one remaining out of eight or nine, that once belonged to this Bishopric; nor is this likely long to out live the rest, unless the generosity of our good Diocesan should dispose him seasonably to rescue it from ruin.

Again; did you see what very sorry and mean cottages (if any) that are left for parsonage and vicarage houses: but in most parishes there are no provisions of any kind for that use, not glebe, nor ground to build upon; but as was said, where there are any, they are commonly so mean and inconvenient, as that the clergy, poor as they are, cannot think them habitable for themselves, and therefore are oblig'd to part with them to any one that will please to rent them; but very often they fall to the sexton's lot, who to get a sorry maintenance, is allowed the privilege of selling ale by the churchyard side. Further, were you to see the general devastation there is of almost all the chapels in the country, which it can't be deny'd, were much more necessary to be kept up here, than in most other places, for the ease and benefit of the people, who in many large parishes are no less than five, six, or seven, or perhaps eight or ten miles distant from their churches; and last of all did you see the forlorn appearance of the parochial churches, and in how pitiful a condition they are kept, it might justly tempt you to imagine from the little care taken of them, that the public and external part of the Christian worship at least, was about to cease or be lain aside here. . .

As the Christian service is thus totally disus'd in some places, there are other some that may be said to be but half serv'd; there being several churches, where we are rarely, if at all meet with preaching, catechising, or administering of the Holy Communion. In others the service of the prayers is but partly read, and that perhaps but once a month, or once in a quarter of a year; nor is it indeed reasonable to expect that they should be better serv'd, while the stipends allow'd for the service of them are so small that a poor curate must sometimes submit to serve three or four churches for ten or twelve pounds a year, and that perhaps when they are almost as many miles distant from each other. And when it is thus with them, with what order, or regularity (can it be suppos'd) are they capable of doing that service? Forc'd they are (now they are ordain'd) to submit to any terms; that is, they must starve, or even be contented with the meanest salaries, and yet drudge and labour for it as far as they are able; and having so little time, and so many places to attend upon, how precipitately, and out of breath are they to read the prayers, or to shorten and abridge them? And what time have they or their congregation to compose themselves for their devotion, while thus forc'd to a kind of perpetual motion, and like hasty itinerants to hurry about from place to place? There is no time fix'd for going to Church, so it be on Sunday, so that the poor man must begin at any time with as many as are at hand, sooner or later, as he can perform his round. He then abruptly huddles over as many prayers as may be in half an hours time, and then returns again to his road fasting (for how earnestly soever his appetite may call for it, it's

seldom that he has time for, or that the impropriators farmer can afford
to give him dinner) till he has dispatch'd his circuit, and that weariness
or darkness obliges him to rest, or perhaps for want of a little necessary
refreshment at home, to go where he ought not, where it's odds but
he will again meet with many of his congregation, who when their
short service is over, are too apt to think themselves at liberty to spend
the remaining part of the day at an ale-house, or at some pastime or
diversion, as they are dispos'd.

This then is the hard case of our poor unhappy curacy-pluralists, the
shameful poverty of single churches obliges them for their subsistence
to undertake the cure of many, by that means they are so straiten'd in
time by hurrying about from one to another, that they have scarce
leisure to read deliberately the prayers at the proper hours of doing it,
much less to preach or catechise, or as much as sometimes for to read
an homily. Such is the faint shadow that remains among us of the public
service of religion. . .

And yet notwithstanding these discouragements, there are, God be
thanked, several clergymen among us, that by their virtue and steady
application, surmount the difficulties they meet with, find means to be
well accomplish'd, and to adorn their station for the sake of well doing,
and to be no less eminent for their care and diligence, than others are
for their neglect and scandal. But alas, the number of them is too unequal
for so great a harvest as they have before them; nor is it to be suppos'd
but that they are, as rare as they are distinguishing in their disposition,
who are so happily resolv'd, as not to be wanting to their duty, even in
spite of ill-usage, and tho' they are neglected and left to herd promiscuously with the lowest or unworthiest of their order, while others, who
attend levies, and not their function, and whose best merit is to be most
importunate, and at hand will seldom fail of being promoted. . .

Nor indeed cou'd it reasonably be expected in some places that there
should be any but for the extraordinary disposition to religion, which
a learned historian observes, prevails among the people of this country;
for whether it be owing to our solitude, or our poverty, or natural
disposition, or to the extraordinary grace of God given us, I know not;
but so it is. There is, I believe, no part of the nation more inclin'd to
be religious, and to be delighted with it than the poor inhabitants of
these mountains. They don't think it too much when neither ways, nor
weather are inviting, over cold and bleak hills to travel three or four
miles, or more, on foot to attend the public prayers, and sometimes as
many more to hear a sermon, and they seldom grudge many times for
several hours together in their damp and cold churches, to wait the

coming of their minister, who by occasional duties in his other curacies, or by other accidents may be oblig'd to disappoint them, and to be often variable in his hours of prayer. And, then also to supply in some measure the want of a more regular public service, there are many, even of the common people, who gladly make the best use of what little knowledge they have gain'd, and take the pains privately, by reading or discoursing to instruct one another in their houses. And it is not uncommon to see servants and shepherds, as they have an opportunity, strive to do these good offices to each other.

[From E. Saunders, *A View of the State of Religion in the Diocese of St David's About the Beginning of the Eighteenth Century. With some account of the causes of its decay.* . . (London, 1721)]

THREE

CONTROVERSIES

1. The Lower House of Convocation addresses the bishops, 1705

The Church of England's official parliament, Convocation, consisted of two houses, the lower House of Clergy and the House of Bishops. Convocation had been largely dormant under James II; under William and Mary in 1689 it met and deliberated the issues facing the Church. The divisions over the oaths of submission to William and Mary and the fraught debates over the right of parliament to overturn a sovereign were such that the King chose to dissolve Convocation. In 1700 another Convocation was called, but the strong Toryism of the clergy created friction with the bishops. In 1705 the same occurred. The Lower House sought to redress grievances, to restore the privileges of the Church which it felt had been eroded by the Toleration Act, and to censure clergy like Edmund Hickeringill and Benjamin Hoadly who advanced views at variance with the Tory clergy. The House of Bishops, led by Archbishop Tenison, denied the right of the Lower House to meet without his approval and to pass such motions.

A letter of the lower house to the archbishop and bishops about books and writing. (Febr. 19)

To the most reverend the president, and the right reverend the bishops in convocation assembled.

The lower House of Convocation think it becomes them to remind your lordships of a motion formerly made by them concerning a bill 'for the more easy and speedy recovery of Church rates,' and to pray your lordships, that till such a bill can be obtained, your lordships would use your best endeavours towards preventing those dilatory and expensive methods of proceeding in courts ecclesiastical, which have been so much complained of on that occasion. . .

In the mean time they think it proper to observe to your lordships, that notwithstanding Her Majesty's pious care to repress and restrain the great enormities of the stage, for which the then lower House moved your lordships without success, that the humble thanks of the Convocation might be given to Her Majesty; yet they find still great reason to complain of the immorality and profaneness of the stage, of which there is a fresh flagrant instance in a profane prologue lately spoken at the opening of the new theatre in the Haymarket, and since printed and published.

They do also look upon themselves as in duty bound to complain to your lordships of the daring insults upon the clergy, the universities, and the constitution itself, continually made by the licentious writers, particularly by the authors of the *Review* and *Observator*, and to pray your lordships' concurrence in an humble representation to Her Majesty of this great grievance and of the mischiefs, which must rebound to our holy Church and religion, if such open assaults upon our order, upon the places of our education, and upon our legal establishment shall continue to be made with impunity.

As likewise to inform your lordships of the scandal given to all good Christians by an assembly of sectaries, under the name of Unitarians, publicly held in the City of London, the teacher whereof is notoriously known to have been convicted of denying the divinity of our blessed Saviour.

And moreover to acquaint your lordships with the late lewd and profane writings of Edmund Hickeringill, rector of St Mary's Colchester, which have brought so great scandal upon our Church and holy order. And they must at the same time declare their grateful sense of the pastoral vigilance and exemplary zeal of the right honourable and right reverend the present Lord Bishop of London, of which he hath given constant proofs in endeavouring to bring such offenders to condign punishment; but hath met with insuperable difficulties therein; the removal of which by such methods, as may be effectual doth, in the opinion of this house, highly deserve the mature consideration of this provincial synod.

They do further propose to your lordships' consideration, what fit methods may (with the same leave and encouragement) be taken by this synod, for inviting and inducing the pastors of the French Protestant churches among us to use their best endeavours with their people for an universal reception of our liturgy; which hath had the approbation of their most eminent divines, hath been long used in several of their congregations within this kingdom, and by Her Majesty's special influence hath been lately introduced into the French congregation held in the chapel near her royal palace.

They do, in the last place, earnestly desire your lordships, that some synodical notice may be taken of the dishonour done to the Church by a sermon preached by Mr Benjamin Hoadly at Saint Lawrence Jewry, Sept. 29, 1705 containing positions contrary to the doctrine of the Church, expressed in the first and second parts of the homily against disobedience or wilful rebellion.

These several heads of information and complaint they are ready to make good by special proofs, whenever your lordships shall be pleased to demand them.

[From E. Cardwell, *Synodalia* (Oxford, 1842)]

2. The trial of Dr Sacheverell, 1710

Henry Sacheverell was chaplain of St Saviour's Southwark and a staunch Tory who sought to attack the Whigs. The trial of Sacheverell for a sermon preached on the text 'in peril among false brethren' in 1709 was the cause of riots and popular disturbance in London for some weeks. The trial of such a leading Tory clergyman, with such widespread support, was a political misjudgement for the Whig government; and by the time Sacheverell was convicted the scene was set for a Tory political take-over. The conviction of Sacheverell, but with the modest sentence of the burning of his sermon which was already a best-seller, and a temporary suspension, was seen as a vindication of him. The account here is by Bishop Gilbert Burnet of Salisbury, a Whig who was attacked in the sermon and naturally opposed Sacheverell.

Dr Sacheverell was a bold insolent man, with a very small measure of religion, virtue, learning, or good sense, but he resolved to force himself into popularity and preferment, by the most petulant railings at dissenters, and low-churchmen, in several sermons and libels, written without either chasteness of style, or liveliness of expression: all was one unpractised strain of indecent and scurrilous language. When he had pursued this method for several years without effect, he was at last brought up by a popular election to a Church in Southwark, where he began to make great reflections on the ministry, representing that the Church was in danger, being neglected by those who govern, while they favoured her most inveterate enemies. At the assizes in Derby (where he preached before the judges) and on the fifth of November (preaching at St Paul's in London) he gave a full vent to his fury, in the most virulent declamation, that he could contrive, upon these words of St Paul's, 'perils from false brethren;' in which, after some short reflections upon popery, he let himself loose into such indecencies, that both the man and the sermon were universally condemned: he asserted the doctrine of non-resistance in the highest strain possible, and said, that to charge the Revolution with resistance, was to cast black and odious imputations on it; pretending, that the late King had disowned it, and cited for the proof of that, some words in his declaration, by which he vindicated himself from a design of conquest. He poured out much scorn and scurrility on the dissenters, and reflected severely on the toleration; he said the Church was violently attacked by her enemies, and loosely defended by her pretended friends: he animated the people to stand up for the defence of the Church, for which he said he sounded the trumpet, and desired them to put on the whole armour of God. The Court of Aldermen refused to desire him to print his sermon; but he did print it, pretending it was upon the desire of Garrard, then Lord Mayor, to whom he dedicated it, with an inflaming epistle at the head of it. The party that opposed the ministry, did so magnify the sermon, that, as was generally reckoned, about forty thousand of them were printed, and dispersed over the nation. The Queen seemed highly offended at it, and the ministry looked on it as an attack made on them, that was not to be despised. The Lord Treasurer was so described, that it was next to the naming him, so a parliamentary impeachment was resolved on; Eyre, then Solicitor-General, and others thought the short way of burning the sermon, and keeping him in prison during the session, was the better method; but the more solemn way was unhappily chosen. . .

Some opposition was made to the motion for impeaching Sacheverell, but it was carried by a great majority. The proceedings were slow, so those who intended to inflame the city and the nation upon that occasion, had time sufficient given them for laying their designs. They gave it out boldly, and in all places, that a design was formed by the Whigs to pull down the Church, and that this prosecution was only set on foot to try their strength; and that, upon their success in it, they would proceed more openly. Though this was all falsehood and forgery, yet it was propagated with so much application and zeal, and the tools employed in it were so well supplied with money (from whom was not then known), that it is scarcely credible how generally it was believed. . .

The clergy did generally espouse Sacheverell as their champion, who had stood in the breach; and so they reckoned his cause was their own. Many sermons were preached, both in London and other places, to provoke the people, in which they succeeded beyond expectation. Some accidents concurred to delay the proceedings; much time was spent in preparing the articles of impeachment: and the answer was by many shifts long delayed: it was bold, without either submission or common respect: he justified every thing in his sermon in a very haughty and assuming style. In conclusion, the Lords ordered the trial to be at the bar of their House; but those who found that by gaining more time the people were still more inflamed, moved that the trial might be public in Westminster Hall, where the whole House of Commons might be present. This took so with unthinking people, that it could not be withstood, though the effects it would have were well foreseen. The preparing Westminster Hall was a work of some weeks.

At last, on the twenty-seventh of February, the trial began. Sacheverell was lodged in the Temple, and came every day with great solemnity in a coach to the Hall; great crowds ran about his coach with many shouts, expressing their concern for him in a very rude and tumultuous manner. The trial lasted three weeks, in which all other business was at a stand, for this took up all men's thoughts. The managers for the Commons opened the matter very solemnly: their performances were much and justly commended. Jekyll, Eyre, Stanhope, King, but above all Parker, distinguished themselves in a very particular manner: they did copiously justify both the Revolution and the present administration. There was no need of witnesses; for the sermon being owned by him, all the evidence was brought from it by laying his words together, and by showing his intent and meaning in them, which appeared from comparing one place with another. When his counsel, Sir Simon Harcourt, Dodds, Phipps, and two others, came to plead for him, they very freely acknowledged the lawfulness of resistance in extreme cases, and plainly justified the Revolution and our deliverance by King William: but they said it was not fit in a sermon to name such an exception; that the duties of morality ought to be delivered in their full extent, without supposing an extraordinary case: and therefore Sacheverell had followed precedents, set by our greatest divines, ever since the reformation, and ever since the Revolution. . .

During the trial, the multitudes that followed him all the way as he came, and as he went back, showed a great concern for him, pressing about him, and striving to kiss his hand. Money was thrown among them, and they were animated to such a pitch of fury, that they went to pull down some meeting-houses, which was executed on five of them, as far as burning all the pews in them. This was directed by some of better fashion, who followed the mob in hackney coaches, and were seen sending messages to them. The word, upon which all shouted, was 'The Church and Sacheverell!' and such as joined not in the shout were insulted and knocked down. Before my own door one, with a spade, cleft the skull of another, who would not shout as they did. There happened to be a meeting-house near me, out of which they drew every thing that was in it, and burned it before the door of the house. They threatened to do the like execution on my house; but the noise of the riot coming to court, orders were sent to the guards, to go about and disperse the multitudes and secure the public peace . . .

When Sacheverell had ended his defence, the managers for the House of Commons replied, and showed very evidently that the words of his sermon could not reasonably bear any other sense but that for which they had charged him. This was an easy performance, and they managed it with great life; but the humour of the town was turned against them, and all the clergy appeared for Sacheverell. Many of the Queen's chaplains stood about him, encouraging and magnifying him; and it was given out that the Queen herself favoured him; though, upon my first coming to town, which was after the impeachment was brought up to the Lords, she said to me that it was a bad sermon, and that he deserved well to be punished for it. All her ministers, who were in the House of Commons, were named to be managers, and they spoke very zealously for public liberty, justifying the Revolution. . .

Some of the bishops spoke in this debate on each side. Hooper, Bishop of Bath and Wells, spoke in excuse of Sacheverell: but Talbot, Bishop of Oxford; Wake, Bishop of Lincoln; Trimnel, Bishop of Norwich; and myself, spoke on the other side. We showed the falsehood of an opinion, too commonly received, that the Church of England had always condemned resistance, even in the cases of extreme tyranny . . . The House of Commons likewise ordered the impious collection of blasphemous expressions that Sacheverell had printed as his justification to be also burnt.

When this mild judgement was given, those who had supported him during the trial expressed an inconceivable gladness, as if they had got a victory; bonfires, illuminations, and other marks of joy appeared, not only in London, but over the whole kingdom.

This had yet greater effects: addresses were set on foot from all the parts of the nation, in which the absolute power of our princes was asserted, and all resistance was condemned, under the designation of anti-monarchical and republican principles: the Queen's hereditary right was acknowledged, and yet a zeal for the Protestant succession was likewise pretended, to make those addresses pass the more easily with unthinking multitudes. Most of these concluded with an intimation of their hopes that the Queen would dissolve the present parliament, giving assurances that, in a new election, they would choose none but such as should be faithful to the crown and zealous for the Church. These were at first more coldly received; for the Queen either made no answer at all, or made them in very general words. Addresses were brought, upon the other hand, magnifying the conduct of the parliament, and expressing a zeal for maintaining the Revolution and the Protestant succession.

In the beginning of April the parliament was prorogued, and the Queen, in her speech thereupon, expressed her concern that there was cause given for that which had taken up so much of their time, wishing that all her people would be quiet and mind their own business; adding, that in all times there was too much occasion given to complain of impiety, but that she would continue that zeal which she had hitherto expressed for religion and for the Church . . .

[From G. Burnet, *History of His Own Time* (London, 1724)]

3. The Occasional Conformity Act, 1711

The new Tory government of 1710 passed the Occasional Conformity Act to bolster the position of the Church of England, by denying those 'occasional' conformers, who took the sacrament in the Church of England as a formality to qualify them for office under the Test Act. Those dissenters who were occasional conformers were thought also to be Whigs and therefore the government accrued party advantage from the Act. The Act was repealed by the Whig regime in 1718, and the repeal itself was the cause of much debate and division among the clergy and bishops.

Occasional Conformity Act, 1711

An Act for preserving the Protestant religion, by better securing the Church of England, as by law established; and for confirming the toleration granted to Protestant dissenters by an Act, entitled, An Act for exempting their Majesties' Protestant subjects, dissenting from the Church of England, from the penalties of certain laws, and for supplying the defects thereof; and for the further securing the Protestant succession, by requiring the practisers of the law in North Britain to take the oaths, and subscribe the declaration therein mentioned. . . .

Be it enacted. . . that if any person or persons either peers or commoners who have or shall have any office or offices civil or military or receive any pay, salary, fee or wages by reason of any patent or grant from or under Her Majesty or any of Her Majesty's predecessors or of her heirs or successors or if any mayor, alderman, recorder, bailiff town clerk, common council man or other person bearing any office of magistracy who by the said recited Acts are obliged to receive the Sacrament of the Lord's Supper according to the rites and usage of the Church of England shall at any time after their admission into their respective offices knowingly or willingly resort to or be present at any conventicle, assembly or meeting for the exercise of religion in other manner than according to the liturgy and practice of the Church of England shall forfeit forty pounds to be recovered by him or them that shall sue for the same in any of Her Majesty's courts. . .

And be it further enacted that every person convicted shall be disabled from thenceforth to hold such office and shall be adjudged incapable to bear any office or employment whatsoever . . .

Provided always and be it further enacted that if any person who shall have been convicted shall after such conviction conform to the Church of England for the space of one year without having been present at any conventicle, assembly or meeting and receive the Sacrament of the Lord's Supper according to the rites and usage of the Church of England at least three times in the year every such person shall be capable of the grant of any the offices or employments aforesaid. . .

And be it further enacted that on or before the fifteenth day of June next, all advocates, writers to the signet, notaries public, and other members of the college of Justice, within Scotland, are hereby obliged to take and subscribe the oath appointed by the Act of the sixth year of Her Majesty's reign [6 Anne, c. 14] before the Lords of Session of the aforesaid part of Her Majesty's kingdom; except such of the said persons who have already taken the same: And if any of the persons aforesaid do refuse to take and subscribe the said oath, as aforesaid, such persons shall be ipso facto adjudged disabled in law to exercise in any manner his said employment or practice.

[From 10 Anne, c. 6]

4. The Schism Act, 1714

The Tory administration of Robert Harley and Henry St John also passed the Schism Act as a means of promoting the Anglican monopoly. The Act, which was passed with an immense majority in the Commons, but only passed the Lords because of the creation of twelve new peers, effectively made the toleration of dissenters' schools a matter of the permission of individual bishops. It was an attempt to rouse the High Church party to action against the dissenters and was an attack on the Toleration Act, which was the true object of the Tories' ire. The Act was repealed by the Whig government in concert with moderate Whig bishops in 1718.

Schism Act, 1714

An Act to prevent the growth of schism, and for the further security of the Churches of England and Ireland as by law, established.

Whereas. . . sundry papists and other persons dissenting from the Church of England, have taken upon them to instruct and teach youth as tutors or schoolmasters, and have for such purpose openly set up schools and seminaries, whereby, if due and speedy remedy be not had, great danger might ensue to this Church and State: for the making the said recited Act more effectual, and preventing the danger aforesaid, be it enacted. . .

That every person or persons who shall keep any public or private school or seminary, or teach and instruct any youth as tutor or schoolmaster, within that part of Great Britain called England the dominion of Wales, or town of Berwick upon Tweed, before such person or persons shall have subscribed so much of the said declaration and acknowledgement, as is before recited [in 13 and 14 Car. II, c. 4], and shall have had and obtained a licence from the respective archbishop, bishop, or ordinary of the place, under his seal of office (for which the party shall pay one shilling, and no more over and above the duties payable to Her Majesty for the same) and shall be thereof lawfully convicted, upon an information, presentment or indictment, in any of Her Majesty's courts of record at Westminster, or at the Assizes, or before justices of Oyer and Terminer, shall and may be committed to the common gaol there to remain without bail or mainprize for the space of three months, to commence from the time that such person or persons shall be received into the said gaol. . .

Provided always, that no licence shall be granted by any archbishop, bishop, or ordinary, unless the person or persons who sue for the same, shall produce a certificate of his or their having received the sacrament according to the usage of the Church of England, in some parish Church, within the space of one year next before grant of such licence, under the hand of the minister and one of the Church-wardens of the said parish, nor until such person or persons shall have taken or subscribed the oaths of allegiance and supremacy, and abjuration, as appointed by law, and shall have made and subscribed the declaration against transubstantiation, contained in the Act [25 Car, II, c. 2] entitled, An Act for preventing dangers which may happen from popish recusants, before the said archbishop, bishop or ordinary, which said oaths and declarations, the said archbishop, bishop or ordinary, are hereby empowered to administer and receive; and such archbishops, bishops, and ordinaries, are required to file such certificates, and keep an exact register of the same. . .

And be it further enacted that any person who shall have obtained a licence and subscribed the oaths, as above appointed, and shall at any time after, during the time of his or their keeping any public or private school or seminary, or instructing any youth as tutor or schoolmaster, knowingly or willingly, resort to any conventicle within England, Wales, or town of Berwick upon Tweed, for the exercise of religion in any other manner than according to the liturgy and practice of the Church of England, or shall be present at any meeting although the liturgy be there used, where Her Majesty (whom God long preserve) and the Elector of Brunswick, shall not there be prayed for in express words, according to the liturgy of the Church of England, except where such particular offices of the liturgy are used, wherein there are no express directions to pray for Her Majesty and the royal family, shall thenceforth be incapable of keeping any public or private school or seminary, or instructing any youth as tutor or schoolmaster.

And be it further enacted that it shall be lawful, to and for the bishop of the diocese, or other proper ordinary, to cite any person or persons whatsoever, keeping school or seminary, or teaching without a licence, as aforesaid, and to proceed against, and punish such person or persons by ecclesiastical censure, subject to such appeals as in cases of ordinary jurisdiction; this Act or any other law to the contrary notwithstanding.

Provided also, That the penalties in this Act shall not extend to any foreigner, or alien of the foreign reformed churches, allowed, by the Queen's Majesty, her heirs or successors, in England, for instructing or teaching any child or children of any such foreigner or alien only, as a tutor or schoolmaster.

Provided always, that if any person who shall have been convicted, as aforesaid, shall, after such conviction, conform to the Church of England, for the space of one year, and receive the sacrament of the Lord's Supper according to the rites and usage of the Church of England at least three times in that year, every such person or persons shall be again capable of having and using a licence to teach school, or to instruct youth as a tutor or schoolmaster, he or they also performing all that is made requisite thereunto by this Act . . .

[From 13 Anne, c. 7]

5. Bishop Hoadly's sermon: 'Christ's Kingdom is not of this world', 1717

The cause of the Bangorian controversy, named after the diocese over which Hoadly presided, was a sermon by Bishop Benjamin Hoadly. Hoadly's sermon was assumed to mean that he did not believe that there should be a Church with any authority. The Bangorian controversy lasted for over three years, and its ferocity was such that Convocation had to be silenced to prevent attacks on the King's favourite bishop. The sermon also formed part of a series of discussions during the century on the nature of relations between the Church and State. There is little doubt that Hoadly saw the privileges of the Church of England as discriminating against dissenters, and that his sermon was a means of emphasizing that view.

'Jesus answered, My Kingdom is not of this World.' St John xviii. 36.
. . .I have chosen those words, in which our Lord himself declared the nature of his own Kingdom. This Kingdom of Christ, is the same with the Church of Christ. And the notion of the Church of Christ, which, at first, was only the number, small or great, of those who believed Him to be the Messiah or of those who subjected themselves to Him, as their King, in the affair of religion; having since that time been so diversified by the various alterations it hath undergone, that it is almost impossible so much as to number up the many inconsistent images that have come, by daily additions, to be united together in it: nothing, I think, can be more useful, than to consider the same thing, under some other image, which hath not been so much used; nor consequently so much defaced. And since the image of His Kingdom, is that, under which our Lord himself chose to represent it: we may be sure that, if we sincerely examine our notion of his Church, by what He saith of his Kingdom, that it is not of this world, we shall exclude

out of it, everything that he would have excluded; and then, what remains will be true, pure, and uncorrupted. And what I have to say, in order to this, will be comprehended under two general heads.

I. As the Church of Christ is the Kingdom of Christ, He himself is King: and in this it is implied, that He is himself the sole law-giver to his subjects, and himself the sole judge of their behaviour, in the affairs of conscience and eternal salvation. And in this sense therefore, His Kingdom is not of this world; that He hath, in those points, left behind Him, no visible, human authority no vicegerents, who can be said properly to supply his place; no interpreters, upon whom his subjects are absolutely to depend; no judges over the consciences or religion of his people. For if this were so, that any such absolute vicegerent authority, either for the making new laws, or interpreting old ones, or judging his subjects, in religious matters, were lodged in any men upon earth; the consequence would be, that what still retains the name of the Church of Christ, would not be the Kingdom of Christ, but the Kingdom of those men, vested with such authority. For, who ever hath such an authority of making laws, is so far a King: and whoever can add new laws to those of Christ, equally obligatory, is as truly a King, as Christ himself is: nay, who ever hath an absolute authority to interpret any written or spoken laws; it is He, who is truly the law-giver to all intents and purposes; and not the person who first wrote, or spoke them.

In human society, the interpretation of laws may, of necessity, be lodged, in some cases, in the hands of those who were not originally the legislators. But this is not absolute; nor of bad consequence to society: because the legislators can resume the interpretation into their own hands, as they are witnesses to what passes in the world; and as they can, and will, sensibly interpose in all those cases, in which their interposition becomes necessary. And therefore, they are still properly the legislators. But it is otherwise in religion, or the Kingdom of Christ. He himself never interposeth, since his first promulgation of his law, either to convey infallibility to such as pretend to handle it over again; or to assert the true interpretation of it, amidst the various and contradictory opinions of men about it. If he did certainly thus interpose, He himself would still be the legislator. But, as He doth not; if such an absolute authority be once lodged with men, under the notion of interpreters, they then become the legislators, and not Christ; and they rule in their own kingdom, and not in His.

It is the same thing, as to rewards and punishments, to carry forward the great end of his Kingdom, if any men upon earth have a right to add to the sanctions of his laws; that is to increase the number, or alter the nature, of the rewards and punishments of his subjects, in matters of conscience, or salvation: they are so far kings in his stead; and reign in their own kingdom, and not in His, so it is, whenever they erect tribunals, and exercise a judgement over the consciences of men; and assume to themselves the determination of such points, as cannot be determined, but by one who knows the hearts; or, when they make any of their own declarations, or decisions, to concern and affect the state of Christ's subjects, with regard to the favour of God: this is so far, the taking Christ's Kingdom out of His hands, and placing it in their own. . .

II. The next principal point is, that, if the Church be the Kingdom of Christ; and this Kingdom be not of this world: this must appear from the nature and end of the laws of Christ, and of those rewards and punishments, which are the sanctions of his laws. Now his laws are declarations, relating to the favour of God in another state after this. They are declarations of those conditions to be perform'd, in this world, on our part, without which God will not make us happy in that to come. And they are almost all general appeals to the will of that God; to his nature, known by the common reason of mankind; and to the imitation of that nature, which must be our perfection. The keeping his commandments is declared the way to life; and the doing his will, the entrance into the Kingdom of Heaven, the being subjects to Christ, is to this very end, that we may the better and more effectually perform the will of God. The laws of this Kingdom, therefore, as Christ left them, have nothing of this world in their view no tendency, either to the exaltation of some, in worldly pomp and dignity; or to their absolute dominion over the faith and religious conduct of others of his subjects; or to the erecting of any sort of temporal kingdom, under the covert and name of a spiritual one. . .

For, if the very essence of God's worship be spirit and truth; if religion be virtue and charity, under the belief of a supreme governor and judge; if true real faith cannot be the effect of force; and, if there can be no reward where there is no willing choice: then, in all or any of these cases, to apply force or flattery, worldly pleasure or pain; is to act contrary to the interests of true religion, as it is plainly opposite to the maxims upon which Christ founded His Kingdom; who chose the motives which are not of this world, to support a Kingdom which is not of this world. And indeed, it is too visible to be hid, that wherever the rewards and punishments are changed, from future to present, from the world to come, to the world now in possession; there, the Kingdom founded by our Saviour is, in the nature of it, so far changed, that it is become, in such a degree, what He professed His Kingdom was not: that is, of this world; of the same sort with other common earthly kingdoms, in which the rewards are, worldly honours, posts, offices, pomp, attendance, dominion; and the punishments are, prisons, fines, banishments, gallies and racks; or something less, of the same sort.

If these can be the true supports of a kingdom which is not of this world; then sincerity, and hypocrisy; religion, and no religion; force, and persuasion; a willing choice, and a terrified heart; are become the same things: truth and falsehood stand in need of the same methods, to propagate and support them; and our Saviour himself was little acquainted with the right way of increasing the number of such subjects, as He wished for. If he had but at first enlighten'd the powers of this world, as He did St Paul; and employed the sword which they bore, and the favours they had in their hands, to bring subjects into his Kingdom; this had been an expeditious and an effectual way, according to the conduct of some of his professed followers, to have had a glorious and extensive Kingdom, or Church, but this was not his design; could be compassed in quite a different way. . .

I will only make two or three observations, grounded upon this: and so conclude.

1. From what hath been said it is very plain, in general, that the grossest mistakes in judgement, about the nature of Christ's Kingdom, or Church, have arisen from hence, that men have argued from other visible societies, and other visible kingdoms of this world, to what ought to be visible, and sensible, in His Kingdom: constantly leaving out of their notion, the most essential part of it, that Christ is King in his own Kingdom; forgetting this King himself, because He is not now seen by mortal eyes; and substituting others in his place, as law-givers and judges, in the same points, in which He must either alone, or not at all, be law-giver and judge; not contented with such a Kingdom as He established, and desires to reign in; but urging and contending, that His Kingdom must be like other kingdoms . . .

2. From what hath been said it appears that the Kingdom of Christ, which is the Church of Christ, is the number of persons who are sincerely, and willingly subjects to Him, as law-giver and judge, in all matters truly relating to conscience, or eternal salvation. And the more

close and immediate this regard to Him is, the more certainly and the more evidently true it is, that they are of his Kingdom. . .

3. This will be another observation, that it evidently destroys the rule and authority of Jesus Christ, as King, to set up any other authority in His Kingdom, to which His subjects are indispensably and absolutely obliged to submit their consciences, or their conduct, in what is properly called religion. There are some professed Christians, who contend openly for such an authority, as indispensably obliges all around them to unity of profession; that is, to profess even what they do not, what they cannot, believe to be true, this sounds so grossly, that others, who think they act a glorious part in opposing such an enormity, are very willing, for their own sakes, to retain such an authority, as shall oblige men, whatever they themselves think, though not to profess what they do not believe, yet, to forbear the profession and publication of what they do believe, let them believe it of never so great importance. . .

The peace of Christ's Kingdom is a manly and reasonable peace; built upon charity, and love, and mutual forbearance, and receiving one another, as God receives us. As for any other peace; founded upon a submission of our honesty, as well as our understandings; it is falsely so called. It is not the peace of the Kingdom of Christ; but the lethargy of it: and a sleep unto death, when his subjects shall throw off their relation to Him; fix their subjection to others; and even in cases, where they have a right to see, and where they think they see, his will otherwise, shall shut their eyes and go blindfold at the command of others; because those others are not pleas'd with their enquiries into the will of their great Lord and Judge.

To conclude, the Church of Christ is the Kingdom of Christ. He is King in his own Kingdom. He is sole law-giver to his subjects, and sole judge, in matters relating to salvation. His laws and sanctions are plainly fixed: and relate to the favour of God, and not at all to the rewards, or penalties, of this world, all his subjects are equally his subjects; and, as such, equally without authority to alter, to add to, or to interpret, his laws so as to claim the absolute submission of others to such interpretation. And all are His subjects, and in his Kingdom, who are ruled and governed by Him, their faith was once delivered by Him. The conditions of their happiness were once laid down by Him. The nature of God's worship was once declared by Him. And it is easy to judge, whether of the two is most becoming a subject of the Kingdom of Christ, that is, a member of his Church; to seek all these particulars

in those plain and short declarations of their King and law-giver himself:
or to hunt after them thro' the infinite contradictions, the numberless
perplexities, the endless disputes, of weak men, in several ages, till the
enquirer himself is lost in the labyrinth, and perhaps sits down in despair,
or infidelity. If Christ be our King, let us show ourselves subjects to
Him alone, in the great affair of conscience and eternal salvation: and,
without fear of man's judgement, live and act as becomes those who
wait for the appearance of an all-knowing and impartial judge; even
that King, whose Kingdom is not of this World.

[A sermon preached before the King at the Chapel Royal, St
James's on Sunday 31 March 1717]

6. William Law's response to Hoadly: Church authority is real but conditional, 1717

Part of the Bangorian controversy, Law's *Letter to the Bishop of Bangor*, from
which the following extract is taken, sought to challenge Hoadly's view that
there was no visible authority left on earth by Christ. Law asserted that there
was a visible authority left on earth, and that the scriptures and the works of
the Apostles were evidence of it. But Law denied that the authority was
absolute, claiming instead that it was a conditional authority. Law's response
to Hoadly makes clear exactly how Hoadly's views impacted on the nature of
English government.

. . .Here you make nothing of that authority which is not absolute; and
yet you think it hard to be told that you have taken away all Church
authority, that which is absolute you expressly deny. And here you say,
that which is not absolute is nothing at all, where then is the authority
you have left? Or how is it that Christ has impower'd any one to act
in His name? Your Lordship fights safe under the protection of the word
absolute; but your aim is at all Church power. And your Lordship makes
too hasty an inference, that because it is not absolute, it is none at all.
If you ask, where you have made this inference, it is on occasion of the
above-mentioned where your Lordship makes it an insignificant which
is only to be obey'd so long as it is not contrary to Scripture.

Your Lordship seems to think, all is lost, as to Church power because
the Doctor does not claim an absolute one; but allows it to be subject
to Scripture: as if all authority was absolute, or else nothing at all. I shall
therefore consider the nature of this Church power, and show, that
though it is not absolute, yet it is a real authority, and is not such a mere

notion as your Lordship makes it. An absolute authority, according to your Lordship is what is to be always obeyed by every individual that is subject to it, in all circumstances. This is an authority that we utterly deny to the Church, but, I presume, there may be an authority inferior to this, which is nevertheless, a real authority, and is to be esteemed as such, and that for these reasons:

First, I hope, it will be allow'd me, that our Saviour came into the world with authority. But it was not lawful for the Jews to receive him, if they thought his appearance not agreeable to those marks and characters they had of him in their Scriptures, may I not here say, my Lord, glorious authority of Christ indeed, to which the Jews ow'd no obedience, till they had examined their Scriptures; and then they obey, not Him, but them!

Again, the Apostles were sent into the world with authority. But yet, those who thought their doctrines unworthy of God, and unsuitable to the principles of natural religion, were obliged not to obey them. Glorious authority indeed, of the Apostles, to whom mankind ow'd no obedience, till they had first examin'd their own notions of God and religion; and then they obeyed, not the Apostles, but them. I hope, my Lord, it may be allow'd, that the Sacraments are real means of grace: but it is certain, they are only conditionally so, if those that partake of them, are endowed with suitable dispositions of piety and virtue. Glorious means of grace of the Sacraments, which is only obtained by such pious dispositions; and then it is owing to the dispositions, and not the Sacraments, now, my Lord, if there can be such a thing as instituted real means of grace, which are only conditionally as instituted real means of Grace, which are only conditionally apply'd, I cannot see, why there may not be an instituted real authority in the Church, which is only to be conditionally obey'd.

Your Lordship has written a great many elaborate pages to prove the English government limited; and that no obedience is due to it, but whilst it preserves our fundamentals; and, I suppose, the people are to judge for themselves, whether these are safe, or not. Glorious authority of the English government, which is to be obeyed no longer than the people think it their interest to obey it.

Will your Lordship say there is no authority in the English government, because only a conditional obedience is due to it, whilst we think it supports our fundamentals? Why then must the Church authority be reckoned nothing at all, because only a rational conditional obedience is to be paid, whilst we think it not contrary to Scripture? Is a limited, conditional government in the State, such a wise, excellent, and glorious constitution? And is the same authority in the Church, such absurdity, nonsense, and nothing at all, as to any actual Power?

If there be such a thing as obedience upon rational motives, there must be such a thing as authority that is not absolute, or that does not require a blind, implicit obedience. Indeed, rational creatures can obey no other authority; they must have reasons for what they do. And yet because the Church claims only this rational obedience, your Lordship explodes such authority as none at all.

Yet it must be granted, that no other obedience was due to the prophets, or our Saviour and his Apostles: they were only to be obey'd by those who thought their doctrines worthy of God, so that if the Church has no authority, because we must first consult the Scriptures, before we obey it; neither our Saviour, nor his Apostles, had any authority, because the Jews were first to consult their Scriptures, and the heathen their reason, before they obey'd 'em. And yet this is all that is said against Church-authority; that because they are to judge of the lawfulness of its injunctions, therefore they owe it no obedience: which false conclusion, I hope, is enough exposed.

[From W. Law, *Letter to the Bishop of Bangor.* . . (London, 1717)]

7. William Warburton's view of the alliance between Church and State, 1736

Warburton, later Bishop of Gloucester, was a controversial writer opposing Wesley, Lowth and others during his career. His greatest work, *The Alliance between Church and State*, was sufficiently popular for it to run to over a dozen editions during the nineteenth century. Looking back at the post-Revolutionary Convention parliament, Warburton's view was derived from Locke, that the Church was a voluntary society. He held that the Church was independent of the State, but in alliance with it for their mutual benefit. An example of such a benefit was the Test Act, enacted by the State to protect the Church.

The Nature of the Union between Church and State

The conferring on the supreme magistrate, the title of head of the Church, is by no means our holy religion. This title hath been misrepresented by the enemies of our happy establishment, as the setting up a legislator, in Christ's Kingdom, in the place of Christ, but it hath been shown, that no other jurisdiction is given to the civil magistrate by this supremacy than the Church, as a mere political body, exercised before the Convention . . .

The aim of the State being, agreeable to its nature, utility, and the aim of the Church, agreeable to hers, truth, from whence we may observe, that as these privileges all took their rise, by necessary consequence from the fundamental article of the Convention, which was, that the Church should serve the State, and the State protect the Church; so they receive all possible addition of strength, from their mutual dependency on one another. This we have cause to desire may be received as a certain mark that our plan of alliance is no precarious arbitrary hypothesis, but a theory founded in reason, and the unvariable nature of things. For having, from the real essence of the two societies, collected the necessity of allying, and the freedom of the compact; we have, from the necessity, fairly introduced it; and, from its freedom, consequentially established every mutual term, and condition of it, so that now if the reader should ask, 'where this charter, or treaty of convention for the union of the two societies, on the terms here delivered, is to be met with', we are enabled to answer him. We say, it may be found in the same archive with the famous original compact between magistrate and people, so much insisted on, in vindication of the common rights of subjects. . .

A Test Law Justified

The necessity of a national religion was, till of late, one of the most uncontested principles in politics. The practice of all nations and the opinions of all writers concurred to give it credit. To collect what the best and wisest authors of antiquity, where the consent was universal, have said in favour of a rational religion, would be endless. We shall content ourselves with the opinion of two modern writers in its favour: who, being professed advocates for the common rights of mankind, will, we suppose, have a favourable hearing, 'This (says one of them) was ancient policy (viz, the union of the civil and religious interests) and hence it is necessary that the people should have a public leading in religion for to deny the magistrate a worship, or take away a national Church, is as mere enthusiasm as the notion which sets up persecution.'

'Toward keeping mankind in order (says the other) it is necessary there should be some religion professed and even established.' Indeed not many, even now, will directly deny this necessity; tho', by employing such arguments against a test as hold equally against an establishment, they open a way, tho' a little more oblique, to this conclusion. But it is that unavoidable consequence of an established Church, in every place where there are diversities of religions, a test law, which makes the judgements of so many revolt; and choose rather to give up an establishment than receive it with this tyrannical attendant. Tho' it appears, at first view, so evident that, when a Church and State are in union, he that cannot give security for his behaviour to both, may with as much reason be deprived of some civil advantages, as he, who, before the union, could not give security to the State alone.

The matter, therefore, of greatest concern remains to be enquired into; namely, how the equity of a test law can be deduced from those principles of the law of nature and nations, by which we have so clearly proved the justice of an established religion. But here, as before in the case of an establishment, it is not our purpose to defend this or that national form or mode, but a test law in general. By which I understand some sufficient proof or evidence required from those admitted into the administration of public affairs, of their being members of the religion established by law.

And, in showing the justice, equity, and necessity of a test law, I shall proceed in the manner I set out, and have hitherto preserved, of deducing all my conclusions, in a continued chain of reasoning, from the simple principles at first laid down.

Hitherto I have considered that alliance, between Church and State, which produces an establishment, only under its more simple form, i.e. where there is but one religion in the State. But it may so happen, that, either at the time of Convention, or afterwards, there may be more than one.

If there be more than one at the time of Convention, the State allies itself with the largest of those religious societies, it is fit the State should do so, because the larger the religious society is, where there is an equality in other points, the better enabled it will be to answer the ends of an alliance; as having the greatest number under its influence, it is scarce possible it should do otherwise; because the two societies being composed of the same individuals, the greatly prevailing religion must have a majority of its members in the assemblies of State; who will naturally prefer their own religion to any other.

With this religion is the alliance made; and a full toleration given to the rest; yet under the restriction of a test law, to keep them from hurting that which is established. . .

> [From W. Warburton, *The Alliance between Church and State*. . .
> (London, 1736)]

8. William Paley's view of an established Church justified by utilitarian ideas, 1785

Archdeacon William Paley of Carlisle wrote *The Principles of Morals and Political Philosophy* in 1785, and received £1,000 for the manuscript. The book was a popular textbook at Cambridge for years and presaged the utilitarian views of the nineteenth century, though unlike Bentham he believed in a supernatural sanction. In this work he advanced the view that the idea of a State Church was one which benefited both the Church and the State and this alone justified the concept.

. . .The authority therefore of a Church establishment is founded in its utility, and whenever, upon this principle, we deliberate concerning the form, propriety, or comparative excellency of different establishments, the single view, under which we ought to consider any one of them, is that of a 'scheme of instruction': the single end we ought to propose by them is, 'the preservation and communication of religious knowledge'. Every other idea, and every other end that have been mixed with this, as the making of the Church an engine, or even an ally of the State; converting it into the means of strengthening or of diffusing influence; or regarding it as a support of regal in opposition to popular forms of government, have served only to debase the institution, and to introduce into it numerous corruptions and abuses.

The argument, then, by which ecclesiastical establishments are defended, proceeds by these steps. The knowledge and profession of Christianity cannot be upheld without a clergy; a clergy cannot be supported without a legal provision; a legal provision for the clergy cannot be constituted without the preference of one sect of Christians to the rest: and the conclusion will be satisfactory in the degree in which the truth of these several propositions can be made out.

If it be deemed expedient to establish a national religion, that is to say, one sect in preference to all others, some test, by which the teachers of that sect may be distinguished from the teachers of different sects, appears to be an indispensable consequence. The existence of such an establishment supposes it: the very notion of a national religion includes that of a test. But this necessity, which is real, hath, according to the fashion of human affairs, furnished to almost every Church a pretence for extending, multiplying and continuing such tests beyond what the occasion justified. For though some purposes of order and tranquillity may be answered by the establishment of creeds and confessions, yet they are at all times attended with serious inconveniences. They check enquiry; they violate liberty; they ensnare the consciences of the clergy by holding out temptations to prevarication; however they may express the persuasion, or be accommodated to the controversies, or to the fears of the age in which they are composed, in process of time, and by reason of the changes which are wont to take place in the judgement of mankind upon religious subjects, they come at length to contradict the actual opinions of the Church, whose doctrines they profess to contain; and they often perpetuate the proscription of sects and tenets, from which any danger has long ceased to be apprehended. . .

After the State has once established a particular system of faith as a national religion, a question will soon occur, concerning the treatment and toleration of those who dissent from it. This question is properly preceded by another, concerning the right which the civil magistrate possesses to interfere in matters of religion at all: for although this right be acknowledged whilst he is employed solely in providing means of public instruction, it will probably be disputed, indeed it ever has been, when he proceeds to inflict penalties, to impose restraints or incapacities, on the account of religious distinctions. They who acknowledge no other just original of civil government, than what is founded in some stipulation with its subjects, are at liberty to contend that the concerns of religion were excepted out of the social compact; that in an affair which can only be transacted between God and a man's own conscience, no commission or authority was ever delegated to the civil magistrate, or could indeed be transferred from the person himself to any other. We, however, who have rejected this theory, because we cannot discover any actual contract between the State and the people, and because we cannot allow an arbitrary fiction to be made the foundation of real rights and of real obligations, find ourselves precluded from this distinction. The reasoning which deduces the authority of civil government from the will of God, and which collects that will from public expediency alone, binds us to the unreserved conclusion, that the jurisdiction of the magistrate is limited by no consideration but that of general utility in plainer terms, that whatever be the subject to be regulated, it is lawful for him to interfere, whenever his interference, in its general tendency, appears to be conducive to the common interest. . .

The justice and expediency of toleration we found primarily in its conduciveness to truth, and in the superior value of truth to that of any other quality which a religion can possess: this is the principal argument; but there are some auxiliary considerations too important to be omitted. The confining of the subject to the religion of the State, is a needless violation of natural liberty, and in an instance in which constraint is always grievous. Persecution produces no sincere conviction, nor any real change of opinion; on the contrary, it vitiates the public morals, by driving men to prevarication, and commonly ends in a general though secret infidelity, by imposing, under the name of revealed religion, systems of doctrine which men cannot believe, and dare not examine: finally, it disgraces the character, and wounds the reputation of Christianity itself, by making it the author of oppression, cruelty, and bloodshed.

Under the idea of religious toleration I include the toleration of all books of serious argumentation; but I deem it no infringement of religious liberty to restrain the circulation of ridicule, invective, and mockery upon religious subjects; because this species of writing applies solely to the passions, weakens the judgement, and contaminates the imagination or its readers; has no tendency whatever to assist either the investigation or the impression of truth; on the contrary, whilst it stays not to distinguish the character or authority of different religions, it destroys alike the influence of all.

Concerning the admission of dissenters from the established religion to offices and employments in the public service, which is necessary to render toleration complete, doubts have been entertained with some appearance of reason. It is possible that such religious opinions may be holden as are utterly incompatible with the necessary functions of civil government; and which opinions consequently disqualify those who maintain them from exercising any share in its administration. There have been enthusiasts who held that Christianity has abolished all distinction of property, and that she enjoins upon her followers a community of goods. With what tolerable propriety could one of this sect be appointed a judge or a magistrate, whose office it is to decide upon questions of private right, and to protect men in the exclusive enjoyment of their property? It would be equally absurd to entrust a military command to a Quaker, who believes it to be contrary to the Gospel to take up arms. This is possible; therefore it cannot be laid down as an universal truth, that religion is not in its nature a cause which will justify exclusion from public employments. When we examine, however, the sects of Christianity which actually prevail in the world, we must confess, that with the single exception of refusing to bear arms, we find no tenet in any of them, which incapacitates men for the service of the State. It has indeed been asserted that discordancy of religions, even supposing each religion to be free from any errors, that affect the safety or the conduct of government, is enough to render men unfit to act together in public stations. But upon what argument, or upon what experience is this assertion founded? I perceive no reason why men of different religious persuasions may not sit upon the same bench, deliberate in the same council, or fight in the same ranks, as well as men of various opposite opinions upon any controverted topic of natural philosophy, history, or ethics . . .

The result of our examination of those general tendencies, by which every interference of civil government in matters of religion ought to be tried, is this: 'That a comprehensive national religion, guarded by a few articles of peace and conformity, together with a legal provision for the clergy of that religion; and with a complete toleration of all dissenters from the established Church, without any other limitation or exception, than what arises from the conjunction of dangerous political dispositions with certain religious tenets, appears to be, not only the most just and liberal, but the wisest and safest system, which a State can adopt: in as much as it unites the several perfections which a religious constitution ought to aim at – liberty of conscience with means of instruction; the progress of truth with the peace of society; the right of private judgement with the care of the public safety'.

[From: W. Paley, *The Principles of Morals and Political Philosophy*
(London, 1785)]

RELIGION OUTSIDE THE ESTABLISHMENT

1. The concern of the Anglican clergy, 1692 and 1698

The two letters presented here were received by Archbishop John Sharp of York from clergy in his diocese. Their concerns are those which must have confronted many Anglican clergy, and suggest some of the problems confronting Anglican clergy. The first, from the Revd Robert Banks, is concerned with the time taken for the reading of banns three times, and the attraction to parishioners to migrate to be married by nonconformist ministers. The second letter, from the Revd William Stephenson, is concerned with how best he should try to convert a Quaker to Anglicanism. The reply of Archbishop Sharp to these enquiries has not survived.

1.

Hull, March 6, 1692

May it please your Grace;

I hope your Grace will pardon me, if beg your Grace's advice in a matter that relates to the discharge of my duty. In short the case is this: there have been several couples since I came to this parish who have had the matrimonial banns thrice published, and because they are not asked out before the prohibited times in which the ecclesiastical court will now allow us to marry them without licence; they have upon our refusal gone to be married by the nonconformist minister, whereby we not only lose our dues, but usually our parishioners too, who are too often by this means seduced to a coventicle.

I have at present several persons in my parish that were published the third time last Sunday, and some of them came this morning to desire me to marry them, telling me that if according to the laws of

God and the Church (having been thrice published) they could not be married here, they must take some other course, and if it proved sinful, it would lie at my door; I desired them to stay till next Monday at which time I would give them an answer (whether they will do so, or no, I know not) but if I then comply not with their desire (which I dare not do without your Grace's permission) I fear they will, in this time of liberty, desert our communion as others have done on the like occasion. I know I may cite them and run them to an excommunication, but that only fixes them in their separation and renders the regaining them next to impossible.

My Lord, I am as tender of infringing the wholesome laws and constitutions of this excellent Church, as any person whatsoever, but really, my Lord, I understand not on what Canon of our Church, or law of the land this prohibition is founded; I suppose on neither but upon an old Canon of the Church of Rome and published about the same time the clergy were prohibited marriage. . . Or if it be forbidden by the Church of England I know not why upon every trifling occasion it should be dispensed with (as 'tis daily by the surrogates who grant licences) contrary to the constitutions: Eliz: 1597. Or if it may be so dispensed as *I* desire much more reasonable at this time, especially when a too rigorous insisting upon this ill-grounded custom will give men great opportunities of forsaking our Church and running into Schism. . .

May it please your Grace, your Grace's most dutiful and obliged humble servant,
Robert Banks

2.

[A leading nonconformist] is lately returned from London, and has brought a wife among us; and is so great a bigot that (as I am informed since the Visitation) he by the assistance of his brotherhood at Pontefract Sessions (being the 3rd of May) has obtained an order for a meeting house in our town, which I fear may be of dangerous consequence. I was under some apprehension of this before, and the method I resolved upon about it was this: first to discourse the young man privately and by clear proofs from the Holy Scripture, and the force of reason to endeavour to convince him of his errors and seduce him to his duty. This attempt I have frequently made, but altogether in vain, and my ill success herein has discouraged me from hopes of better success from the second which was this: to desire the presence and assistance of some neighbouring ministers at the Quakers' first great meeting to see if they could prevail upon any of the Quakers to renounce their errors, or discourage the fraternity from meeting. But considering the prejudices these weak people labour under, and their obstinate deafness to all reason and arguments which make against the errors, I am afraid this will do them as little service as the former; and therefore the last thing I resolved to do was this: to take along with me to the meeting two or three of the ablest men and best affected to the Church in my parish, and before these to expose the errors and enthusiasm of these schismatics, and to show them what little reason they or any other in my parish have to leave our Church and herd with such unreasonable creatures.

But before I proceed any further herein, I humbly desire your Lordship's direction and assistance, and whatever you shall please to command shall be religiously observed by

My Lord, your most dutiful son and most obedient servant
William Stephenson
Rawmarsh
May 10, 1698

> [From A. T. Hart, *The Eighteenth Century Country Parson* (Shrewsbury: Wilding & Sons, 1955)]

2. Numbers of dissenters in early eighteenth-century England and Wales: Dr Evans's list, 1715

The second column in Table 4.1 was compiled by Dr John Evans about 1715; the data in the first column are derived from estimates made from the baptismal registers of dissenting congregations. The information is perhaps as problematic as helpful, since it often excludes Quakers and other smaller denominations as well as some of the smaller communities; nevertheless these figures are the best available evidence of the strength and regional distribution of dissent in the period. A more detailed estimate of dissenter numbers by denomination is provided in Tables 4.2 and 4.3, taken from Michael Watts's modern study.

Table 4.1   Comparison between the evidence of the dissenting
registers and the Evans list

	Size of community estimated from baptismal registers	Number of hearers according to Evans MS
Berkshire		
Newbury, Independent (1710–14, 1716–20)	473	400
Cambridgeshire		
Cambridge, Independent (1710–14,1716–29)	485	1100
Cheshire		
Hyde, Presbyterian (1711–21)	548	674
Macclesfield, Presbyterian (1719–28)	437	500
Cumberland		
Hudlesceugh, Independent (1703–12)	373	235
Denbigh		
Wrexham, Presbyterian (1713–17)	313	230
Devon		
Chudleigh, Presbyterian (1712–21)	270	250
Honiton, Presbyterian (1701–10)	590	600
Moretonhampstead, Presbyterian (1710–19)	767	600
Plymouth, Presbyterian (1720–29)	357	500
Tavistock, Presbyterian (1710–19)	393	600
Durham		
Sunderland, Presbyterian (1720–29)	487	400
Essex		
Brentwood, Presbyterian (1710–19)	323	300
Rookwood Hall, Presbyterian (1710–19)	393	500
Gloucestershire		
Stroud, Independent (1716–25)	303	500
Hampshire		
Gosport, Independent (1710–19)	1497	1000
Portsmouth, Presbyterian (1710–19)	730	800
Herefordshire		
Bromyard, Presbyterian (1710–19)	107	200
Hereford, Presbyterian (1720–29)	147	150
Kent		
Canterbury, Presbyterian (1712–20)	133	500
Dover, Presbyterian (1711–18)	362	300
Lancashire		
Chipping and Newton-in-Bowland (Yorks), Presbyterian (1711–17, 1719, 1721–22)	493	150
Elswick, Presbyterian (1718–27)	227	290
Leicestershire		
Hinckley, Presbyterian (1710–19)	607	480
Leicester, Presbyterian and Independent (1713–22)	647	580
Lincolnshire		
Gainsborough, Independent (1710–19)	253	250

	Size of community	Number of hearers
London		
Bethnal Green, Presbyterian (1716–25)	57	200
Hand Alley, Presbyterian (1710–19)	1180	1000
Monmouthshire		
Abergavenny, Independent (1719–22)	150	280
Nottinghamshire		
Nottingham, Presbyterian (1710–19)	1100	1400
Nottingham, Independent (1713–22)	470	468
Oxfordshire		
Henley, Independent (1720–29)	317	450
Shropshire		
Oldbury, Presbyterian (1716–17, 1719–25)	370	400
Shrewsbury, Independent (1696–1705)	220	150
Whitchurch, Presbyterian (1709–11)	392	300
Somerset		
Bath, Presbyterian (1720–29)	220	300
Bristol, Broadmead and Pithay Baptist, burials (1710–19)	1573	1200
South Petherton, Presbyterian (1704–13)	683	450
Taunton, Presbyterian (1717–26)	933	2000
Staffordshire		
Tamworth, Presbyterian (1715–24)	147	180
Suffolk		
Bury St Edmunds, Presbyterian (1710–19)	600	700
Debenham, Presbyterian (1710–19)	347	250
Hadleigh, Presbyterian (1710–19)	167	250
Ipswich, Independent (1722–31)	530	500
Sudbury, Presbyterian (1710–18)	370	400
Walpole, Independent (1710–13, 1717–22)	503	350
Woodbridge, Independent (1714–22)	400	350
Wrentham, Independent (1706–15)	150	400
Surrey		
Dorking, Presbyterian (1711–1827)	357	200
Mortlake, Presbyterian (1720–29)	130	100
Sussex		
Brighton, Presbyterian (1710–19)	680	560
Westmorland		
Kendal, Presbyterian (1710–13, 1720–25)	207	100
Yorkshire		
Cottingham and Swanland, Independent (1713–20)	795	800
Leeds, Independent (1700–9)	417	800
Northowram, Presbyterian (1710–19)	853	500
Sheffield, Presbyterian (1726–35)	943	1163
Stannington, Independent (1719–28)	257	350

Table 4.2   Estimates of dissenting numbers in early eighteenth-century England

		Presbyterians			Independents		
	Estimated Population	*No. of congs.*	*Hearers*	*% of population*	*No. of congs.*	*Hearers*	*% of population*
Bedfordshire	54,760	0	0	0.00	2	1600	2.92
Berkshire	76,280	13	3070	4.02	3	960	1.26
Buckinghamshire	83,420	9	2580	3.09	1	500	0.60
Cambridgeshire	80,950	6	1480	1.83	9	2410	2.98
Cheshire	111,700	18	8100	7.25	0	0	0.00
Cornwall	116,970	11	1190	1.02	1	350	0.30
Cumberland	67,730	9	1360	2.01	2	550	0.81
Derbyshire	103,720	25	4270	4.12	2	550	0.53
Devon	253,150	57	18,220	7.20	7	3580	1.41
Dorset	89,550	20	5090	5.68	2	880	0.98
Durham	85,500	6	1270	1.49	0	0	0.00
Essex	169,570	22	7730	4.56	13	6420	3.79
Gloucestershire	137,790	16	4360	3.16	9	1660	1.20
Hampshire	124,670	14	4400	3.53	10	2500	2.01
Herefordshire	71,440	7	1190	1.67	1	200	0.28
Hertfordshire	76,630	6	1690	2.21	6	2500	3.26
Huntingdonshire	38,320	1	500	1.30	4	940	2.45
Kent	193,310	19	4990	2.58	3	600	0.31
Lancashire	196,120	42	16,630	8.48	3	1370	0.70
Leicestershire	88,090	17	2750	3.12	5	1400	1.59
Lincolnshire	192,620	9	1510	0.78	1	250	0.13
Middlesex and London	581,180	38	13,480	2.32	23	6280	1.08
Monmouthshire	29,200	0	0	0.00	9	1180	4.04
Norfolk	233,450	5	1930	0.83	11	3870	1.66
Northamptonshire	116,350	6	2550	2.19	13	4500	3.87
Northumberland	121,660	23	6570	5.40	3	1150	0.95
Nottinghamshire	79,590	14	3420	4.30	3	850	1.07
Oxfordshire	86,930	8	2600	2.99	1	450	0.52
Rutland	15,580	2	370	2.37	0	0	0.00
Shropshire	114,200	8	1620	1.42	1	150	0.13
Somerset	201,090	48	13,630	6.78	2	500	0.25
Bristol	28,170	2	2100	7.45	1	500	1.77
Staffordshire	112,560	25	4560	4.05	0	0	0.00
Suffolk	184,380	16	4590	2.68	16	4200	2.28
Surrey and Southwark	168,360	14	4870	2.89	10	2110	1.25
Sussex	101,220	16	2360	2.33	5	850	0.84
Warwickshire	100,510	12	3700	3.68	2	440	0.44
Westmorland	29,680	3	330	1.11	2	290	0.98
Wiltshire	122,650	16	4780	3.90	4	790	0.64
Worcestershire	101,420	8	2880	2.84	1	40	0.04
Yorkshire	501,200	46	10,270	2.05	12	2570	0.51
Totals	5,441,670	637	179,350	3.30	203	59,940	1.10

Particular Baptists			General Baptists			Quakers		
No. of congs.	Hearers	% of population	No. of congs.	Hearers	% of population	No. of congs.	Hearers	% of population
15	2830	5.17	2	120	0.22	9	560	1.02
6	1290	1.69	1	200	0.26	12	610	0.80
6	790	0.95	8	1050	1.26	15	740	0.89
4	440	0.54	5	830	1.03	14	330	0.41
5	210	0.19	2	120	0.11	12	880	0.79
2	480	0.41	0	0	0.00	12	410	0.35
2	230	0.34	0	0	0.00	20	1080	1.59
0	0	0.00	1	110	0.11	9	330	0.32
12	3170	1.25	0	0	0.00	14	640	0.25
3	660	0.74	2	310	0.35	23	350	0.39
1	180	0.21	0	0	0.00	9	520	0.61
4	1080	0.64	7	1120	0.66	30	1730	1.02
13	2400	1.74	0	0	0.00	22	960	0.70
13	1080	0.87	3	360	0.29	16	530	0.43
1	200	0.28	0	0	0.00	5	120	0.17
10	3130	4.08	2	180	0.23	23	900	1.17
1	50	0.13	2	190	0.50	6	570	1.49
6	1260	0.65	21	3630	1.88	16	670	0.35
6	810	0.41	0	0	0.00	22	1460	0.74
4	460	0.52	6	470	0.53	23	630	0.72
0	0	0.00	12	2360	1.23	22	990	0.51
11	3280	0.56	8	2040	0.35	23	8140	1.40
7	2080	7.12	0	0	0.00	4	90	0.31
3	470	0.20	3	420	0.18	22	1690	0.72
15	1720	1.48	8	820	0.70	12	340	0.29
0	0	0.00	0	0	0.00	7	160	0.13
0	0	0.00	4	200	0.25	13	530	0.67
4	230	0.26	2	110	0.13	14	780	0.90
1	80	0.51	0	0	0.00	3	30	0.20
1	40	0.04	1	50	0.04	3	90	0.08
9	1470	0.73	3	940	0.47	35	740	0.37
2	1200	4.26	0	0	0.00	1	1720	6.11
1	180	0.16	1	110	0.10	10	170	0.15
0	0	0.00	0	0	0.00	11	600	0.33
6	1740	1.03	5	910	0.54	10	2450	1.46
2	130	0.13	7	1130	1.12	13	360	0.36
4	690	0.69	1	200	0.20	20	690	0.69
0	0	0.00	0	0	0.00	12	470	1.58
12	3620	2.95	3	320	0.26	21	620	0.51
7	1520	1.50	1	300	0.30	15	730	0.72
7	1320	0.26	1	200	0.04	89	4100	0.82
206	40,520	0.74	122	18,800	0.35	672	39,510	0.73

Table 4.3 Estimates of dissenting numbers in early eighteenth-century Wales

		Presbyterians			Independents		
	Estimated population	No. of congs.	Hearers	% of population	No. of congs.	Hearers	% of population
Anglesey and Caernarvonshire	38,270	0	0	0.00	2	250	0.65
Breconshire	26,700	1	150	0.56	4	1200	4.49
Cardiganshire	18,020	1	250	1.39	2	1000	5.55
Carmarthenshire	34,430	17	4750	13.80	2	1350	3.92
Denbighshire	38,670	2	285	0.74	0	0	0.00
Flintshire	19,640	1	25	0.13	0	0	0.00
Glamorgan	43,400	1	?	?	6	2060	4.75
Merioneth	17,450	0	0	0.00	1	150	0.86
Montgomeryshire	28,650	1	120	0.42	3	300	1.05
Pembrokeshire	29,860	1	500	1.67	3	480	1.61
Radnorshire	14,660	0	0	0.00	3	850	5.80
Totals	309,750	25	6080	1.96	26	7640	2.47

3. Oxford students give an account of the early Methodists at Oxford, 1732 and 1734

These letters give an insight into early Methodism in Oxford. The first is George Whitefield's account of his time in the Holy Club in Oxford after 1732, a wholly sympathetic account. The second is an account written in January 1734 by Richard Morgan, a young Irish undergraduate, to his father. The letter is an account of his tutor, John Wesley. Morgan had anticipated enjoying his time in Oxford, even bringing a greyhound with him so he could indulge in hare coursing. In fact, Wesley encouraged him to become part of the Holy Club. Morgan hated this, and threatened to leave the University rather than continue under Wesley's tutelage. The final letter is that of John Wesley to Morgan's father written the following day in his own defence.

1. George Whitefield

I had not been long at the University before I found the benefit of the foundation I had laid in the country for a holy life. I was quickly solicited to join in their excess of riot with several who lay in the same room; God, in answer to prayers before put up, gave me grace to withstand them; and once, in particular, it being cold, my limbs were

Particular Baptists			Quakers		
No. of congs.	Hearers	% of population	No. of congs.	Hearers	% of population
0	0	0.00	0	0	0.00
1	400	1.50	1	?	?
1	?	?	1	?	?
3	900	2.61	4	?	?
1	150	0.39	1	20	0.05
0	0	0.00	0	0	0.00
5	1600	3.69	2	?	?
0	0	0.00	3	?	?
0	0	0.00	6	?	?
1	?	?	4	70	0.23
2	1000	6.82	2	40	0.27
14	4050	1.31	24	?	?

[© Michael R. Watts 1978. Reprinted from Michael R Watts, *The Dissenters*, vol. 1, by permission of Oxford University Press]

so benumbed by sitting alone in my study because I would not go out amongst them, that I could scarce sleep all night. But I soon found the benefit of not yielding; for when they perceived they could not prevail, they let me alone as a singular, odd fellow. . .

I now began to pray and sing psalms thrice every day, besides morning and evening, and to fast every Friday, and to receive the Sacrament at a parish church near our college, and at the Castle, where the despised Methodists used to receive once a month. The young men so called, were then much talked of at Oxford. I had heard of, and loved them before I came to the University, and so, strenuously defended them when I heard them reviled by the students, that they began to think that I also in time should be one of them. For above a twelvemonth my soul longed to be acquainted with some of them, and I was strongly pressed to follow their good example, when I saw them go through a ridiculing crowd to receive the Holy Eucharist at St Mary's. At length, God was pleased to open a door. It happened that a poor woman in one of the workhouses had attempted to cut her throat, but was happily prevented. Upon hearing of this, and knowing that both the Mr Wesleys were ready to every good work, I sent a poor aged apple-woman of our college to inform Mr Charles Wesley of it, charging her not to discover who sent her. She went; but, contrary to my orders, told my name; he having heard of my coming to the Castle and a parish-church Sacrament, and having met me frequently walking by myself, followed the woman when she was gone away, and sent an invitation to me by her, to come to breakfast with him the next morning. . .

From time to time Mr Wesley permitted me to come unto him, and instructed me as I was able to bear it. By degrees, he introduced me to the rest of his Christian brethren. . .

I now began, like them, to live by rule, and to pick up the very fragments of my time, that not a moment of it might be lost. . . Like them, having no weekly Sacrament, (although the rubric required it,) at our own college, I received every Sunday at Christ Church. I joined with them in (keeping the stations by) fasting Wednesdays and Fridays. . .

The first thing I was called to give up for God, was what the world calls my fair reputation. I had no sooner received the Sacrament publicly on a week-day at St Mary's, but I was set up as a mark for all the polite students that knew me to shoot at.

(By this they know that I was commenced Methodist; for though there is a Sacrament at the beginning of every term, at which all, especially the seniors, are, by statute, obliged to be present, yet so dreadfully has that once faithful city played the harlot, that very few masters, no undergraduates (but the Methodists) attended upon it. Mr Charles Wesley (whom I must always mention with the greatest deference and respect,) walked with me, (in order to confirm me,) from the church even to the college, I confess, to my shame, I would gladly have excused him; and the next day, going to his room, one of our Fellows passing by, I was ashamed to be seen to knock at his door. . . Soon after this, I incurred the displeasure of the Master of the college, who frequently chid, and once threatened to expel me, if ever I visited the poor again. Being surprised by this treatment, and overawed by his authority, I spake unadvisedly with my lips, and said, if it displeased him, I would not; my conscience soon pricked me for this sinful compliance; I immediately repented, and visited the poor the first opportunity;. . . My tutor, being a moderate man, did not oppose me much, but thought, I believe, that I went a little too far. He lent me books, gave me money, visited me, and furnished me with a physician when sick. In short he behaved in all respects like a father. . .)

I daily underwent some contempt at college. Some have thrown dirt at me; others, by degrees, took away their pay from me; and two friends that were dear unto me, grew shy of, and forsook me. . .

The devil also sadly imposed upon me in the matter of my college exercises. Whenever I endeavoured to compose my theme, I had no power to write a word, nor so much as tell my Christian friends of my inability to do it; Saturday being come, (which is the day the students give up their compositions,) it was suggested to me that I must go down into the hall and confess I could not make a these, and so publicly suffer, as if it were for my Master's sake. When the bell rung to call us, I went to open the door to go downstairs, but feeling something give me a violent inward check, I entered my study, and continued instant in prayer, waiting the event; for this my tutor fined me half a crown. The next week Satan served me in like manner again; but having now got more strength, and perceiving no inward check, I went into the hall. My name being called, I stood up, and told my tutor I could not make a thesis. I think he fined me a second time; but, imagining that I would not willingly neglect my exercise, he enquired whether any misfortune had befallen me, or what was the reason I could not make a theme? I burst into tears, and assured him that it was not out of contempt of authority, but that I could not act otherwise. Then, at length, he said he believed I could not; and, when he left me, told a friend, (as he very well might) that he took me to be really mad. . .

2. Richard Morgan to his father

. . .There is a Society of gentlemen, consisting of seven members, whom the world calls Methodists, of whom my tutor is President. They imagine they cannot be saved if they do not spend every hour, nay minutes, of their lives in the service of God. And to that end they read prayers every day in the common jail, preach every Sunday, and administer the sacrament once every month. They almost starve themselves to be able to relieve the poor and buy books for their conversion. They endeavour to reform notorious whores and allay spirits in haunted houses. They fast two days in the week, which has emaciated them to that degree that they are a frightful sight. One of them had like to have lost his life lately by a decay, which was attributed to his great abstinence. They rise every day at five of the clock, and till prayers, which begin at eight, they sing psalms and read some piece of divinity. They meet at each other's rooms at six of the clock five nights in the week, and from seven to nine read a piece of some religious book. In short, they are so particular that they are become the jest of the whole University.

When I came to college, my tutor gave me two rules in writing, which he expected I should follow. The first was to have no company but what he approved of, and the second to read no books but of his choosing. In compliance with the first, I have spent every evening of their meeting from seven to nine in their company till I received your letter; from six to seven they read over the petitions of poor people and relieve their wants, dispose of pious books, and fix the duties of the ensuing day. They told me very solemnly that, when I had acquired a pretty good stock of religion, they would take me in as an assistant. When we are all met, my tutor reads a collect to increase our attention; after that a religious book is read all the time we are together. They often cry for five minutes for their sins; then lift up their heads and eyes, and return God thanks for the great mercies He has showed them in granting them such repentance, and they laugh immoderately as if they were mad. The greatest blessing next to that is being laughed at by the world, which they esteem a sufficient proof of the goodness and justness of their actions, for which they also return thanks as aforesaid. Though some of them are remarkable for eating very heartily on gaudy-days, they stint themselves to two pence meat, and a farthing bread, and a draught of water when they dine at their own expense; and as for supper, they never eat any. There is a text in the Revelation which says that a man had better be very wicked than lukewarm. This Mr Wesley explained thus: that there is no medium in religion; that a man that does not engage himself entirely in the practice of religion is in greater fear of damnation than a notorious sinner. When I considered that I was in the middle state, I grew very uneasy, and was for several days in a kind of religious madness, till I was convinced by a sermon of Dr Young's, which gives those words a quite different meaning.

Mr Wesley often says that it is madness in any man to leave off reading at the end of the eleventh hour if he can improve himself by the twelfth. This rule he expects his pupils to observe. I have not been an hour idle since I came to college but when I walk for my health, which he himself advises. He also expects that I should spend a hour every day before prayers in reading Nelson's works, which I have complied with. He has lectured me scarce in anything but books of devotion. He has given me a book of Mr Nelson to abridge this Christmas. By becoming his pupil I am stigmatised with the name of a Methodist, the misfortune of which I cannot describe. For what they reckon the greatest happiness, namely, of being laughed at, to me is the greatest misery. I am as much laughed at and despised by the whole town as any one of them, and always shall be so while I am his pupil. The whole College makes a jest of me, and the Fellows themselves do not show me common civility, so great is their aversion to my tutor. In short, labouring under all these disadvantages, I am grown perfectly melancholy, and have got such an habit a sighing, which I cannot avoid, that it must certainly do me great mischief. Soon after I came to college the Rector favoured me with his company, and cautioned me against Mr Wesley's strict notions of religion, and told me that the character of his Society prevented several from entering in the College. You are pleased in both your letters to express a great regard for my welfare; for which I hope you shall find a grateful return in me. And as I myself ought to contribute all in my power thereto, I think it incumbent upon me to inform you that it is my opinion that if I am continued under Mr Wesley I shall be ruined. . .

3. To Richard Morgan snr from John Wesley

Oxon January 15, 1734

Sir, Going yesterday into your son's room, I providentially cast my eyes upon a paper that lay upon the table, and, contrary to my custom, read a line or two of it, which soon determined me to read the rest. It was a copy of his last letter to you; whereby, by the signal blessing of God, I came to the knowledge of his real sentiments, both with regard to myself and to several other points of the highest importance.

In the account he gives of me and those friends who are as my own soul, and who watch over it that I may not be myself a castaway, are some things true: as, that we imagine it is our bounden duty to spend our whole lives in the service of Him, that gave them, or, in other words, 'whether we eat or drink, or whatever we do, to do all to the glory of God'. That, we endeavour, as we are able, to relieve the poor by buying books and other necessaries for them; that some of us read prayers at the prison once a day; that I administer the sacrament once a month, and preach there as often as I am not engaged elsewhere; that we sit together five evenings in a week; and that we observe, in such manner as our health permits, the fasts of the Church. Some things are false, but taken up upon trust, so that I hope Mr Morgan believed them true: as, that we almost starve ourselves; that one of us had like lately to have lost his life by too great abstinence; that we endeavour to reform notorious whores and to lay spirits in haunted houses; that we all rise every day at five o'clock; and that I am President of the Society. And some things are not only false, but I fear were known so to be when he related them as true (inasmuch as he had then had the repeated demonstration of both his eyes and ears to the contrary): such as that the Society consists of seven members (I know no more than four of them); that from five to eight in the morning they sing psalms and read some piece of divinity; and that they are emaciated to such a degree that they are a frightful sight. . .

As strange as it may appear that one present upon the spot should so far vary from the truth in his relation I can easily account, not only for his mistake, but for his designed misrepresentation too. The company he is almost daily with (from whom, indeed, I should soon have divided him, had not your letter's coming in the article of time tied my hands) abundantly accounts for the former, as his desire to lessen your regard for me, and thereby obviate the force of any future complaint, which he foresaw I might some time have occasion to make to you, does for the latter. And, indeed, I am not without apprehension that some such occasion may shortly come. I need not describe that apprehension to you. Be pleased to reflect what were the sentiments of your own heart when the ship that took your son from you loosed from shore; and such (allowing for the superior tenderness of a parent) are mine. Such were my father's before he parted from us; when, taking him by the hand, he said, 'Mr Morgan between this and Easter is your trial for life: I even tremble when I consider the danger you are in; and the more because you do not yourself perceive it.' Impute not, sir, this fear either to the error of my youth or to the coldness of his age. Is there not a cause? Is he not surrounded, even in this recess, with those who are often more pernicious than open libertines? – men who retain something of outward decency, and nothing else; who seriously idle away the whole day, and reputably revel till midnight, and if not drunken themselves, yet encouraging and applauding those that are so. . .

[From G. Whitefield, *A Short Account of God's Dealings with the Rev George Whitefield* (London, 1740); and J. Telford (ed.) *The Letters of John Wesley* (London, 1931), quoted by kind permission of the Epworth Press]

4. John Wesley's conversion, 1738

The following extract is from John Wesley's diary. It covers the events running up to Wednesday 24 May 1738, the date on which Wesley experienced his heart 'strangely warmed'. The diary takes Wesley's spiritual path from his early years, through university and his time in Savannah to contact with the Moravians and then to his conversion.

What occurred on Wednesday the 24th, I think best to relate at large, after premising what may make it though better understood. Let him that cannot receive it, ask of the Father of Lights, that he would give more light to him and me. . .

I believe, till I was about ten years old, I had not sinned away that 'washing of the Holy Ghost' which was given me in baptism, having been strictly educated and carefully taught, that I could only be saved 'by universal obedience, by keeping all the commandments of God'; in the meaning of which I was diligently instructed. And those instructions, so far as they respected outward duties and sins, I gladly received and often thought of but all that was said to me on inward obedience or holiness I neither understood nor remembered. So that I was, indeed, as ignorant of the true meaning of the Law, as I was of the Gospel of Christ.

The next six or seven years were spent at school where, outward restraints being removed, I was much more negligent than before, even of outward duties, and almost continually guilty of outward sins, which I know to be such, though they were not scandalous in the eye of the world. However, I still read the Scriptures, and said my prayers, morning and evening; and what now hoped to be saved by, was 1. Not being so bad as other people. 2. Having still a kindness for religion. And 3. Reading the Bible, going to Church, and saying my prayers.

Being removed to the University, for five years, I still said my prayers, both in public and in private, and read, with the Scriptures, several other books of religion, especially comments on the New Testament. Yet I had not all this while so much as a notion of inward holiness; nay, went on habitually and (for the most part very contentedly) in some or other known sin; indeed, with some intermission and short struggles, especially before and after the Holy Communion, which I was obliged to receive thrice a year. I cannot well tell what I hoped to be saved by now, when I was continually sinning against that little light I had, unless by those transient fits of what many divines taught me to call repentance. . .

Removing soon after to another college, I executed a resolution, which I was before convinced was of the utmost important, shaking off at once all my trifling acquaintance. I began to see more and more the value of time. I applied myself closer to study. I watched more carefully against actual sins; I advised others to be religious, according to that scheme of religion by which I modelled my own life. But meeting now with Mr Law's *Christian Perfection* and *Serious Call*, (although I was much offended at many parts of both, yet) they convinced me more than ever of the exceeding height, and breadth, and depth of the law of God; the light flowed in so mightily upon my soul, that every thing appeared in a new view I cried to God for help, and resolved not to prolong the time of obeying him as I had never done before. And by my continued 'endeavour to keep his whole law' inward and outward, 'to the utmost, of my power,' I was persuaded that I should be accepted of him, and that I was even then in a state of salvation.

In 1730, I began visiting the prisons, assisting the poor and sick in town, and doing what other good I could, by my presence or my little fortune, to the bodies and souls of all men. To this end I abridge myself of all superfluities, and many that are called necessaries of life. I soon became a by-word for so doing, and I rejoiced that 'my name was cast out as evil.' The next spring I began observing the Wednesday and Friday fasts, commonly observed in the ancient Church; tasting no food till three in the afternoon. And now I know not how to go any further. I diligently strove against all sin. I omitted no sort of self-denial which I thought lawful; I carefully used, both in public and in private, all the means of grace at all opportunities. I omitted no occasion of doing good: I for that reason suffered evil. And all this I know to be nothing, unless as it was directed toward inward holiness. Accordingly this, the image of God, was what I aimed at in all, by doing his will, not my own. Yet when, after continuing some years in this course, I apprehended myself to be near death, I could not find that all this gave me any comfort, or any assurance of acceptance with God. At this I was then not a little surprised, not imagining I had been all this time building on the sand, nor considering that 'other foundation can no man lay, than that which is laid by God, even Christ Jesus'. . .

In this refined way of trusting to my own works, and my own righteousness, (so zealously inculcated by the mystic writers) I dragged on heavily, finding no comfort or help therein, till the time of my leaving England. On shipboard, however, I was again active in outward works; where it pleased God, of his free mercy, to give me twenty-six of the Moravian brethren for companions, who endeavoured to show me a more excellent way. But I understood it not at first. I was too learned and too wise. So that it seemed foolishness unto me. And I continued preaching and following after and trusting in that righteousness, whereby no flesh can be justified. . .

All the time I was at Savannah I was thus beating the air. Being ignorant of the righteousness of Christ, which by a living faith in him bringeth salvation 'to every one that believeth,' I sought to establish my own righteousness, and so laboured in the fire all my days. I was now, properly under the law. I know that the law of God was spiritual; I consented to it, that it was good. Yea, I delighted in it, after the inner man. Yet was I carnal, sold under sin. Every day was I constrained to cry out, 'What I do, I allow not; for what I would, I do not; but what I hate, that I do; to will is indeed present with me; but how to perform that which is good, I find not. For the good which I would, I do not, but the evil which I would not, that I do. I find a law, that when I would do good, evil is present with me; even the law in my members, warring against the law of my mind, and still bringing me into captivity to the law of sin.'. . .

In my return to England, January, 1738, being in imminent danger of death, and very uneasy on that account, I was strongly convinced that the cause of that uneasiness was unbelief, and that the gaining a true, living faith, was the one thing needful for me. But still I fixed not this faith on its right object: I meant only faith in God, not faith in or through Christ. Again, I knew not that I was wholly void of this faith; but only thought I had not enough of it. So that when Peter Bohler, whom God prepared for me as soon as I came to London, affirmed of true faith in Christ, (which is but one,) that it had those two fruits inseparably attending it, 'Dominion over sin, and constant peace from a sense of forgiveness,' I was quite amazed, and looked upon it as a new Gospel. If this was so, it was clear, I had not faith. But I was not willing to be convinced of this. Therefore I disputed with all my might, and laboured especially where the sense of forgiveness was not: for all the Scriptures relating to this, I had been long since taught to construe away, and to call all Presbyterians who spoke otherwise. Besides, I well saw no one could (in the nature of things) have such a sense of forgiveness, and not feel it. But I felt it not. If then there was no faith without this, all my pretensions to faith dropped at once . . .

I continued thus to seek it, (though with strange indifference, dullness, and coldness, and usually frequent relapses into sin) till Wednesday, May 24. I think it was about five this morning that I opened my Testament on those words: 'There are given unto us exceeding great and precious promises even that ye should be partakers of the divine nature.' (2 Pet. i. 4.) Just as I went out, I opened it again on those words: 'Thou art not far from the kingdom of God.' In the afternoon I was asked to go to St Paul's. The anthem was, 'Out of the deep have I called unto thee, O Lord: Lord, hear my voice. O let thine ears consider well the voice of my complaint. If thou, Lord, will be extreme to mark what is done amiss, O Lord, who may abide it? But there is mercy with thee; therefore thou shalt be feared. O Israel, trust in the Lord: for with the Lord there is mercy, and with him is plenteous redemption. And he shall redeem Israel from all his sins.'

In the evening I went very unwillingly to a society in Aldersgate Street, where one was reading Luther's preface to the Epistle to the Romans. About a quarter before nine, while he was describing the change which God works in the heart through faith in Christ, I felt my heart strangely warmed. I felt I did trust in Christ, Christ alone, for salvation; and an assurance was given me, that he had taken away my sins, even mine, and saved me from the law of sin and death.

I began to pray with all my might for those who had in a more especial manner despitefully used me and persecuted me. I then testified openly to all there what I now first felt in my heart. But it was not long before the enemy suggested, 'This cannot be faith; for where is thy joy?' Then was I taught, that peace and victory over sin are essential to faith in the Captain of our salvation; but, that as to the transports of joy that usually attend the beginning of it, especially in those who have mourned deeply, God sometimes giveth, sometimes withholdeth them, according to the counsels of his own will.

After my return home, I was much buffeted with temptations; but cried out, and they fled away. They returned again and again. I as often lifted up my eyes, and he sent me help from his holy place. And herein I found the difference between this and my former state chiefly consisted. I was striving, yea, fighting with all my might under the law, as well as under grace; but then I was sometimes, if not often, conquered: now, I was always conqueror.

[From F. W. Macdonald (ed.), *The Journal of the Revd John Wesley* (London, 1939), by permission of J. M. Dent]

5. John Wesley's defence, 1739

In 1739, John Wesley, visiting Bath, was handed a copy of *A Caution Against Religious Delusion* which attacked Methodists, as his followers were becoming widely called. Wesley's answer to the author was perhaps the pithiest defence of his position in the early years of Methodism. The defence is a mixture of open acknowledgement of the accusation made of him and denial of the wilder charges. Wesley freely indicates that he is not responsible for George Whitefield's views, though he does defend them.

Having 'A Caution against Religious Delusion' put into my hands about this time, I thought it my duty to write to the author of it; which I accordingly did, in the following terms:-

Reverend Sir,

1. You charge me (for I am called a Methodist, and consequently included within your charge) with 'vain and confident boastings; rash, uncharitable censures; damning all who do not feel what I feel; not allowing men to be in a salvable state, unless they have experienced some sudden operation, which may be distinguished as the hand of God upon them, overpowering as it were the soul; with denying men the use of God's creatures, which He hath appointed to be received with thanksgiving, and encouraging abstinence, prayer, and other religious exercises, to the neglect of the duties of our station.' 'O Sir, can you prove this charge upon me? The Lord shall judge in that day!'

2. I do indeed go out into the highways and hedges, to call poor sinners to Christ; but not in a tumultuous manner; not to the disturbance of the public peace, or the prejudice of families, Neither herein do I break any law which I know; much less set at nought all rule and authority. Nor can I be said to 'intrude into the labours' of those who do not labour at all, but suffer thousands of those for whom Christ died to 'perish for lack of knowledge.'

3. They perish for want of knowing that we, as well as the Heathens, 'are alienated from the life of God;' that 'every one of us,' by the corruption of our inmost nature, 'is very far gone from original righteousness;' so far that 'every person born into the world deserveth God's wrath and damnation;' that we have by nature no power either to help ourselves, or even to call upon God to help us; all our tempers and works in our natural state being only evil continually. So that our coming to Christ, as well as theirs, must infer a great and mighty change. It must infer not only an outward change, from stealing, lying, and all corrupt communication; but a thorough change of heart, an inward renewal in the spirit of our mind. Accordingly, 'the old man' implies infinitely more than outward evil conversation, even 'an evil heart of unbelief,' corrupted by pride and a thousand deceitful lusts. Of consequence, the 'new man' must imply infinitely more than outward good conversation; even a good heart, 'which after God is

created in righteousness and true holiness': 'a heart full of that faith which, working by love, produces all holiness of conversation.'

[From F. W. Macdonald (ed.), *The Journal of the Revd John Wesley* (London, 1939), by permission of J. M. Dent]

6. Wesley's sermon on salvation by faith

These extracts from a sermon by John Wesley address one of the central themes of Methodism: 'Salvation by Faith'. The sermon was preached at the University Church in Oxford in 1738, a month after his conversion. It encapsulates the nature of his belief in justification and salvation. Its interest is in the emphasis that Wesley places on sin. It was a message that he frequently returned to, making Methodism a gospel for the sinner.

. . .Now, God requireth of a heathen to believe, 'that God is. . . a rewarder of them that diligently seek Him'; and that He is to be sought by glorifying Him as God, by giving Him thanks for all things, and by a careful practice of moral virtue, of justice, mercy, and truth, toward their fellow creatures, a Greek or Roman, therefore, yea, a Scythian or Indian, was without excuse if he did not believe thus much: the being and attributes of God, a future state of reward and punishment, and the obligatory nature of moral virtue, for this is barely the faith of a Heathen.

Nor, secondly, is it the faith of a devil, though this goes much farther than that of a Heathen. For the devil believes, not only that there is a wise and powerful God, gracious to reward, and just to punish; but also, that Jesus is the Son of God, the Christ, the Saviour of the world. So we find him declaring, in express terms, 'I know Thee who Thou art; the Holy One of God' (Luke iv. 34). Nor can we doubt but that unhappy spirit believes all those words which came out of the mouth of the Holy One; yea, and whatsoever else was written by those holy men of old, of two of whom he was compelled to give that glorious testimony, 'These men are the servants of the most high God, who show unto you the way of salvation'. Thus much, then, the great enemy of God and man believes, and trembles in believing – that God was made manifest in the flesh; that He will 'tread all enemies under His feet'; and that 'all Scripture was given by inspiration of God'. Thus far goeth the faith of a devil.

Thirdly, the faith through which we are saved, in that sense of the word which will hereafter be explained, is not barely that which the

Apostles themselves had while Christ was yet upon earth; though they so believed on Him as to 'leave all and follow Him'. Although they had then power, to work miracles, to 'heal all manner of sickness, and all manner of disease' yea, they had then 'power and authority over all devils', and, which is beyond all this, were sent by their Master to 'preach the kingdom of God'.

What faith is it then through which we are saved? It may be answered, first, in general, it is a faith in Christ: Christ, and God through Christ, are the proper objects of it. Herein, therefore, it is sufficiently, absolutely distinguished from the faith either of ancient or modern heathens, and from the faith of a devil it is fully distinguished by this: it is not barely a speculative, rational thing, a cold, lifeless assent, a train of ideas in the head; but also a disposition of the heart. For thus saith the Scripture, 'With the heart man believeth unto righteousness'; and, 'If thou shalt confess with thy mouth the Lord Jesus, and shalt believe with thy heart that God hath raised Him from the dead, thou shalt be saved'. . . .

He that is, by faith, born of God sinneth not (1) by any habitual sin; for all habitual sin is sin reigning; but sin cannot reign in any that believeth. Nor (2) by any wilful sin; for his will while he abideth in the faith, is utterly set against all sin, and abhorreth it as deadly poison. Nor (3) by any sinful desire; for he continually desireth the holy and perfect will of God; and any tendency to an unholy desire, he by the grace of God, stifleth in the birth. Nor (4) doth he sin by infirmities, whether in act, word, or thought; for his infirmities have no concurrence of his will; and without this they are not properly sins. Thus, 'he that is born of God doth not commit sin'. And though he cannot say he hath not sinned, yet now 'he sinneth not'. . . .

This then is the salvation which is through faith, even in the present world: a salvation from sin, and the consequences of sin, both often expressed in the word justification; which, taken in the largest sense, implies a deliverance from guilt and punishment, by the atonement of Christ actually applied to the soul of the sinner now believing on Him, and a deliverance from the whole body of sin, through Christ formed in his heart. So that he who is thus justified, or saved by faith, is indeed born again, he is born again of the Spirit unto a new life, which 'is hid with Christ in God'. He is a new creature: old things are passed away: all things in him are become new. And as a new-born babe he gladly receives the 'sincere milk of the word, and grows thereby'; going on in the might of the Lord his God, from faith to faith, from grace to grace, until at length, he comes unto 'a perfect man, unto the measure of the stature of the fullness of Christ' . . .

At this time, more especially, will we speak, that 'by grace are ye saved through faith', because, never was the maintaining this doctrine more seasonable than it is at this day, nothing but this can effectually prevent the increase of the Romish delusion among us. It is endless to attack, one by one, all the errors of that Church. But salvation by faith strikes at the root, and all fall at once where this is established. It was this doctrine, which our Church justly calls the strong rock and foundation of the Christian religion, that first drove Popery out of these kingdoms; and it is this alone can keep it out. Nothing but this can give a check to that immorality which hath 'overspread the land as a flood'. Can you empty the great deep, drop by drop? Then you may reform us by dissuasives from particular vices. But let the 'righteousness which is of God by faith' be brought in, and so shall its proud waves be stayed. Nothing but this can stop the mouths of those who 'glory in their shame, and openly deny the Lord that bought them'. They can talk as sublimely of the law, as he that hath it written by God in his heart. To hear them speak on this head might incline one to think they were not far from the kingdom of God: but take them out of the law into the gospel; begin with the righteousness of faith; with Christ, 'the end of the law to every one that believeth'; and those who but now appeared almost, if not altogether, Christians, stand confessed the sons of perdition; as far from life and salvation (God be merciful unto them!) as the depth of hell from the height of heaven . . .

[From J. Wesley, *A Sermon Preached at St Mary's, Oxford before the University on 11 June 1738*]

7. John Gambold bemoans the methods of preachers, 1743

John Gambold was an Oxford Methodist and vicar of Stanton Harcourt, Oxfordshire. He gave up his living in 1742 to tour Wales, during which he wrote the following letter to Howell Harris on his views on religion in Wales. The small number of preachers who attracted Gambold's approbation, and the difficulties they encountered in preaching mass sermons on the topics which might be better said face to face were clearly those which many dissenters met. The dangers of preaching what should be the content of private discussion is the subject of the rest of the letter.

Almost everywhere, I think the preachers are forc'd to do all & answer every purpose with souls, in their public sermons; being too few, not having leisure, opportunity, &c. to apply to them in private such advice & discipline as would be proper. They have observ'd, that upon their preaching the free grace & mercy to sinners, thro' faith in Jesus, some hypocrites have started up, with carnal pride or with a bad life pretending to faith. To detect & convince these the worthy preachers have subjoin'd in most of their sermons, (since they could come at them no other way) reproofs to the hypocrites, & an enumeration of the many many ways one may deceive himself in the Christian cause, & what proofs one must endeavour to see in himself to make him sure. All this I don't doubt they had rather speak distinctly & separately to each man's face, to whom it was applicable & wholesome, & fix it on him in private; & lead every soul on by such measures of discipline as was suitable to his particular case; but wanting opportunity for this, as I said before, they are forc'd to do it in public discourses. Whereby (which they can't help as matters stand) these inconveniences often happen.

1. Tender hearted upright poor people take the reproofs & terrors to themselves in ignorance & humility, & so become discourag'd; while the hypocrites, to whom such words were due, put them off from them & are untouch'd.

2. Many, by such large casuistical treating of things, get a form of knowledge in the head, especially the acute reasoning people of this country, which fatally hides from them & covers the emptiness & deadness of their hearts: (& by the way, the eagerness about theological niceties, & the measuring all grace & improvement by the readiness & skill in speaking of divine things upon several occasions, is an evil that wants to be remedied in Wales.)

3. By hearing severity so quickly & constantly added after mildness in all public discourses, the people are generally very apt to confound the law & the gospel in their own ideas & apprehensions, & more yet in their spirit & temper; & this bondage of mind, & secret resting on their own works in some view or other, is equally plain & painful to see in very many of them . . .

[From G. M. Roberts (ed.) *Selected Trevecca Letters 1742–1747*
(Caernarvon, 1956), by permission of the Presbyterian Church of
Wales Historical Society]

8. Bishop Gibson of London's hostility to Methodism, 1744

In 1744 Bishop Edmund Gibson of London published *Observations upon the Conduct and Behaviour of a Certain Sect usually distinguished by the Name of Methodists*. It was a strong attack on the Methodists for their breach with Church rules and authority. For an ecclesiastical canonist like Gibson, this was perhaps the worst transgression of which the Methodists were capable. Nevertheless, Gibson also charged the Methodists with doctrines that concerned him.

This new sect of Methodists have broken through all those provisions and restraints; neither regarding the penalties of the laws which stand in full force against them nor embracing the protection which the Act of Toleration might give them. And, not content with that, they have had the boldness to preach in the fields and other open places, and by public advertisements to invite the rabble to be their hearers; notwithstanding an express declaration in a statute (Car. II, c. 1) against assembling in a field, by name. . .

But now these wholesome rules are not only broken through, but notoriously despised by the new sect of Methodists; who leaving their own parish churches where they are known, come from several quarters, in very great numbers, to receive the communion at other churches, where they are not known; and between whom and the minister there is no manner of relation.

This is a practice which may justly be complained of by the ministers of the churches to which they resort in that irregular manner; as it puts such ministers under the difficulty, either of rejecting great numbers as unknown to them, or administering the Sacrament to great numbers, of whom they have no knowledge.

Besides the main irregularities which are justly charged upon these itinerant preachers, as violations of the laws of Church and State; it may be proper to enquire, whether the doctrines they teach, and those lengths they run, beyond what is practised among our religious societies, or in any other Christian Church; be a service or a disservice to religion? To which purpose, the following queries are submitted to consideration. . .

Qu. Whether, in particular, the carrying the doctrine of justification by faith alone to such a height, as not to allow, that a careful and sincere observance of moral duties is so much as a condition of our acceptance with God, and of our being justified in his sight; whether this, I say, does not naturally lead people to a disregard of those duties, and a low esteem of them; or rather to think them no part of the Christian religion?. . .

Qu. Whether a gradual improvement in grace and goodness, is not a better foundation of comfort, and of an assurance of a new birth, than that which is founded on the doctrine of a sudden and instantaneous change; which if there be any such thing, is not easily distinguished from fancy and imagination; the workings whereof we may well suppose to be more strong and powerful, while the person considers himself in the state of one who is admitted as a candidate for such a change, and is taught in due time to expect it?

Qu. Whether, in a Christian nation, where the instruction and edification of the people is provided for, by placing ministers in certain districts, to whom the care of the souls within those districts is regularly committed. It can be for the service of religion, that itinerant preachers run up and down from place to place, and from county to county, drawing after them confused multitudes of people, and leading them into a disesteem of their own pastors, as less willing or less able to instruct them in the way of salvation: an evil, which our Church has wisely provided against in the ordination of priest, by expressly limiting the exercise of the powers conferred upon him of preaching the word of God, and administering the Holy Sacraments. . .

[From E. Gibson, *Observations upon the Conduct and Behaviour of a Certain Sect usually distinguished by the Name of Methodists* (London, 1744)]

9. Howell Harris's fears for the hostility evangelical ministers faced, 1748

In this letter, written to Thomas Boddington, the manager of George Whitefield's affairs in London in 1748, Harris gives an insight into the efforts he had devoted to preaching in Wales and the hostility he faced. Harris's letter shows some of the effects of the exhaustion he felt. The letter is particularly interesting since Harris clearly saw hostility to Methodism as based on class interest and the majority of the brethren as oppressed by the gentry.

'Tis now about nine weeks since I begun to go round south & north Wales, & this week I came home from my last journey round north Wales – I have now visited in that time thirteen counties & travelled mostly 150 miles every week, & discoursed twice every day & sometimes three & four times a day: & this last journey I have not taken off my clothes for seven nights & travelled from one morning to ye next evening without any rest, above a hundred miles, discoursing at twelve or two in ye morning on ye mountain, being oblig'd to meet at that time, by reason of persecution – one man being made ye week before I went there to pay 20£ near Wrexham, to Sr W. W Wynne, & several of ye hearers 5£ & some 10£ yt had pd before, this being ye third time poor people have been serv'd thus in yt neighbourhood for assembling together; & now there was only one of our brethren went to prayer with some of ye neighbours in ye family Sr W, triumphed over ye poor people & said we have send for law against him but Cd find none.

Lord answer for thyself & appear in thy own cause – I had in another place, viz Bala, a blow on my head with violence enough to slit my head in two but I rec'd no hurt – such crowds I never saw coming to hear & more glory among ye people, many hearts & doors have been lately opened; & several lately which we know of have been awakened, & ye Lord seems to turn His face towards ye rich. . .

[From G. M. Roberts (ed.) *Selected Trevecca Letters 1747–1794* (Caernarvon, 1962), by permission of the Presbyterian Church of Wales Historical Society]

10. Phillip Doddridge's accounts of nonconformity, 1740s

The following accounts, from Phillip Doddridge's correspondence, present a picture of Presbyterianism in the 1740s. Doddridge is perhaps best known for the dissenting academy he ran at Northampton, a description of which forms part of his letter to Daniel Wadsworth of Hartford, Connecticut. The second letter is to Doddridge from John Barker in 1747 (o.s.), giving an account of an attempt at comprehension between the Church of England and Presbyterianism, which came to nothing. However the letter recounts a free interchange with Archbishop Herring of Canterbury and suggests something of the amicable relations between men of differing religious opinions.

1. Phillip Doddridge to Daniel Wadsworth

. . .The State of our affairs don't furnish out any very remarkable history, but I bless God that what I have to write is of a very comfortable nature. I question not but you have other correspondents who are more capable of informing you of the state of the dissenting interest in general both in London and the country in this Southern part of our island, and therefore I shall not touch upon it, any further than to tell you I don't think it's much on the decay, except in those places into which the Arian & Pelagian doctrines have been introduced which is chiefly tho' not only in the Western and Southern Counties. Yet even here there is a secret strength. . . As for these parts, I bless God religion is in a very flourishing state; we are generally moderate Calvinists. . . we have ten officers, besides the pastor, i.e. four elders and six deacons, of these elders which will perhaps surprise you, one was many years a clergyman in the established Church, but discouraged in his attempts to do good there, and desiring further instructions in the Gospel, he laid aside his office and became first a member, and then an officer in the Church under my pastoral care, he often preaches in the neighbouring congregations, and is an excellent man, another of our elders was a Baptist lay preacher, in the town for some time, who meeting with some unkind treatment from some of his people is settled with us, and is a very amicable and useful member, of our body. A third is the Reverend and worthy Mr Job Orton a young minister, whom I had the honour to educate, he is my assistant both in the Academy and congregation, and is perhaps one of the best of preachers and of men. A fourth is a very modest humble serious Christian who teaches a charity school lately erected amongst the Dissenters in this place. These four with our six deacons, who are also men of great wisdom and eminent piety and moderation, constitute a little council which meets once a month to consider the affairs of the congregation (& of elders once a week), but pretend to no judicial power at all, all public acts being done by the whole Church. And I bless God they are always conducted with great unanimity, friendship and decorum. Our Church consists of about 230 members of which about 130 have been admitted since I became their pastor. . . God has of late given us a sensible revival. . . As to my Academy, sir, it consists of about thirty six and the number of pupils have been about this for some time, of these twelve are on the foundation of a gentleman of whom I doubt not but you have heard, i.e. William Coward Esquire late of Walthamstow in Essex who left £18 a year a piece to twenty five students for ever, there were great debates in Chancery about the will, but they are all happily determined in our favour and the execution of the trust is lodged in the hands of those great and excellent men Dr Watts, Dr Guise and Mr Neal with whose names and characters you, sir, can't but be very well acquainted thro' the divine goodness I have every year the pleasure to see some plants taken out of my nursery and set in neighbouring congregations where they generally settle with a unanimous consent, and that to a very remarkable degree in some very large and once divided congregations. . . I have at present a greater proportion of pious and ingenious youths under my care than I ever before had. . . they carry on a kind of public worship in neighbouring villages repeating and praying on the Lord's day evening, in assemblies to which often most of the inhabitants of the town resort. . . I will not sir trouble you at present with a large account of my method of academical education, only would observe that I think it of vast importance to instruct them carefully in the Scriptures, and not only endeavour to establish them in the great truths of Christianity, but to labour to promote their practical influence on their hearts; for which purpose I frequently converse with each of them alone, and conclude the conversation with prayer. This does indeed take up a great deal of time; but I bless God it's amply repaid in the pleasure I have in seeing, my labour is not in vain in the Lord. Most of the lectures I read are such as I myself draw up, specially in Algebra; Jewish antiquities; Pneumatology, Ethicks, Divinity and the manner of preaching, and the pastoral care in its several branches. . .

When you ask me my opinion on the Methodists indeed sir I find it difficult to give it you so shortly, in the general I think them very good men but that they have carried some matters to extremes. A great deal of good they have undoubtedly done, but I fear Satan has even from thence taken some advantage against a few of them, puffing up with spiritual pride, as if the whole stress of the Christian cause lay entirely upon their shoulders, errors to be sure they have amongst them, of one kind or another, because there are frequent contradictions amongst them. . .

2. To Phillip Doddridge from John Barker

As for the Comprehension so much talked of in town & country the utmost of that matter is this, Mr Chandler while his meeting place was shut up made a visit to his friends at Norwich, & there happened to hear the Bishop [Gooch] give a charge to his clergy which he tho't not very candid one [his] expression appeared to him invidious (viz.) that the heads of the rebellion were Presbyterians, as appeared by those Lords in the Tower sending for Presbyterian confessors. Upon Mr Chandler's return to London he wrote a letter to Dr Gooch complaining of his charge & particularly of that expression; his letter was writt very handsomely, & it bro't a very civil respectful answer, after Gooch came to town Chandler at his desire made him a visit, in which they had much discourse & amongst other things, there was talk of a Comprehension. This visit was follow'd at Gooch's desire with another where the B[ishop] of Salisbury [Sherlock] was present who soon discover'd his shrewdness, but said our Church, Mr Chandler, consists of three parts, Doctrine, Discipline, & Ceremonies. As to the last, they should be left indifferent as they are agreed on all hands to be. As to the second – our discipline, said he, is so bad that no one knows – your articles My Lord must be express'd in Scripture words. And the Athanasian creed be discarded &c, both the Bishops answer'd they wish'd they were rid of that creed & had no objection to altering the articles into Scripture words. But what should we do about reordination. To this Mr Chandler made such a reply as he judg'd proper, but I think granted more than he ought, he said none of us would renounce his Presbyterian ordination, but if their Lordships meant only to impose their hands on us, & by that rite recommend us to public service in their society or constitution, that perhaps might be submitted to. But when he told me this I said perhaps not, no by no means that being in my opinion a virtual renunciation of our ordination which I apprehend not only as good but better than theirs. The two Bishops at the conclusion of the visit, requested Mr Chandler to wait on the Archbishop [Herring] which he did, & met Gooch there by accident. The Archb[ishop] receiv'd him well & being told by Gooch what Ch[andler] & he had been talking on (viz.) a Comprehension said 'a very good thing'. He wish'd it with all his heart, & the rather because this was a time which called upon all good men to unite against infidelity & immorality which threatened universal ruin & added he was encouraged to hope from the piety learning & moderation of many dissenters that this was a proper time to make the attempt. But, may it please your Grace, said Gooch, Mr Chandler says the articles must be alter'd into the words of Scripture. And why not reply'd the Archbishop. It is the impertinencies of men thrusting their words into articles instead of the words of God, that have occasion'd most of the divisions in the Christian Church from the beginning of it to this day. The Archb[ishop] added that the bench of bishops seem'd to be of his mind that he should be glad to see Mr Chandler again but was then oblig'd to go to court, and this is all. I have smiled at some who seem rightly frighted at this affair are very angry with Mr Chandler & cry out 'we won't be comprehended we won't be comprehended' one would think they imagin'd it was like being electrify'd or inoculated for the smallpox.

[From G. E. Nuttall (ed.), *The Calendar of Correspondence of Phillip Doddridge DD (1702–1751)* (HMC, 1979). Crown copyright is reproduced with the permission of the Controller of Her Majesty's Stationery Office]

11. The debate on the Jewish Naturalisation Act, 1753

In July 1753 Henry Pelham introduced the Jewish Naturalisation Bill into the Commons. The Bill passed through both houses. However the public clamour which followed in the wake of the passage of the Act – on the mistaken assumption that it naturalized *all* Jews – was sufficient to force the government to repeal the Act in the following year. The first two extracts below are from the debate in July 1753: William Northey MP opposed the measure primarily on the grounds that the naturalization of Jews would erode native Britons' birthrights; the Prime Minister, Henry Pelham, supported it on more rational grounds. The third extract is from Bishop Thomas Secker of Oxford's speech in favour of the repeal of the law in 1754. The speech is a model of pragmatism and supports repeal as long as it didn't also repeal the denial of the right of Jews to be Church patrons.

1753: Mr William Northey rose and said:

Sir: I hope some of the gentlemen, who are advocates for this Bill, will rise up and inform the House, what terrible crime the people of this kingdom have committed; for I must suppose, that they have been guilty of some heinous offence because we have of late had some sort of Bill offered every year to parliament for depriving them of their birthright: I say, depriving them Sir; for the communication reaches a taking it away from those who had before the sole right to it. Attempts have formerly been made to rob them of their birthright as Englishmen, but this Bill I must look on as an attempt to rob them of their birthright as Christians. . . .

Sir, when I saw we should not give away our birthright for nothing, I must suppose, that we might sell it for something; and I am warranted in this supposition from what is told us by our histories. The Jews never did obtain the protection or countenance of the crown, even for living and trading in this kingdom, without a very valuable consideration; and our histories tell us, that they offered 500,000£. to Oliver

Cromwell for a naturalisation. Moreover, I have heard, that they offered a much larger sum both in the reigns of King William and Queen Anne. . .

The Bill being patronised by those who pretend to be friends to His Majesty and his family, and should the Bill pass this House, I hope he will make the proper use of it; for whatever offence the people of this country may have committed against some of our ministers, I am sure they have not of late committed any offence against His Majesty or his illustrious family. On the contrary, their ready submission to all the additional loads that have of late years been laid upon them, and in particular the zeal they showed upon a late memorable occasion, for the support of our present happy establishment, entitles them to all the favours that can be bestowed by the Crown, and surely, much more to that of being preserved in the possession of that privilege which belongs to them as Englishmen and as Christians. But a notion has of late years been propagated by some notional gentlemen, that the birthright of an Englishman is a right which is so far from being worth preserving, that it is prejudicial to the community, and that therefore it ought to be abolished; for so it will be, should it ever be granted to all those who are not by their religion declared enemies to the continuance of our present royal family upon the throne of these kingdoms.

1753: Mr Pelham:
. . .As to what has been said, Sir, about Christianity being a part of our establishment, and that we ought not to allow the professed enemies of our ecclesiastical establishment to come and live amongst us, no more than we would allow the professed enemies of our civil establishment to come and live amongst us, it is an argument that goes a great deal too far: not only Christianity, but Christianity as professed and practised by the Church of England, is a part of our establishment: will any gentleman say, that we ought not to allow any person to live amongst us, that will not in every punctilio conform to the profession and practice of the Church of England? Surely, Sir, I am not to look upon every man as my enemy who differs from me in opinion upon any point of religion. This would be a most unchristian way of thinking; therefore I must think, that the Jews are in much the same case with the other dissenters from the Church of England: we ought not to look on them as enemies to our ecclesiastical establishment, but as men whose conscience will not allow them to conform to it; therefore we may, in charity we ought to, indulge them so far as not to endanger thereby our ecclesiastical establishment; and from them we have less danger to

fear than from any other sort of dissenters, because they never attempt to make converts, and because it would be more difficult for them to succeed in any such attempt. Nay, we know, that by the strict tenets of their religion, every man is excluded from it who is not of the seed of Israel; and as they cannot intermarry with a strange woman we need not fear their having success in converting our women.

From the Jews, therefore, we have nothing to fear with respect to our ecclesiastical establishment, and as to our civil establishment, they are by the laws now in being sufficiently excluded from ever having any share in it; for unless they become Christian, they cannot be so much as excisement or custom-house officers. . .

I am surprised to hear the Bill opposed by any gentleman who has ever complained of the decay of our trade, or of the insupportable burden of our debts and taxes; and I am the more surprised, when I consider the chimerical apprehensions upon which this opposition is founded: as if by naturalising a few Jews our constitution was to be unhinged, our liberties sacrificed, and the Christian religion extirpated. I should be extremely sorry, if I thought that any gentleman could be serious when he endeavours to possess us with such apprehensions, because I should from thence conclude, that both our religion and our constitution stood upon a very unstable foundation; but as I am convinced that no man of sense can be serious when he talks so, I fear no danger to either from this Bill; and as it will certainly be of some, and maybe of very great advantage to this country, I shall be for its passing into a law.

1754: The Bishop of Oxford:

My lords; as there is no precept of Christianity that forbids us to allow the Jews to live amongst us, I thought religion very little concerned in the question, whether they should be permitted to be naturalised, without being under any necessity to do what even they cannot think right for them to do; for though they may not think it a profanation of any religious institution to partake of the holy Sacrament of the Lord's Supper, yet they must think it immoral to dissemble so far as to pretend to be Christians, which they must do before the most profligate clergyman will administer it to them. Therefore if religion was any way concerned, it was in favour of the Bill brought in last session, and from daily experience I was convinced, that the most successful, and I am sure, the best way of making converts, is to treat those who differ from us with that mildness and universal benevolence which our holy religion so strongly recommends. This induced me to give my consent to the passing of that Bill into a law, especially as care had been taken to prevent any Jew naturalised by that Act, or by any other method, from intermedling in any affairs relating to the Church, which I looked upon as a considerable point gained in favour of our religion, as many Jews may become naturalised by means of the American Act, and as several considerable lawyers have given it as their opinion, that Jews born here is to all intents and purposes a natural born subject, and entitled to all those rights and privileges which any other subject, who is not of the established Church, is by his birth entitled to.

This, my lords, was then my opinion, and I have not yet met with any good reason for altering it; but as the Act has given offence to so many of our Christian brethren, and as I do not think it a matter of very great importance either to religion or the state, I shall in this case be ready, as I shall always be in cases which I do not think of the utmost importance, to sacrifice my opinion to the satisfaction of my Christian brethren. For this reason, I shall be ready to consent to the repeal of that part of the late act which permits Jews to be naturalised, but I cannot consent to the repeal of that part of it which disables any Jew to purchase advowsons, or any thing that may give him a right to intermeddle in affairs relating to the Church; and therefore I cannot agree to the leaving out the exception or proviso contained in the Bill now before us; for though no Jew should ever be naturalised by parliament, yet many of them will certainly be naturalised by means of the American Act, and if all Jews born here are to be deemed natural born subjects, we can make no doubt but that many of them will purchase land estates with advowsons annexed. . .

But now, my lords, suppose that every Jew patron should take care to present a clergyman of the most undoubted qualification and unblemished character; yet his being presented to the living by a Jew would be a derogation to his character among the people, as we may certainly suppose from the popular clamour raised against the Act now proposed to be repealed; and this would prevent his having that weight and authority among the people of his parish, which every clergyman ought to have. Then, my lords let us consider, that in this kingdom there are many donatives over which, if they have not been augmented, the bishop has no power either as to the presentation or as to visitation: nay, he cannot so much as compel the patron to present or fill up the vacancy, any other way than by ecclesiastical censures which are no but too little regarded by Christians, and would certainly be held in contempt by Jews; therefore we may suppose, that if they should acquire the right to such donatives, they would never fill up the vacancies, but apply the income to the support of their own rabbis.

[From W. Cobbett, *The Parliamentary History of England*. . .

(London, 1813)]

12. Samuel Davies's account of Presbyterianism in England, 1754

Samuel Davies was a young American Presbyterian preacher travelling in England and Scotland to raise funds for the new College of New Jersey (later Princeton University). Davies's diary of the mission gives us an insight into the divided and disunited state of the denomination in England.

Wednesday July 3. Waited on Mr Somervile and Mr Turner, ministers in Berwick; and proposed the business of my mission. The former has given up his charge, partly on account of his indisposition, and partly on account of the divisions in his congregation, occasioned by one that was formerly his assistant. The latter has but a small part of his former congregation, the rest having chosen his assistant, Mr Monteith, for their minister and rejected him, because he would not receive him for his co-pastor. These reasons discouraged them from soliciting collections for me. I applied to Mr Monteith, who gave me some ground to hope he would raise a public collection. I went to visit Mr Thompson, minister of Spittal, about a mile from Berwick, but could not see him. However, I waited on Mr Hatton, the principal man in his congregation, and secured his interest, and wrote to Mr Thomson, begging he would endeavour to have a congregational collection. . .

Berwick had two large congregations of dissenters formerly, but they are sadly weakened by their divisions. The place is surrounded with high walls and mounts, and has sundry garrisons. The ruins of the old castle are very majestic. The bridge is near as long as that of London, and contains fifteen arches . . .

The dissenting ministers here have so generally imbibed Arminian or Socinian sentiments, that it is hard to unite prudence and faithfulness in conversation with them. They are many of them gentlemen of good sense, learning, candour, and regular in their morals, entertaining and instructive companions and friends to the liberty of mankind. But what shall I say? They deny the proper divinity and satisfaction of Jesus Xt, on which my hopes are founded. They ascribe a dignity and goodness to human nature in its present state, contrary to my daily sensations: and they are not so dependent upon divine influences, as I find I must be. Are they or I mistaken? Is the mistake, in such circumstances, essential? It is with the utmost reluctance I would admit the conclusion; and yet I cannot avoid it. The denial of the divinity of Xt introduces an essential innovation into the Xn system: and yet the greatest number of the dissenting ministers under the Presbyterian name in England, as far as I have observed, have fallen into that error, and the people love to have it so; and what will be the end of these things? It is a strong presumption with me against these new doctrines, that I have observed, wherever they prevail, there practical, serious religion, and generally the dissenting interest too, declines, and people become careless about it. Some of them go off into the Ch of England, and others fall into deism. And it is matter of complaint, that the deists generally, if not universally, are of the Whig party, and join the low-Churchmen. Alas! how are the principles of liberty abused!

[From G. W. Pilcher, *The Revd Samuel Davies Abroad, 1753–1755* (Urbana, IL, 1967), by permission of the University of Illinois Press]

13. Oxford University expels six Methodists, 1768

In 1768 the Vice-Chancellor of Oxford expelled six students from St Edmund Hall from the University, following a charge made by Mr Higson, the Vice-Principal of the Hall, against them of Methodism. Higson supported the charge with evidence before the Vice-Chancellor. The following sentences were read to the students in the chapel of St Edmund Hall. The expulsions appear to be not simply a result of their Methodist tendencies; the class and level of education of the students appeared to be a factor in the judgements.

The sentences read by the Vice-Chancellor were as follows: –
It having appeared to me, D. Durell, Vice-Chancellor of the University of Oxford, and undoubted Visitor of St Edmund Hall within the said University, upon due information and examination, that James Matthews, of the said Hall, had been originally brought up to the trade of a weaver, and afterwards followed the low occupation of keeping a tap-house, and that afterwards having connected himself with known Methodists, he did without any the least proficiency in school knowledge, enter himself of St Edmund Hall, aforesaid, with a design to get into Holy Orders; and that he still continues to be wholly illiterate, incapable of doing the statutable exercises of the Hall, and

consequently more incapable of being qualified for Holy Orders, for which he had lately offered himself a candidate. Moreover, it having appeared by his own confession that he had frequented illicit conventicles held in a private house in the City of Oxford. Therefore, I, D. Durell, by virtue of my visitatorial power and with the advice and opinion of the Rev. Thos. Randolph, D.D., President of C.C.C. and Margaret Professor of Divinity in this University, and of the Rev. Thos. Fothergill, D.D., Provost of Queen's College, and of the Rev. Thos. Nowell, D.D., Principal of St Mary Hall and Public Orator, and of the Rev. Francis Atterbury, M.A., Senior Proctor of this University, my several Assessors regularly appointed on this occasion, do expel the said James Matthews from the said Hall, and do hereby pronounce him expelled.

It having also appeared to me that Thomas Jones, of St Edmund Hall, had been brought up to the trade of a barber, which occupation he had followed very lately, that he had made but a small proficiency in learning, and was incapable of performing the statutable exercises of the said Hall; and, moreover, it having appeared by his own confession that he had frequented illicit conventicles in a private house in this town, and that he had himself held an assembly for public worship at Wheat-Aston, in which he himself, though not in Holy Orders, had publicly expounded the Holy Scriptures to a mixed congregation, and offered up extempore prayers. – Therefore, I, D. Durell, by virtue, etc., do expel the said Thomas Jones from the said Hall, and hereby pronounce him also expelled. . .

It having also appeared to me that Benjamin Kay, of the said Hall, by his own confession, had frequented illicit conventicles in a private house in this town, where he had heard extempore prayers frequently offered up by one Hewett, a staymaker. Moreover, it having been proved by sufficient evidence that he held methodistical principles, viz., 'the doctrine of absolute election; that the spirit of God works irresistibly, that once a child of God always a child of God'. That he had endeavoured to instil the same principles into others and exhorted them to continue steadfastly in them against all opposition. – Therefore, I, D. Durell, by virtue, etc., do expel the said Benjamin Kay from the said Hall, and hereby pronounce him also expelled.

It having also appeared to me that Thomas Grove, of St Edmund Hall, aforesaid, though not in Holy Orders, had by his own confession lately preached to an assembly of people called Methodists in a barn, and had offered up extempore prayers in that congregation. – Therefore, I, D. Durell, by virtue of my visitatorial power and with the advice and opinion of each and every one of my Assessors, the reverend persons before-named, do expel the said Thomas Grove from the said Hall, and hereby pronounce him also expelled.

[From S. L. Ollard, *The Six Students of St Edmund Hall expelled from the University of Oxford in 1768* (Oxford, 1911)]

14. The burial of a dissenting child, 1770

In 1770 Mr Evans, the vicar of Marshfields, refused to bury a child in the parish churchyard on the grounds that she was a dissenter and not therefore entitled to burial in the churchyard. The Dissenting Deputies took the matter to Bishop Barrington of Llandaff, whose response, reported by the Deputies and presented here, was more sympathetic than that of the vicar. Bishop Barrington's response to the Deputies was typical of the growing tolerance and understanding between the denominations.

The Bishop received them very politely, and said that he was very sorry that any clergyman in his diocese should be so little of the gentleman and Christian and so ignorant of the laws of his country as to be guilty of such a piece of misbehaviour. That he looked upon himself as greatly obliged to the gentlemen concerned for not prosecuting Mr Evans without giving him [the Bishop] this notice, and since they had acted so genteelly, he begged they would grant him this further indulgence, not to commence any prosecution till he had wrote to him (which he said he would do forthwith) insisting on an acknowledgement of his error to the widow, and promising to bury all the Dissenters in his parishes for the future, and that if he should then continue obstinate in his refusal the Bishop said he should be prosecuted in his court for such neglect of his duty. . .

Mr Evans's response was that if it had been baptised by any regular dissenting minister he would bury it, but that he did not look upon the gentleman who christened it as such, he not having been ordained by any regular dissenting minister only by one who was a mason, and therefore desired they would bury the child in their own ground which they refused. The Bishop added that he could not say this was a sufficient excuse and that therefore he would write again to Mr Evans directing him for the future to bury all the dissenters in his parishes without asking any questions, and hoped the committee would write to Mrs Daniel and her friends recommending candour and moderation to them.

[From *The Sketch of the Protestant Dissenting Deputies.* . . (London, 1813)]

15. The Church's attitude to relief, 1779–81

The attitude of the bishops to relief for dissenters and for Catholics was that they were both part of a wider tolerance of other Christian denominations. In this account of the attitudes at the time of the Catholic and Dissenters' Relief Acts it is clear that Bishop Porteus of Chester felt that subscription to an oath of allegiance was a vital prerequisite to toleration. The extract also suggests that some Protestant dissenters were unhappy at the relief for Catholics. Perhaps most significant of all is Porteus's account of the interest of the House of Lords in the issue of whether the Catholic population was on the increase.

On the 10th of March 1779, a motion was made in the House of Commons, for leave to bring in a Bill for the further relief of Protestant Dissenters; the purport of which was to exempt them from subscription to the Articles, and to entitle them to the full benefit of the Act of Toleration, on their taking the oaths of Allegiance and Supremacy, and subscribing the Declaration against Popery. To this the Bench had no objection; but were at the same time of opinion, that in a Christian country none ought to be allowed to preach or teach without some formal acknowledgement of their being Christians and Protestants, and that they will make the Scriptures the rule of their faith and practice. Upon this principle it was agreed to move an amendment to the Bill, containing a declaration to that effect, and with the exception of a few expressions, the same with that proposed by the Dissenters themselves, on a former application to Parliament in 1773. In the Bishop's papers, I find the following reasons assigned for the part which he himself took in this question.

'On the most mature consideration' he says, 'I am clearly of opinion that some declaration was proper and necessary, and that for several reasons. First, because the English clergy in general, and many of the laity, would have been, and I think justly, exceedingly dissatisfied, had the Bishops consented to unlimited indulgence of religious opinions, without any declaration at all.

Secondly, When any one applies for liberty to preach and teach, the State has a right to know what the leading principles of his religion are, in order to be assured that they contain nothing injurious to civil society, or to the established form of Government.

Thirdly, If there be no declaration, not only Protestant Dissenters, but Mahometans, Deists, Atheists and Pagans, will by this Bill be entitled to preach and teach their opinions with impunity; for any of these may pretend to be Protestant Dissenters. And although these may be connived at, as they now are, so long as they behave peaceably and inoffensively, yet I apprehend the legislature would not choose to give them a legal toleration . . .'

Whilst the government and the Church of England were acting with this moderation towards the Protestant Dissenters, it was reasonable that some indulgence should be shown to the Roman Catholics; and accordingly in the course of this year an Act was passed, repealing a severe, oppressive law, which had been enacted against them in the reign of King William. But this measure, though sanctioned on the same principles of charity, and grounded on the same policy was very differently received. . . .

A Protestant Association, as it was called, was formed in London, the avowed design of which was to oppose the progress of Popery, and to counteract the effects of the late Act, which was affirmed to be of the most dangerous tendency. It was stated that several Popish schools, and mass houses, which had before been kept private, were made public; that many new ones were opened in several parts of the Metropolis, and that the numbers resorting to them greatly increased. At the same time the Association disclaimed persecution, as contrary to the Christian rule, and professed to make use of no other means, but what were clearly consistent with moderation and prudence . . .

Early in 1781, the returns to an inquiry, which the House of Lords had ordered to be made, into the number of Papists in England and Wales, were laid upon the table: when Earl Ferrers, who had moved for that inquiry, observed, that it appeared evidently from these returns, that there had been a very considerable increase of Papists in this kingdom, and particularly in the Diocese of Chester. 'In that Diocese,' he said, 'the number in 1717, was 10,308; in 1767, it was 25,139; and at this time the number given in to the House amounts to 27,228. He therefore submitted to their Lordships, whether it would not be highly expedient to lay such restrictions upon the Catholics, as might, consistently with the true principles of liberality and candour, prevent their further increase. He was no friend to persecution; but he believed the spirit of Popery was not changed: and if it was allowed to spread in the minds of the multitude without control, the worst consequences at a future period might be justly apprehended.'

This proposition, as the facts on which it rested, referred principally to his own Diocese, made it necessary for the Bishop to reply; and he has left the following abstract, as the substance of his speech on that occasion. 'As the discussion of this subject appeared to me exceedingly dangerous, and as I well knew that there was no just ground for dreading any increase of Popery, I thought it right to say something in answer to Lord Ferrers; and undertook to prove, that his statement of the number of Catholics in the Diocese of Chester in the year 1717, was extremely erroneous, having been taken only from very inaccurate returns to Bishop Gaskell's visitatorial inquiries, and not from any parliamentary survey, which alone could be depended upon: that two such surveys had been lately taken of the number of Papists in England and Wales, one in 1767, the other in 1780; that the number returned at the former period was 67,916, at the latter, 69,376; that the increase therefore, in these thirteen years, throughout the whole kingdom, was only 1460, and that this was owing entirely, not to the increase of Popery, but to the increase of population: that I had in my own possession, in consequence of inquiries made upon the subject, very convincing proofs, that in the diocese of Chester alone there had been within the last sixty years an increase of more than 250,000 souls, and that this would more than account for the progress which Popery had made in that See. Upon the whole I contended, that, considering the great increase of general population in this realm, the Catholics were a decreasing rather than an increasing quantity, and that there was therefore no ground for the alarms, which some well-meaning but certainly not well-informed people had taken on that subject. These observations were satisfactory to the House, and Lord Ferrers withdrew his motion . . .'

[From R. Hodgson, *The Works of the Rt Revd Beilby Porteus DD. . . With His Life* (London, 1811)]

16. John Wesley breaks from the Church of England, 1784

In 1784, after a long debate within Methodism, John Wesley took the dramatic step of ordaining Richard Whatcoat and Thomas Vasey, and of appointing Thomas Coke as superintendent of Methodists in America. Coke was already in Anglican priests' orders, but Wesley's action, including the laying on of hands and the signing of a deed (below) which referred to his own providential calling, suggested he was separating from the Church. His action in ordaining 'elders', as Whatcoat and Vasey were called, for America and later for Scotland was defended by Wesley at the Methodist Conference in 1786 (the second extract) as forced upon him by extraordinary circumstances and not affecting the status of Methodism within the Church of England. Wesley's determination to 'live and die a member of the Church of England' was expressed in 1789, a year before he died, but in spite of his denials the seeds of schism had been sown.

1. The Appointment of Whatcoat and Vasey

'To all to whom these presents shall come, Jo. Wesley, late fellow of Lincoln College in Oxford, Presbyter of ye Church of England, sendeth greeting.

Whereas many of ye people in ye Southern Provinces of North America, which desire to continue under my care, and still adhere to ye doctrines and discipline of ye Church of England, are greatly distressed for want of ministers, to administer ye Sacraments of Baptism and ye Lord's Supper, according to ye usage of ye said Church: and whereas there does not appear to be any other way of supplying them with ministers:

Know all men, that I, John Wesley think myself to be providentially called at this time, to set apart some persons for ye work of the ministry in America. And therefore under ye protection of Almighty God, and with a single eye to his glory, I have ye day set apart for ye said work, by ye imposition of my hands and prayer (being assisted by two other ordained ministers) Rich'd Whatcoat and Thomas Vasey, men whom I judge to be well qualified for that great work. And I do hereby recommend them to all whom it may concern, as fit persons to feed ye flock of Xt, and to administer Baptism and the Lord's supper according to the usage of ye Church of England. In testimony whereof I have this day set my hand and seal, this second day of September, 1784.'

2. Minutes of the Methodist Conference, 1786

Those who had been members of the Church had none either to administer the Lord's Supper or to baptise their children. They applied to England over and over, but it was to no purpose. Judging this to be a case of real necessity I took a step which for peace and quietness I had refrained from taking for many years: I exercised that power which I am fully persuaded the Great Shepherd and Bishop of the Church has given me. I appointed three of our labourers to go and help them, by not only preaching the word of God, but likewise administering the Lord's Supper and baptising their children . . .

After Dr Coke's return from America many of our friends begged I would consider the case of Scotland, where we had been labouring so many years and had seen so little fruit of our labours. Multitudes indeed have set out well, but they were soon turned out of the way, chiefly by their ministers either disputing against the truth or refusing to admit them to the Lord's Supper, yea, or to baptise their children, unless they would promise to have no fellowship with the Methodists. . .

To prevent this I at length consented to take the same step with regard to Scotland which I had done with regard to America. But this is not a separation from the Church at all. Not from the Church of Scotland, for we were never connected therewith, any further than we are now: not from the Church of England, for this is not concerned in the steps which are taken in Scotland. Whatever then is done either in America or Scotland is no separation from the Church of England. I have no thought of this: I have many objections against it. It is a totally different case.

[From British Library Add. Mss. 41,295E, by permission; and from *Minutes of the Methodist Conference* (London, 1786)]

17. Silas Told's experiences as a Methodist convert, 1786

Silas Told was, as a young man, a bound apprentice on a slave ship. His experiences on board, his shipwreck and capture by pirates and the scenes of murder, pestilence, privations and sacrifices form the first part of his autobiography. However, back in England, as he recounts in this section, he was converted by John Wesley and became first a schoolmaster and later, for over twenty years, a preacher to those condemned to execution. Wesley wrote in the preface to Told's autobiography that it contained 'many instances of divine Providence'.

In July, 1740, Mr Charles Casper Greaves, a young bricklayer. . . asked me to go with him that evening to hear the Rev. Mr Wesley at the Foundry. I begged him, for God's sake, never to ask me questions of that kind any more, for I was determined never to go thither; and said, if my wife should come to know it, she would never forgive me, he said no more; but in that instant, God began to work powerfully upon my soul, then the eye of my mind saw the Son of God sitting on His throne to judge the world, and such peace resting upon me as tongue cannot express. I found my spirit now much united to Mr Greaves, and therefore related my experience to him, I then proposed going with him to hear the Rev. Mr Wesley. . . Exactly at five o'clock a whisper ran through the congregation, 'Here he comes! here he comes!' I had a curiosity to see his person. He passed through the pulpit, and, having his robes on, I expected he have begun with the Church service; but, to my astonishment, he began with singing a hymn, with which I almost enraptured; but his extempore prayer was unpleasant, as I thought it favoured too much of the first Epistle general of St John, 12, 13 'I write unto you, little children, because your sins are forgiven you,' &c. The enemy now suggested that he was a Papist, as he dwelt so of Scripture many times before, yet I never understood we were to know our sins forgiven on earth; supposing that it referred only to those to whom the Apostle was then writing, as I had never heard this doctrine preached in the Church, however, my prejudice quickly abated; and I plainly saw I could never be saved without knowing my sins were forgiven; and the spirit of God sealed every word upon my heart, at the close of the discourse, however strange it may appear, a small still voice entered my heart with these words, 'This is the truth!' and instantly I felt it in my soul. My friend Greaves, observing my attention to the sermon, asked me how I liked Mr Wesley. I replied, 'As long as I live I will never part from him,' I now broke off at a stroke from my old acquaintances in iniquity, who mocked and derided me exceedingly, and one of my most intimate acquaintances said to me, 'What, Told! are you commenced a Whitefieldite? As sure as ever you were born, if you follow them you are damned.' But the heavier my persecutions were, the more abundantly I rejoiced, and found such love and union to my ministers, and companions in tribulation, that nought but death could make a separation, I had now to encounter with my wife and family, with whom for many years I had lived peaceably; but they, perceiving an alteration in my behaviour, suspected that I had been among the Methodists. My wife, though a worthy, honest woman, yet an entire stranger to this light, one day exclaimed very warmly, and said, 'What the d——l possesses you? I hope you have not been among the Methodists, I'll sacrifice my soul rather than you shall go among those miscreants.' I gave her for answer, 'If you are resolved to sacrifice your soul, I am resolved, God willing, to join them,' At which she said no more, nor ever opposed my going to hear the word . . .

In the year 1744. . . Mr Wesley requested my undertaking to teach the charity-children at the Foundry-School; but being fixed with Mr Bembow, I refused it. A few days after, Mr Hogg returned, and, together with a repetition of his former message, said that Mr Wesley positively insisted upon it I then believed it was my duty to comply with his desires, and therefore. . . as they never had an assistant [who] executed their commands with such attention. . . I dared not to reject. . .

The day after I was established in the Foundry-School, collected threescore boys and but the society being poor, could not grant me more than ten shillings per week, this, however, was sufficient for me, as they boarded and clothed my daughter. Having the children under my care from five in the morning till five in the evening, both winter and summer, sparing no pains, with the assistance of an usher and four monitors, I brought near forty of them into writing and arithmetic, I continued in the school seven years and three months, and discharged two hundred and seventy-five boys, most of whom were fit for any trade.

In the year 1744, while I attended the children one morning at the five o'clock preaching, Mr Wesley took his text out of the twenty-fifth chapter of St Matthew, the forty-first and following verses. When he read these words, 'I was sick, and in prison, and ye visited me not,' as I was sensible of my negligence, in never visiting the prisoners during the course of my life, I was filled with horror of mind beyond expression. This drew me well nigh into a state of despondency, as I was totally unacquainted with the measures requisite to be pursued for that purpose. However, the gracious God, two or three days after, sent a messenger to me in the school, who informed me of ten malefactors that were under sentence of death, and would be glad of any of our friends who could make it convenient to go and pray with them. . .

This was the first time of my visiting the malefactors at Newgate, and of my attending them to the place of execution; and it was not without much shame, because I perceived the greater part of the populace considered me as one of the sufferers, When we came to the fatal tree, Lancaster lifted up his eyes thereto, and said, 'Blessed be God!' then prayed extempore in a very excellent manner, and the others behaved with great discretion, John Lancaster had no friend to procure him a proper interment; so that when they had hung the usual time, and were cut down, the surgeon's mob secured his body, and carried it over to Paddington. . . This gave birth to a great riot in the neighbourhood, which brought an old woman, who had lived in the house, down stairs, when she saw the corpse at the step of the door, she cried out, 'Lord, here is my Son, John Lancaster!' This being spread abroad, the Methodists made a collection, and got him a shroud and a coffin. . .

[From Silas Told, *The Life of Mr Silas Told, written by himself* (London, 1786)]

POPULAR RELIGION

1. The separation of the sexes in church, *c.* 1690

The seating of men and women on different sides of a church, separating family members from one another, was still a practice to be found in churches in the late seventeenth and eighteenth centuries, and was adopted by some Methodist congregations later on. Services at the chapel royal under William III adopted the custom; in the extracts presented here, Sir George Wheler cites the prayerbook of Edward VI as a source for the practice, and bemoans its fall to disuse.

. . .The promiscuous mixture of men and women together in our assemblies, is an abuse crept in, not meant by our first reformers, as is manifest from the first Common Prayer Book of Edward VI and the Order in many Country Churches to this day . . .

I believe this division of sex was formerly in our churches: for in many country churches (where the grandees have not deformed them, by making some High and some Low, to be tenements to their whole families) is yet to be seen . . . the right and left hand seats for the women the seats for the men being next to the chancel, and the seats for the women next from the middle-doors to the belfry; with an alley up to the middle of the church; and another cross that to the north and south doors.

[From George Wheler, *The Protestant Monastery* (London, 1698); and *An Account of the Churches of the Primitive Christians* (London, 1689)]

2. Irreverent behaviour in church: *The Tatler*, 1710 and *The Guardian*, 1713

These two extracts from popular London journals suggest that the growing sociability of eighteenth-century society, and the movement of worship from the domestic sphere into the public arena, did not always promote decorous and respectful behaviour in church. Irreverent behaviour was not new: in the years after the Restoration walking in churches during services and congregations reacting to sermons with signs of approval or disapproval were common and the subject of episcopal censure.

1. *The Tatler*

Mr Bickerstaff:

Observing that you are entered into a correspondence with Pasquin, who is, I suppose, a Roman Catholic, I beg of you to forbear giving him any account of our religion or manners, until you have rooted out certain misdemeanours even in our churches. Among other, that of bowing, saluting, taking snuff, and other gestures. Lady Autumn made me a very low courtesy the other day from the next pew, and, with the most courtly air imaginable called herself [a] miserable sinner. Her niece, soon after, saying, 'Forgive us our trespasses', courtesied with a gloating look at my brother. He returned it, opening his snuff-box, and repeating yet a more solemn expression. I beg of you, good Mr Censor, not to tell Pasquin anything of this kind, and to believe this does not come from one of a morose temper, mean birth, rigid education, narrow fortune, or bigotry in opinion, or from one in whom time has worn out all taste of pleasure. I assure you, it is far otherwise, for I am possessed of all the contrary advantages; and, I hope, wealth, good humour, and good breeding, may be best employed in the service of religion and virtue; and desire you would, as soon as possible, remark upon the above-mentioned indecorums, that we may not long transgress against the latter, to preserve our reputation in the former.

Your humble servant, Lydia.

2. *The Guardian*

. . .I go sometimes to a particular place in the city, far distant from mine own home, to hear a gentleman, whose manner I admire, read the liturgy. The other morning I happened to rise earlier than ordinary, and thought I could not pass my time better, than to go upon the admonition of the morning bell, to the church prayers at six of the clock. I was there the first of any in the congregation, and had the opportunity, however I made use of it, to look back on all my life, and contemplate the blessing and advantage of such stated early hours for offering ourselves to our Creator, and prepossess ourselves with the love of Him, and the hopes we have from Him, against the snares of business and pleasure in the ensuing day. But whether it be that people think fit to indulge their own ease in some secret, pleasing fault, or whatever it was, there was none at the confession but a set of poor scrubs of us, who could sin only in our wills, whose persons could be no temptation to one another, and might have, without interruption from any body else, humble, lowly hearts, in frightful looks and dirty dresses, at our leisure. When we poor souls had presented ourselves with a contrition suitable to our worthlessness, some pretty young ladies in mobs, popped in here and there about the church, clattering the pew door after them, and squatting into a whisper behind their fans. Among others, one of Lady Lizard's daughters, and her hopeful maid, made their entrance: the young lady did not omit the ardent form behind the fan, while the maid immediately gaped round her to look for some other devout person, whom I saw at a distance very well dressed; his air and habit a little military, but in the pertness, not the true possession, of the martial character. This jackanapes was fixed at the end of a pew, with the utmost impudence, declaring, by a fixed eye on that seat (where our beauty was placed) the object of his devotion. This obscene sight gave me all the indignation imaginable, and I could attend to nothing but the reflection, that the greatest affronts imaginable are such as no one can take notice of. Before I was out of such vexatious in advertence to the business of the place, there was a great deal of good company now come in. There was a good number of very jaunty slatterns, who gave us to understand, that it is neither dress nor art to which they were beholden for the town's admiration. Besides these, there were also by this time arrived two or three sets of whisperers, who carry on most of their calumnies by what they entertain one another within that place, and we were now altogether very good company. There were indeed a few, in whose looks there appeared a heavenly joy and gladness upon the entrance of a new day, as if they had gone to sleep with expectation of it. For the sake of these, it is worth while that the church keeps up such early matins throughout the cities of London and Westminster; but the generality of those who observe that hour, perform it with so tasteless a behaviour, that it appears a task rather than a voluntary act . . .

[From *The Tatler*, no. 140 (1709–10); and *The Guardian*, no. 65 (1713)]

3. A poorly-trained clergyman, 1734

For the most part, the Anglican clergy of the eighteenth century were of a growing social status and of a growing educational attainment. However, it was possible for someone who was not a graduate to be ordained as a 'literate'. Such was Owen Bulkeley, curate of Llanddeusant in Anglesey. The account of Bulkeley's life given here suggests that bishops were often dependent upon the recommendation of others for who would be a suitable clergyman. However, in cases such as Bulkeley's a parish was saddled with an inadequate parson.

Owen Bulkeley of Gronant read in this church today & preach'd . . . This Owen Bulkeley was six years ago but a common labourer, nothing even of a school scholar, & Owen Lloyd of Llansadwrn being then parson of Llanddeusant, and a lazy worthless man, not being able to get a curate to serve ye three churches of Llanddeusant, Llanfairynghornwy & Llanbabo for the pitiful wages of £14 a year (for he would not give any more) by which means (he living at Bangor at his ease & serving in no Church), these three churches were in a manner neglected for ye space of two or three months, except it was that somebody came very seldom to ruffle them over the prayers of the church (as we had ours by this fellow today) the parishioners by this time beginning to grumble, and all the country besides crying shame, Owen Lloyd had then no remedy but either to read there himself (which to be sure was too much slavery for so great & good a man as he) or to pay £20 a year to a curate for serving it, which was certainly too much and very hard upon the poor Priest, for then he could not clear above £50 a year which was but a small pension to live upon at Bangor, considering the care of several hundreds of souls that were committed to his charge, whom he very punctually & affectionately visited once every year at Midsummer, but in order to have this living served for little or nothing, Hugh Wms the late Member for this County, at ye recommendation of John Owen Presaddfed & Lewis Trysclwyn (for Robert Bulkeley Gronant this fellow's brother was married to Lewis Tryselwyn's sister, & always a hearty voter & well wisher of Hugh Wms) in order to get this fellow bread after a more idle manner than before, by his industry, got Owen Lloyd to write by this Owen Bulkeley to London to Bishop Sherlock then Bishop of Bangor to get this fellow ordained deacon & priest & to be his curate, John Presaddfed and Tryselwyn writing the same time to Hugh Wms to wait upon the Bishop with the same request, which was accordingly granted, but I presume without any, manner of examination, for if ye Bishop had examined him 'tis impossible he could have been ordained, but ordained he was . . .

[From G. N. Evans, *Religion and Politics in Mid-Eighteenth Century Anglesey* (Cardiff, 1953), by permission of the University of Wales Press]

4. A funeral wake, *c.* 1735

Funerals were one of the rites of passage that were as important in the eighteenth century as earlier and later times. Night funerals, funeral sermons, processions and rings were all features of the eighteenth century's response to death. In this extract, written about 1735 probably by Bishop Hare, the Welsh custom of a wake is described. The practices of a wake and of condolence (literally to eat bread together) were widespread in the period.

The night before a dead body is to be interred, the friends and neighbours of the deceased resort to the house the corpse is in, each bringing with him some small present of meat, bread, or drink, (if the family be something poor) but more especially candles, whatever the family is; and this night is called *wyl nos*, whereby the country people seem to mean a watching night.

Whenever anybody comes into the room where a dead corpse lies, especially the *wyl nos*, and the day of its interment, the first thing he does he falls upon his knees by the corpse and saith the Lord's prayer.

Pence and half-pence, in lieu of little rolls of bread, (which heretofore generally and by some still are given on these occasions,) are now distributed to the poor, who flock in great numbers to the house of the dead before the corpse is brought out, when the corpse is brought out of the house, and laid upon the bier, and covered before it be taken up, the next of kin to the deceased, widow, mother, daughter, or cousin, (never done by a man,) gives cross over the corpse to one of the poorest neighbours two or three white loaves of bread and a cheese with a piece of money stuck in it, and then a new wooden cup of drink, which some will require the poor body that receives it immediately to drink a little of. When this is done, the minister (if present) saith the Lord's prayer, and then they set forward towards church. And all along, from the house to the church-yard, at every cross way, the bier is laid down, and the Lord's prayer renewed; and so when they come first into the church-yard, and before any of the verses appointed in the service to be said.

In some places there is a custom of ringing a little bell before the corpse from the house to the church-yard. If it should happen to rain while the corpse is carried to church, 'tis reckoned to bode well for the deceased, whose bier is wet with the dew of heaven. When a corpse is carried to church from any part of the town the bearers take care to carry it so that the cross may be on their right hand, nor will they bring the corpse to the church-yard any other way but through the south gate. There is also a custom of singing psalms on the way as the corpse is carried to church.

At church nothing is done but as directed by the rubric, besides that, evening service is read with the office of burial. At those words, 'we commit this body to the ground,' the minister holds the spade and throws in the earth first.

The minister goes to the altar and there saith the Lord's prayer, with one of the prayers appointed to be read at the grave; after which, the congregation offer upon the altar, or on a little board the rails of the altar, their benevolence to the officiating minister. A friend of the deceased is appointed to stand at the altar, observing who gives, and how much. When all have given, he tells the money with the minister, and signifies the sum to the congregation, thanking them for all their good will.

The people kneel and say the Lord's prayer on the graves of lately deceased friends for some Sundays after their interment, and this is done generally upon their first coming into the church, and after that they dress the grave with flowers.

[From *The British Magazine*, vol. 7 (1835)]

5. Music in church, and its difficulties, 1749–52

Music in English churches had evolved by the eighteenth century from psalmody and plainsong to anthems and hymns, in which the eighteenth century was especially rich. The problem for parochial music was the poor training that many musicians had received and the quality of the instruments; combined, the effects of a tuneless cacophony could be to reduce the edifying effect of worship. The extracts from the parish register of Hayes, near London, suggest the difficulty sometimes attendant on the provision of music in churches in the eighteenth century.

'Feb. 11, 1749. The company of singers, by the consent of the ordinary, were forbidden to sing any more by the minister, upon account of their frequent ill-behaviour in the chancel, and their ordering the carpenter to pull down part of the belfry without leave from the minister and churchwardens.'

On another day, March 18: 'The clerk gave out the 100th Psalm, and the singers immediately opposed him, and sung the 15th and bred a disturbance. The clerk then ceased.'

And under 1752 it is enter'd: 'Robert Johnson buried, and a sermon preached to a noisy congregation.' But these were not the only cases of insubordination which disturbed the Rector's mind; for on one occasion, when the Acton ringers came over, the churchwarden ordered the belfry door to be broken open for them to ring 'contrary to the canon and leave of the minister . . . the ringers and other inhabitants disturbed the service from the beginning of prayers to the end of the sermon, by ringing the bells, and going into the gallery to spit below a fellow came into Church with a pot of beer and a pipe, smoking in his own pew until the end of the sermon.'

[From T. F. Thiselton-Dyer, *English Social Life as told by the Parish Registers* (London, 1898)]

6. A dean resents the public nature of cathedral life, 1750

In 1746 at the age of 33, Spencer Cowper, son of Lord Cowper, became Dean of Durham through the good offices of his family. The young dean found his residence in the north a great tedium, and in the two extracts here at the start and end of his month's residence at the cathedral suggests the reasons why. The dean, as the leading officer of the cathedral, was expected to maintain a public role, to give hospitality, to preside over the chapter and fulfil all the administrative duties of the cathedral. However much he resented it, Dean Cowper was a great public figure and had to resign himself to the public nature of his role.

Durham. Sept 28 1750

. . .As this is the eve of my residence, I cannot say I am in the best or pleasantest humour in the world. Hitherto I have lived almost as quiet and snug as at Pansanger, and excepting one day w'ch his Honour Lumley and family thought fit to interrupt that quiet, I think I have pass'd my days without more interruptions than you, though you boast much, have done at Althorp. But tomorrow this scene changes for the reverse. Beadsmen, jurymen and justices fill up this week to come, and the two next, prebendaries and minor canons divide amongst themselves: the long book will be produced in the morning, with the column for the day most curiously laid out in circles from top to bottom. But you know all this so well, that the very hinting it will revive the memory of its whole progress . . .

Thank God, I am now enter'd into the last week of residence, the noble mayor and corporation were to have been my guests today, but they have excused themselves, and my table now is open to all the riff-raff corny can pick up.

[From E. Hughes (ed.), *The Letters of Spencer Cowper Dean of Durham 1746–1774* (Surtees Society, 1956), by permission]

7. Religion and politeness, 1760

The idea of politeness developed in the eighteenth century. It became a feature of social differentiation, allowing the middle and upper classes to assert their separation from the common herd. It also lubricated the social processes of an increasingly complex society. Religious observance was one of those occasions on which courtesy, respect and refinement were able to be expressed. The extract, an account of a charity sermon in 1760, suggests that ceremony and piety often complemented each other.

. . .We met at Northumberland House, and set out in four coaches. Prince Edward, Colonel Brudenel his groom, Lady Northumberland, Lady Mary Coke, Lady Carlisle, Miss Pelham, Lady Hertford, Lord Beauchamp, Lord Huntington . . . Lord Hertford at the head of the Governors with their white staves met us at the door and led the Prince directly to the chapel, where before the altar was an armchair for him, with a blue damask cushion, a prie-dieu, and a footstool of black cloth with gold nails. We sat on forms near him. There were Lord and Lady Dartmouth, in the odour of devotion, and many city ladies. The chapel was dressed with orange and myrtle . . . Prayers then began, psalms and a sermon, the latter by a young clergyman, one Dodd; who contributed to the popish idea one had imbibed by haranguing entirely in the French style, and very eloquently and touchingly. He apostrophised the lost sheep, who sobbed and cried for their souls – so did my Lady Hertford and Fanny Pelham . . . In short it was a very pleasing performance, and I got the most illustrious [Prince] to desire it might be printed. We had another hymn and then were conducted to the parlour, where the Governors kissed the Prince's hand . . .

[From J. Walkins, *Horace Walpole's Letters* (London, 1819)]

8. The Church and rates: extracts from Winchcombe vestry minute book, 1763–99

The extracts from the vestry book of the parish of Winchcombe, in Gloucestershire, in the second half of the eighteenth century are representative of many such records. The vestry charged the church rate, which was the source of money spent in these records, on the landowners of the parish; the vestry also chose the churchwardens for the year. Country parishes, like Winchcombe, were often open vestries – at which all ratepayers were represented – and their duties included payment of a range of officials and the oversight of roads and the poor.

Jan. 8, 1764. Ordered that a new pew be erected for the Excise officer and a rate made to pay for it.

November 27, 1764. Rate of 4/- on everyone possessing £100, and of 2/- on every labourer to repair of highways.

December, 1771. John Smith to make new clock with quarters and put the chimes in good repair for £30, with a handsome hand without on the South side of the Tower, finding all materials except the dial plate and keep in repair for 7 years at 5/- a year.

April 18, 1776. For the future the churchwardens shall not expend more at the Visitation in eating and drinking than 5/- per man.

March 5, 1776. Organ loft of no manner of service. Ordered to be pulled down and rebuilt and eight pews to be erected and fitted up.

July, 1783. £28 levied to pay the organist's salary.

November 5, 1786. Churchwardens to put in execution an act for preventing and punishing vice, prophaneness and immorality.

July 1788. Whereas Rachel wife of William Phillips is insane and not kept under confinement but suffered to go at large, the houses and effects of several persons in the said borough are thereby liable to be destroyed by fire. We therefore order the churchwardens to take and deliver her to the Workhouse.

July, 1789. John Chadborn to teach 40 boys every Sunday for £6 10s 0d and to have 8/– extra for firing. Mary Clark and Sarah Cartwright to teach 30 girls (at 1/6 a week each) every Sunday and 8/– for firing.

March 12th, 1790. Ale for the ringers on account of his Majesty's recovery from his late indisposition 6/–. Ale for the Singers Xmas last 10/–. Ale for the singers by reason of his Majesty's recovery. 10/6.

November 5, 1790. To Ed. Mason at 3 several times for teaching the children to sing in the church. 15/– For velvet wherewith the pulpit cloth was made £12 8s 3d. For making same 4/–.

March 12, 1791. David Harvey carriage of a load of stone for repairing the church walls 5/–. John Crook for crying the damage done to the churchyard wall 1/–.

February 28th, 1794. To Rev. J. J. Lates for a hood pertaining to Master of Arts £1 11s 6d.

January 15th, 1798. William Seabright who is very ill and also his wife having 4 young children be allowed 2/6 per week.

1799. Richard Warner of Leachlade and his wife to superintend the poor and live in the Workhouse at £28 a year and provide such ale, beer, butter, sugar, tea and butchers meat as himself and wife or either of them shall or may have occasion to buy or use if the meat in the said Workhouse may not be thought by him sufficient.

September 6, 1799. John Chadbourn Vestry Clerk to have 8 guineas for the extraordinary service and attendance he has done for and served the parish for the two last years.

> [From A. T. Hart, *The Eighteenth Century Country Parson*
> (Shrewsbury: Wilding & Sons, 1955)]

9. Religion and society at Bath, 1766

The following extracts from the Revd John Penrose's letters from Bath, where he and his family went to enjoy the waters, illustrate many of the features of worship in the fashionable spas. The first extract indicates how religious observance could form part of the fashionable 'round', like the pump rooms: to see and be seen was as important as the worship. The second extract shows how charity sermons harnessed condescension and patronage to the demands of fashionable activity. The third passage mentions the remarkable use of sedan chairs in church, which must have combined the very worst of private and public worship. The fourth extract shows that it was not only the industrial northern towns which were poorly served by church accommodation; the new resorts had as serious a problem with church seatings. The fifth extract shows how fashionable worship did not mean that the dogmas of the Church were lost: the Restoration of Charles II was celebrated with great show and display in Bath.

1.

. . .This morning, while Mamma and [your] Sister were at the Abbey, I was conducted by Mrs Leigh to the Pump-Room. I went the sooner, partly, because when Church is over, there is a vast crowd of people assemble there, and, partly, because Mr Chantor Snow made me an offer of part of his chaise, at half hour after twelve. For this offer I accepted of, and had a very agreeable airing, five miles on the lower Bristol Road, in gentle weather, and the Chantor very sociable. There was but little company in the Pump-Room, as I wished; but one was Dr Barnard, Bp. of Londonderry in Ireland . . . While I was at the Pump-Room, and on my jaunt, Mamma was at Church. She says, the number of communicants was like that at Gluvias; as many gentlemen as ladies (that is uncommon elsewhere,) some few poor persons, and (what she was pleased to see) one footman with a shoulder-knot. I believe, the people frequent the churches, as well as the assembly rooms for I spoke with no less than four this day, who were at St James's Church, and offered money for a seat, but could not be admitted for want of room: tho' in this church, there is no sermon mornings, only prayers. Your Mamma hath had a ticket presented to her, to gain admittance to Lady Huntingdon's Chapel. It is a message-card with this inscription:

'Strait is the Gate and narrow is the Way which leadeth unto Life and few there be that find it. Mat. 7. 14. This ticket admits the Bearer to a seat in my Chapel' S. Huntingdon. Seal. March 16 1766.'

2.

Sunday, Apr. 27.

. . .Glorious weather this day; I have been three times at the Pump-Room, twice at the Abbey, twice on the parade with your Mamma (who has a great cold in her head) and Fanny. The gentleman, who preached in the morning, was Dr Goodall, a gentleman possessed of several ecclesiastical dignities, but I know not where . . . It was an occasional sermon for the Bath Hospital, which was erected between twenty; and thirty years ago for the reception of sick poor from all parts of the Kingdom, such whose disorders are particularly Bath cases. The building is capacious enough to admit upwards of an hundred patients: but the subscriptions and benefactions will not maintain more than seventy; for which reason the governors do not think it advisable at present to admit more than that number. A collection towards this useful charity was made this morning at the Abbey and all other places of public worship in Bath, except Lady Huntingdon's Chapel. At the Abbey was collected £65; at Queen Square Chapel £36; at St. James's Church £30; at Cross Bath Chapel, £6. What at other places I have not heard; nor what was gathered in the afternoon at the Abbey; for there a collection was made both parts of the day. It was a very affecting sight to see all the patients ranged in two lines, the men on one side, the women on the other, making a lane from the outer door of the Abbey to the door of the inner part, where service is performed, for the mayor and magistrates and all the congregation to pass through. Eight beadles, in an uniform dress, (brown great coats, with yellow capes, and sleeves turned up with yellow,) with each a staff in his hand with a brass knob at the top attended them. And when they went from Church, they all walked two and two very orderly, four beadles with staves preceding, then the men patients, then two more beadles, then the women patients, then the other two beadles closing the procession. In the same manner we saw them come to Church in the afternoon . . .

3.

. . .The morning was very fine, but it hath been a moist afternoon: yet I have been at the Abbey, where I read prayers, and afterwards (as usual) at the Pump-Room. I have drank more water, since I have been here, than in many years before. I may have told you so before, for what I know; for keeping no memorandum of what I write, it is not unlikely but I may use tautology. Last Sunday at Church, a lady was brought in a sedan, and placed before the reading desk in the Abbey, and remained in it all service time. This is no uncommon thing. And this morning another lady, the same; and, after prayers, was carried up to the communion table to be churched (for women are churched there) and did not come out of the sedan at all . . .

4.

. . .You have seen in the newspapers, that the foundation stone is laid of an Octagon Chapel to be built here in Milsom Street: and it is but needed. Bath is so enlarged, that the places of public worship will not contain a tithe of the inhabitants, and strangers resorting hither. At the Chapel in Queen-Square, a stranger cannot get a sitting under half a crown a time, or a guinea for the season: the inhabitants themselves, to have a seat, must pay a guinea a year each person. So numerous as the people here are, of some sort or other, here is no place of burial but in the churches; or none worth mentioning: and the fees for breaking ground in churches monstrous high, ten pounds at the Abbey. So all the poor, and middling people, nay all except the rich and great, are carried, when dead to the churchyards of Widcombe or chiefly at Bathwick, two neighbouring parishes on the other side the river Avon, which is crossed in a ferry-boat; and four or five shillings are paid as a fee for breaking the ground.

5.

. . .This morning, being the day of the Restoration of K Charles II: the day, in which the ecclesiastical and civil constitution was restored: a day, which all true members of the Church of England ought to celebrate with religious joy; was ushered in, with ringing of bells from the three towers of the Abbey of St Michael's and St James's Churches; not only the boys and girls, but the chairmen, collier's horses, coach-horses, etc. are adorned with oaken leaves; large oaken boughs stand up in the front of most houses; the Union Flag was displayed, on top of the Abbey-Tower; Mr Mayor in his scarlet gown, attended by the magistrates, and preceded by his officers and the city music went to church in solemn state, where an excellent sermon, proper to the occasion, was preached by Mr Taylor, (his Text Psal. XC v.2 former part): prayers were read by Dr Warner a clergyman of Bath. You cannot think, how I was pleased to see the day so well observed: and I am sure, Mrs Nevill must have respected the preacher to her dying day if she had heard how he run down the Usurper Cromwell . . .

[From B. Mitchell and H. Penrose (eds), *Letters from Bath 1766–1767 by the Revd John Penrose* (Gloucester: Alan Sutton Publishing Ltd (an imprint of Sutton Publishing Ltd), 1990), with permission]

10. Northern contempt for religion, 1778

In 1778, Thomas Hest, the seventy-year-old vicar of Warton, commented on a spirit of contempt for religion that he felt had become prevalent. It was exactly the sort of complaint that Victorian historians have used in condemning the levels of piety and respect for religion. Doubtless it is possible to find such attitudes at any time and place in English history.

. . .We have alas many who have no regard for religion, who commonly absent themselves from the public worship of God, some I believe, thro' indolence, others thinking themselves witty, employ their talents in ridiculing the Scriptures, and laughing at those who are disposed to be serious . . . for what reformation can be expected from the rising generation, when they have daily before their eyes such very bad examples of their own wicked and profane parents.

[From Chester Diocesan Record Office, Articles for Visitation, EDV/7/2, no. 350, with the permission of Cheshire County Council; quoted in J. Addy, *Sin and Society* (London, 1989)]

11. Sunday amusements, 1780s

During the eighteenth century attitudes to Sundays changed. The full-blown sabbatarianism of the nineteenth century was unknown, and once Sunday service was over entertainment and amusement were widely enjoyed. George III, a devout and conservative sovereign, enjoyed music on Sundays and satisfied himself that there was no reason why he should not. Hannah More regarded the King's enjoyment of bands as a poor example to the boys of Eton, and there is some evidence that George III did not expect the Archbishop of Canterbury to follow his example, having apparently criticized him for amusements at Lambeth on Sundays. The extract describes Bishop Porteus's attempts to raise Sunday activities to a more spiritual plane.

. . .'The beginning of the winter of 1780,' he observes, 'was distinguished by the rise of a new species of dissipation and profaneness. A set of needy and profligate adventurers, finding every day, and almost every hour, of the week occupied by some amusement or other, bethought themselves of trying what might be done on a Sunday. It was a novel and a bold attempt, but not the less likely to succeed in this country and in these times. They therefore opened and publicly advertised two different sorts of entertainment for the Sunday evening. One of these was at Carlisle House, and was called a Promenade. The other was a meeting at public rooms hired for the purpose, and assumed the name of Christian Societies, Religious Societies, Theological Societies, Theological Academies, &c. The professed design of the former was merely to walk about and converse, and take refreshments, the price of admission being three shillings: but the real consequence, and probably the real purpose of it, was to draw together dissolute people of both sexes, and to make the Promenade a place of assignation: and, in fact, it was a collection of the lowest and most profligate characters that could possibly be assembled together from every part of London. It gave offence, not only to every man of gravity and seriousness, but even to young men of gaiety and freedom, several of whom I have heard speak of it with abhorrence. Nay, even foreigners were shocked and scandalised at it, considering it a disgrace to any Christian country to tolerate so gross an insult on all decency and good order.

The business, or, as it should be rather called, the amusement proposed at the Sunday Debating Societies, was to discuss passages of Scripture, which were selected and given out for that purpose; when every one present, ladies as well as gentlemen, were to propose their doubts, receive explanations, and display their eloquence on the text proposed. It was to be, in short, a school for Metaphysics, Ethics, Pulpit Oratory, Church History, and Canon Law. It is easy to conceive what infinite mischief such debates as these must do to the younger part of the community, who, being unemployed on this day, would flock to any assembly of this sort; would look upon every doubt and difficulty started there as an unanswerable argument against religion, and would go home absolute sceptics, if not confirmed unbelievers. Thus, as the Promenade tended to destroy every moral sentiment, the theological assemblies were calculated to extinguish every religious principle; and both together threatened the worst consequences to public morals.

It was therefore highly necessary to put a speedy and effectual stop to such alarming evils. I mentioned it early in the winter to several persons of rank and authority, and waited a considerable time in the hope, that some one of more weight and influence than myself, would have stood forth on this occasion. But the [parliamentary] session being now far advanced, and finding no one inclined to take the matter up, it became absolutely necessary to do something; and I therefore resolved to try what my own exertions would do. I first consulted several eminent lawyers, as well as the principal acting magistrates in Westminster, in order to know, whether either the statute or the common law, as they now stood, was sufficient to check this evil. They all assured me that both were insufficient, and that nothing but an Act of Parliament, framed on purpose, could effectually suppress it. In consequence of this opinion, I applied to a legal friend, and with his assistance got a proper Bill sketched out, which I afterwards showed to Lord Bathurst, President of the Council, and to Sir John Skinner, Lord Chief Baron of the Exchequer; and it was afterwards communicated to the Lord Chancellor Thurlow, and Lord Mansfield. After it had received their approbation, I applied to the Solicitor General, Mr Mansfield, who undertook to move it in the House of Commons; and Sir William Dolben agreed to second it. This they did on the 3rd of May 1781, and the Bill was entitled "An Act for preventing certain abuses and profanations on the Lord's Day, commonly called Sunday." It was violently opposed in its different stages through the House by several members, particularly Mr Wilkes; but it passed without a division. On the second reading of the Bill in the House of Lords, it was opposed principally by the Duke of Manchester, who thought that there were not sufficient proofs of the mischievous tendency of the Sunday evening amusements . . .

A division then took place on the commitment of the Bill, which was carried by a majority of 26; and it afterwards passed without further opposition.'

In this manner did the Bishop, by his own energy and perseverance, carry through Parliament an Act, which by its judicious provisions effectually checked a most wicked and licentious system, calculated to produce the worst consequences to religion and to public morals.

[From R. Hodgson, *The Works of the Rt Revd Beilby Porteus DD . . . With His Life* (London, 1811)]

12. The start of Sunday schools, 1783

Sunday schools were founded by Robert Raikes in Gloucester in 1783. Raikes was a journalist and the son of a clergyman. Raikes had been horrified by the conditions in Gloucester gaol, but felt that prisoners were a lost cause; he turned his attention to the children living in squalor in the city streets. Like a number of other people at this time his solution to idleness and unruly behaviour by children was Sunday schools. Raikes's achievement was to make the Sunday school movement a national initiative, rather than a series of isolated local activities. The letter produced below, addressed by Raikes to Colonel Townley of Sheffield, who was interested in the Gloucester initiative, gives an account of the start of the movement.

My friend the Mayor has just communicated to me the letter which you have honoured him with, inquiring into the nature of Sunday-schools. The beginning of this scheme was entirely owing to accident. Some business leading me one morning into the suburbs of the city, where the lowest of the people, (who are principally employed in the pin manufactory) chiefly reside, I was struck with concern at seeing a group of children, wretchedly ragged, at play in the streets. I asked an inhabitant whether those children belonged to that part of the town, and lamented their misery and idleness. 'Ah! sir,' said the woman to whom I was speaking, 'could you take a view of this part of the town on a Sunday, you would be shocked indeed, for then the street is filled with multitudes of these wretches, who, released that day from employment, spend their time in noise and riot, playing at "chuck", and cursing and swearing in a manner so horrid as to convey to any serious mind an idea of hell, rather than any other place. We have a worthy clergyman', said she '[the] curate of our parish, who has put some of them to school but upon the Sabbath they are all given up to follow their own inclinations without restraint, as their parents, totally abandoned in themselves, have no idea of instilling into the minds of their children principles to which they themselves are entire strangers.'

This conversation suggested to me that it would be at least a harmless attempt, if it were productive of no good, should some little plan be formed to check the deplorable profanation of the Sabbath. I then inquired of the woman if there were any decent, well-disposed women in the neighbourhood who kept schools for teaching to read. I presently was directed to four. To these I applied, and made an agreement with them to receive as many children as I should send upon the Sunday, whom they were to instruct in reading and in the Church catechism. For this I engaged to pay them each a shilling for their day's employment. The women seemed pleased with the proposal. I then waited on the clergyman before mentioned and imparted to him my plan. He was so much satisfied with the idea that he engaged to lend his assistance by going round to the school on a Sunday afternoon to examine the progress that was made and to enforce order and decorum among such a set of little heathens.

[From B. Rodgers, *The Cloak of Charity* (London, 1949), by permission of Routledge and Kegan Paul]

13. Easter arrangements, 1786

At Easter 1786, the parson at Hampsthwaite published his arrangements for the services, visiting, worship, and tithes during the Eastertide. For many people Easter was one of the few occasions on which they received communion, and on which bishops asked for numbers receiving communion in their visitations. Clergy also received Easter offerings from their parishioners. These features of Easter as the major festival of the Church were a strong survival in the eighteenth century, and many congregations were swelled to their peak at Easter.

I give notice to all the parishioners within ye p'ish of Hampsthwaite that I intend (God willing) to administer ye Blessed Com. on those days following, viz., Palm Sunday, Good Friday, Easter Even, Easter day in the [church], and here will be sermons and homilies on Good Friday and Easter Even by myself or some other, and I pray do not drive all till last day. On Tuesday in Passion Week at Thornthwaite Chapel. On Monday morning after Palm Sunday to ye sick and lame of Holme Sinders Hills. On Tuesday morning, before I begin at Chapel, to the sick and lame people of Thornthwaite and Padside. On Wednesday morning to ye sick of ye Hamlet of Birtsw'th and Felicliffe, and on Thursday morning to ye Ham't of Hamp. Ye Churchwardens are to give notice ye night before to attend in ye Hambletts.

I desire all ye parishioners of this parish to take notice and others not of ye parish that are concerned, that they come and reckon and pay their . . . [tithes] betwixt [now] and Easter day to me or some other I shall appoint the reck'g will be taken in ye Church.

I shall be at home or in ye Church every day after now until Easter except Monday and Tuesday in Passion Week, when I am to be at Larence Buck's to retain ye reck'g and compts of all persons that live within the compass of Sinders Hills.

I desire the Church wardens will take notice, as much as in them lies, of those persons that do wilfully absent ymselves from Sacrament, that are above 16 years of age. I give notice I will take no reck'gs: nor any for me, on Sunday morn: nor on Good Friday morning nor on Saturday morning.

The Churchwardens are to provide bread and wine on those days I have appointed, at ye charge of ye p'ish. If any person be able to go or ride to Church or Chapel let them not expect me at their houses.

A great sickness I fear this ensuing year. I pray God's Blessing from plag: and pestilence – Ld grant me health amongst my wife and children, I fear sad things will befall this land this year.

[From T. F. Thiselton-Dyer, *English Social Life as told by the Parish Registers* (London, 1898)]

14. Daily worship in the eighteenth century

Table 5.1 (see pp. 156–9) shows the practice of daily worship in London churches in 1692, 1708, 1714, 1732, 1746 and 1824. The information suggests that the eighteenth century was a period of growth, at least in London, of daily worship. Clearly throughout the century a number of London churches provided daily worship, which they had not previously provided.

Table 5.1 A table showing the hours of daily prayer in and about the cities of London and Westminster

	1692		1708	
	M	E	M	E
All Hallows, Barking	8		8s 9w	
All Hallows, Staining				
St Andrew's Holborn	6 & 11	3	6s 7w	3
			11	
St John's Chapel				
St Andrew's Undershaft	6		6s 7w	
St Anne's Westminster	11	4	7 & 11	4 & 7
St Antholin's Watling St	6		6	
St Austin's by St Paul's School		6		3
St Bartholomew the Great	10		11	
St Bartholomew the Less	11	8	11	
St Bartholomew Exchange				7
St Bennet Grace Church	11	3		
St Botolph Aldersgate	10	3	9	3
St Botolph Bishopsgate			8s 9w	7
St Bridget Fleet St	11	8	11	8
Bloomsbury Chapel, Great Russell St				
Charterhouse	10	5s 2w	10	5s 2w
Christchurch, Newgate	11	5s 3w	11	5s 3w
St Christopher Threadneedle St	6	6	6	6
St Clement Danes	10	3 & 8	10	3 & 8
St Dionis Backchurch	8	5	8s 9w	5
Drapers Alms Houses				
Duke St Chapel				
St Dunstan's Stepney	11	6s 3w	11	6s 3w
St Dunstan's West	7 & 10	3	7	3
St Edmund Lombard St	11	7	11	7
Ely House	10	4		
St George's Chapel Queen's Square				
St George's Bloomsbury				
St Giles' Cripplegate				
St Giles' in the Fields	10	3	10	3
Bloomsbury Chapel	11	3		
Great Queen St				
Gray's Inn Chapel	11	3 or 5		
St George's Hanover Square				
Conduit St Chapel				
Audley St Chapel				
Hoxton Hospital				
Islington Alms House				
St James' Westminster	11	4	6 & 11	3 & 6
King St Chapel				
Berwick St				
St James' Chapel	6 & 11	4		
St James' Clerkenwell	10	2 (Sat)	11	2 (Sat)
St John Wapping	8		8s 9w	
St Katherine Tower	11			

| 1714 | | 1732 | | 1746 | | 1824 | |
M	E	M	E	M	E	M	E
8	7	9	7	9	7		
				11	4		
6s 7w	3	6s 7w	3	11	3	11¼	3¼
11		11					
				11	4		
6s 7w	6	6s 7w	6	6s 7w	6		
6s 7w	4 & 6	6s 7w	4 & 6	6s 7w	4 & 6		
11		11		11			
6s 7w		6s 7w		6s 7w			7
11	5	11					
11		11		10 or 11			
	6		7				
11	3	11	3	11	3		
11	7	11	6				
11	8	11	8	11	7¼		
11	3						
11	5s 2w			11	4s 3w		
11	5s 3w	11	5s 3w	11	5s 3w		
6	6	6	6	6	6		
11	3 & 8	11	3	11	3 & 7		
			8s 7w				
8s 9w	5	8s 9w	5	8s 9w	5		
8s 9w							
11	4						
11	6s 3w	11	6s 3w	11	6s 3w	11	
7	3	7	3				
11	7	11	7		7w		
8	4						
(if bishop be in residence)							
11	4	11	4	11	4		
		11	4	11	4		
	8	11	8	11	7		
10	3	10	3	10	4	11	
11	3						
four times daily				11			
11	3w 5s			11	5s 3w		
		11	5	11	5	11	
				11	4		
				11			
11	5s 3w						
11	4						
6s 7w	3 & 6	6s 7w	3	6s 7w	3 & 6	7 & 11	6
11		11	6s 7w	11			
				11	6		
11	5			11	5		
8 & 11	5						
11	2 (Sat)	11		11		11	
8s 9w	5s 3w	8s 11w		11	8		
11		11		11			

Table 5.1 continued

	1692		1708	
	M	E	M	E
King's St Chapel				
St Lawrence Jewry	11	8	11	8
St Leonard Shoreditch				
Asks Chapel				
Lambeth Chapel				
London House Aldergate	10	3		
London Workhouse Bishopsgate St				
Lincoln's Inn	11	5		
Ludgate Prison				
St Magnus London Bridge				
St Margaret's Westminster	10	6	10	6
Duke St Chapel				
Queen Square Chapel				
Chapel in the Broadway				
St Martin's in the Fields	6	5	6s 7w	5
Oxenden Chapel				
Hog Lane Chapel				
St Martin's Ludgate	11	3	11	6
St Mary's Aldermanbury	11			
St Mary le Bow	8	5		
St Mary le Strand				
St Mary Magdalen, Old Fish St	6			
St Mary Magdalen, Bermondsey				
St Mary Woolnoth, Lombard St	11	5	11	5
St Michael's Queenhithe				
St Michael's Basinghall				5
St Michael's Crooked Lane				
St Nicholas Cole Abbey				
Oxford Chapel Marylebone				
St Paul's Covent Garden	6 & 10	3 & 6	6 & 10	3 & 6
St Paul's Shadwell				
St Peter's Cornhill	11	4		
Queen's Bench Prison				
St Sepulchre's	7	3	6	3
Skinner's Alms Houses				
Somerset House Chapel				
St Stephen's Coleman St			11	
St Stephen's Walbrook	11	5		
St Swithun London Stone	11	4	11	5
Temple Church	8 or 7	4		
St Thomas Hospital Chapel				
Trinity Chapel Bond St				
Tuttlefields Chapel, Westminster				
Palmer's Almshouses				
St Vedast's Foster Lane				
Whitehall Chapel				

[From J. Wickham Legg, *English Church Life from the Restoration to the Tractarian Movement* (London, 1914)]

1714		1732		1746		1824	
M	E	M	E	M	E	M	E
6s 7w	3 & 6			11	6		
11							
6	8	11	7	11	7		
		11		11			
		11	3	11	5s 3w		
7s 8w	2 & 9						
12							
6	6						
11	5			11	5		
10							
11	8						
	6s 7w				6		
				11	4		
11w	4			(11 summer only)			
				9	3½		
6s 7w	5	6s 7w	5	6s 7w	6	6s 7w	6
				11		11	
10							
11							
11	6	11	6	11	6		
8	5	8	5	8	5		
7s 8w	5						
11		11		11			
11	5	10	4s 3w	10	4s 3w		
	6		6		6		
	5		4		6w		
					8		
		11		11			
				11	5		
7w 6s	3 & 6	6 & 10	3 & 6	6 & 10	3 & 6		
10							
11	5s 3w						
11	4	11	4	11	4		
7							
6s 7w	3s 4w	6 & 7	3 & 4	6	3½	7	3
11							
11	4			11	4		
11		11	6	11			
11							
11	5	11	5	11	4		
8 or 7	4	8 or 7	4	8 or 9	4 or 3		
	3						
11	3						
9	5s						
	4 or 3w						
11							
	6				6		
11	5			11	5		

15. Church courts, discipline and penance in the eighteenth century

Historians tend to take the view that church courts, usually those of the archdeacon, which corrected immorality and irregular behaviour died out in the eighteenth century. The 'bawdy court', as it was often known, seemed less appropriate for a society which was developing looser ties of social deference, wage labour, geographical and social mobility and new attitudes to morality. However, the extracts from a range of church court records presented below suggest that the disciplinary authority of the Church was not eroded as easily or quickly as is thought, and that moral justice was still sought from the Church. Fornication, bastardy, public penance for sin and irreverent behaviour are the three items recorded here. What is as significant as the attitudes they contain are the dates of the cases, two of which occur late in the century.

Thame, Oxfordshire, 1718. We present Mary Towsin late of Thame, [a] single woman for being delivered of a male bastard child. We present Thomas West for being the reputed father of the sd. bastard child who does now provide for the said child. [Statement presented to court follows:] 'We whose names are hereunto subscribed being parishioners of Thame in the county of Oxon do hereby certify to all whom it may concern that we are of opinion that the bearer Thomas West of our parish who hath lately been presented for being the reputed father of a bastard child begotten on the body of Mary Towsen is not guilty thereof notwithstanding the fame that hath been spread abroad of his being the father thereof and that he is a very honest person and never suspected for any unchastity or dishonesty (for that he hath lived in service in one place for twenty years and upwards) till this fact was discover'd by the said Mary Towsen herself who was in hopes by that means to gain him for her husband he being a single man and that we have been informed she has been a loose and scandalous person before and since she came to live at Thame.' [Signed by the vicar, churchwardens, overseers and 25 parishioners: charge dismissed.] . . .

South Cerney, Gloucestershire, 1785. A schedule of penance to be performed by William Stephens in the parish church of South Cerney on Sunday the sixteenth day of January, 1785: 'Whereas the said William Stephens stands judicially convicted by his own confession that he has been guilty of the foul sin of fornication. It is therefore ordered by the Archdeacon of Gloucester that he shall come to the said Church at the tolling of the bell for Morning or Evening Service . . . and shall stand in the porch . . . until the first lesson is ended bareheaded and barefooted and having a white sheet over his wearing apparel and a white rod in his hand and shall ask forgiveness of all that pass by him, and after the first lesson is ended he shall come into the said Church and stand in some eminent place near the reading desk . . . and shall make an humble confession of his fault saying . . . I William Stephens do in the presence of God and this congregation confess and acknowledge with shame and confusion of face that not having the fear of God before mine eyes and being seduced by the temptation of the Devil and mine own filthy lusts I have been guilty of the foul sin of fornication' [Later entry:] 'This is to certify that the above named William Stephens did perform a public penance . . .'

1799. ' . . .That Thomas Ibbotson should be suspended from the office of parish clerk, without forfeiting the wages, until after the 10th day of February then next, being the first Sunday in Lent; that he do not approach the Sacrament of the Lord's Supper on that day, that, by the prayers of Lent, he might be fitted for it at the festival of Easter; and, lastly, that, on the first Sunday of the ensuing Lent, he should stand during service until the Nicene creed was read, before the font under the gallery, and there depart to a private seat, after having read distinctly the following acknowledgement, viz.

"I, Thomas Ibbotson, do acknowledge that, on the day of the Feast of Circumcision, I behaved very irreverently in the House of God: that I interrupted the divine service, and conducted myself in such a manner, both in the church and out of it, as to give just cause of offence to the congregation then present: that I was led to this misconduct by resentment, and not being perfectly sober at the time, for which I beg pardon of Almighty God, and do promise to order myself with greater sobriety and decency for the time to come".'

[From P. Hair, *Before the Bawdy Court* (London: Paul Elek, 1971); and J. Wickham Legg, *English Church Life from the Restoration to the Tractarian Movement* (London, 1914)]

THE ESTABLISHED CHURCH

1. Thomas Wilson's duties as Bishop of Sodor and Man, 1697–1755

Bishop Thomas Wilson was one of the most conscientious bishops of the eighteenth century. His appointment to the diocese of Sodor and Man in 1697 was made by the Earl of Derby who was hereditary sovereign of the island, and to whom Wilson was chaplain. Wilson devoted himself to the diocese, and spent the remainder of his (long) life as its bishop. His was not a meek conception of episcopal and clerical duty, however. His high expectations of himself as bishop as well as of his clergy, and his determination to supervise them closely, are all evident in this account of his life.

He was continually devising or executing plans of piety and benevolence, suited to the condition and exigencies of the people committed to his charge. Though the revenues of the bishopric at that period are said not to have exceeded 300£ per annum in money, yet in the hands of frugality and charity, they were found sufficient for every purpose. The wants of the poor were principally supplied out of the produce of the demesne. The fleece and the sheaf were in a state of constant requisition, and the most effectual means were adopted for multiplying both. As the Bishop had a poor drawer in his bureau for the reception of all monies dedicated to charitable uses, so he had a poor chest in his barn, for the reception of corn and meal, designed for the relief of the indigent. This chest he was in the habit of frequently inspecting, that he might be satisfied it was filled even up to the brim. At a season of unusual scarcity in the island, when, according to custom, he was inspecting the poor man's repository, he found it almost empty, whilst the family-chest was abundantly supplied. He expressed great displeasure on the occasion, and gave a strict charge to the steward of his house, that whoever were neglected, the poor should not. He regarded the claims of the poor as sacred, and made provision for every species of want and distress. When corn was measured for the poor, he gave express orders to his steward not to stroke it, as is usual, but to give heaped measure. He often conversed with the objects of charity who applied for relief, and minutely enquired into the circumstances of their case. One day a pauper, who had a large family, calling at Bishop's Court, was asked by the Bishop how he contrived to get food for his children. 'May it please your Lordship (says he) I go round with my bag from house to house, and generally get a herring from each housekeeper. This is our food; and as to drink, we quench our thirst at the nearest stream of water.'

'Poor man! (says the Bishop) that is hard fare; but mind you call here whenever you pass this way, and you shall get your bag filled.' Many a bag was filled, and many a family sustained by provisions from the stores of this generous friend of the poor. . .

The medical knowledge which the Bishop acquired in his youth was profitable to many. He acted in a great measure as the physician of his diocese. The poor from all quarters, who were sick of divers diseases, flocked to Bishop's Court for relief, as the pool of Bethesda. No talent which a good man possesses remains long unemployed . . .

To the religious education of children, he attended in a peculiar manner. He regarded the improvement of the parochial schools as an object of high importance, and was unwearied in his endeavours to render them extensively useful . . .

Bishop Wilson took considerable pains to acquire a knowledge of the Manx. In the latter part of his life, he is said to have spoken and read it without much hesitation, and to have taken pleasure in addressing the peasantry in the usual Manx phrases of salutation. Like good Bishop Bedel, he saw the necessity of instructing the people in the language which they best undertook, and was therefore solicitous to furnish them with plain and useful instructions in their native tongue . . .

The Bishop regularly held an annual convocation of his Clergy, at which he addressed them affectionately and earnestly on their pastoral duties, and on the most effectual means of discharging them. . . The following selection from these charges may serve to show the reader with what fidelity and zeal the Bishop discharged this important part of his office.

Bishop's Court, June 9th 1715

'My Brethren,

The last time we met in convocation, I recommended to you the necessity of bringing all our people to family devotions, if ever we expect to see a reformation of manners, or serious religion amongst us.

It concerns me to know how far your care and pains have been used to introduce this godly practice.

The most effectual way to do this, will be for every clergyman to be able to show his Bishop (when it is required of him) a particular register of every family in his parish, with the times when he visited any of them, and in what state he found them, and what hopes he had of reforming what he found amiss in any of them. . .

I intend, God willing, to visit every one of my brethren personally this summer. I shall be well pleased to find that this intimation has had its effect, and that I have not said this to no purpose. In the mean time, I am ready to show any one who desires it, what I mean by a book of parish duties, which I think so necessary to be kept by every clergyman who would faithfully discharge his duty.

I told you just now, that I intend this summer to see every church in the diocese, God enabling me. I hope that I shall find the parochial libraries entire and in good order; the registers regularly kept; the churches, church-houses and chancels in good order, as become the houses of God. And all other things, particularly the schools, in such order, as may satisfy me, and all reasonable people. . .

Now, if any amongst us shall think these duties too great a trouble to be performed, or not worthy of so much pains, and so neglect them, which God forbid; all one can say is, that every such person will surely be accountable to God for what he has now been put in mind of, and for the loss of many a soul, and for the loss of his own soul at last; from which judgement good Lord deliver every one of us, for Jesus Christ's sake, Amen. . .'

Bishop Wilson was in the habit of proposing candidates for holy orders to the clergy at the annual convocation for their approbation, and of strongly recommending to the pastors of the Church, to have a watchful eye over the life and conversation of such candidates, that when they were called on to sign their testimonials, they might do it with a safe conscience. He was undoubtedly solicitous to preserve the purity and sanctity of the sacred order, that they might in all things approve themselves as the ministers of God, and 'both by their life and doctrine set forth his true and lively word. . .' Few more effectual means could have been adopted to prevent the admission of persons of this description into the holy ministry, than the precaution which Bishop Wilson recommended.

[From H. Stowell, *The Life of Thomas Wilson* (London, 1819)]

2. Bishop Edmund Gibson's proposals for church reform, 1724

Bishop Gibson, perhaps the greatest churchman of the eighteenth century, made two proposals for church reform in 1724. The first of these was to institute Whitehall preacherships appointed from the two universities to reward and distinguish clergy at the two universities who were loyal to the House of Hanover (Oxford and Cambridge both having strong Jacobite elements which might be diminished by the measure). The Whitehall preachership was taken up by the government with alacrity, and survived till 1890. The second proposal was a more radical proposal for reform, to establish a new system of church appointments. Gibson was appalled that in spite of crown patronage over a significant number of livings there was only modest support for the Hanoverian succession. His response was to take the crown appointments out of the hands of politicians, who sought short-term advantage, and insist that all crown appointments should be given only to residents of the dioceses in which they fell. The idea was that this would promote expectations among the diocesan clergy and a strong adherence to the crown among them. The King indicated his approval of the measure by an Order in March 1724, but the scheme came to nothing as successive politicians sought to continue party advantage by appointing clergy of their hue to livings in the gift of the crown.

No. 1. A Proposal,

(1) For removing a complaint that so little notice is taken by ye government of the King's friends in ye two Universities: and at ye same time,

(2) For supplying a great defect in the preaching duty in His Majesty's Chapel at Whitehall. . .

Let twenty-four persons, being fellows of colleges in the two Universities, and the best scholars and best preachers that can be found among the King's friends there (that is to say twelve out of each University and two for each month) be appointed preachers at ye Chapel at Whitehall. Let a salary be settled of £20 for each man for his attendance: in all £480 per annum; or rather, if it might be, a salary of £30 to each (in all £720 per annum). £10 to defray ye charge of preparing for ye journey, and coming up and going down, and of living in London: gratuity for doing the duty at Whitehall, and for the great service done to the King and his government in ye University to which he belongs.

Let them continue in that office as long as they continue fellows, or till they be made chaplains to ye King and no longer; and as they die or leave their fellowships or are made chaplains at St James', let other worthy men, of each University respectively and qualified as above, succeed them in the duty at Whitehall; and let it be understood from ye beginning that it is intended to be carried on so in perpetuity.

Advantages of such Establishment.

(1) A salary bestowed for such a service will carry with it not only profit but honour, and will be more creditable and have better effects than a private pension in money.

(2) The King's friends in ye two Universities will see themselves regarded by ye Court; and ye more directly and visibly as this Chapel has an immediate relation to ye Court.

(3) The brightest and most learned persons among them will be brought forth from time to time, into ye eye of ye world, and become known to ye bishops and be better acquainted with them.

(4) Some of these preachers may be thought proper to be made chaplains to the King: and when the station at Whitehall appears to be a step to that, it will make it a greater mark of favour, and also ye succession at Whitehall will be quicker. In this way a succession of able men and good preachers will be always growing up for ye high offices in ye Church.

(5) By being in London, during their month's attendance, they will see and hear many things which will enable them at their return to answer objections against ye Administration, and confute ye lies and misrepresentations of ye enemy upon their own knowledge and observation.

(6) In this way of encouragement there will be no colour to complain of inroads upon the rights or government of ye Universities, which is an objection that other ways which been thought of, are liable to. Nor will there be any need of having recourse to Parliament to effect this.

2. Promotions by Dioceses

Considering the great number of ecclesiastical benefices which are in
the gift of ye King, the Lord Chancellor and the Chancellor of the
Duchy [of Lancaster] in all parts of England; how comes it to pass that
in ye space of six and thirty years which have passed since the time of
the Revolution, the clergy of England are not more attached to ye
interest of ye Protestant succession and the Royal Family?

Because those promotions have not been so ordered and disposed of
in such way as to create a general dependence, and raise a general
expectation among ye clergy; but have been bestowed uncertainly and
as it were, by chance, and been understood to fall only to ye share of
the favourites of particular persons in power and office; and by
consequence have had no influence, nor raised any expectation,
excepting in such favourites only. From whence several evils have
ensued. . .

Remedy. A resolution to be taken and in a proper manner notified,
that ye parochial livings in ye gift of the King, of the Lord Chancellor
and of ye Chancellor of the Duchy, which are not given to chaplains
in ordinary of ye King or to ye domestic chaplains of ye said Chancellors
respectively, will be bestowed upon clergymen officiating at ye time
when the vacancy happens, by virtue of institution or licence, within
ye diocese to which such benefice belongs; or to such persons in the
two Universities as are natives of the diocese and are in Holy Orders
at ye time when ye vacancy happens.

Results.
(1) This will make ye body of ye clergy of every diocese esteem all
benefices of ye forementioned patronage which are within their
dioceses, to be in effect their own property; and every one who thinks
his condition may be bettered by any particular vacancy or vacancies
in view, will have his eye upon them and put himself in proper methods
to obtain them; whereas in ye present method of disposing of these
favours, a benefice. . . raises no more expectation among ye clergy of
ye diocese or even of the neighbourhood, where it lies, than if it were
a hundred miles off and in any other diocese of England.

(2) The expectation being thus raised by vacancies in view, the clergy
will take all proper methods to recommend themselves to such of ye

nobility and gentry as are in ye interest of ye government, and are known to have credit above; and the bishops of the several dioceses who are now for the most part in the interest of the government, and who will be consulted of course concerning ye characters and behaviour of ye clergy who shall be candidates, will be much more regarded by their clergy and have a greater influence over them in all matters relating to ye service of ye government, especially ye young clergy, who either remain in ye Universities, or are come fresh from it to curacies, and have no preferment and who are now generally most noisy against ye government, will then become expectants of favour from the Crown upon ye prospect of particular vacancies in their eye. And as ye smaller benefices in ye gift of ye seals are very numerous and dispersed all over the nation, and though small, are certain, and more desirable than curacies; this would undoubtedly create a great dependence upon ye government as well among the younger clergy of every diocese, as among the natives thereof in ye two Universities. If it be said that care may be taken, without any such limitation to particular dioceses, to bestow ye promotions of ye Crown upon such persons only as are known to deserve well of ye government, ye answer is; that it is not the bestowing the benefice when vacant from whence ye great benefit arises to ye government, inasmuch as that is a favour only to one single person. . . but it is from ye raising a fixed and certain expectation of something directly and immediately within their view, to which the clergy of that diocese are particularity entitled; and from the regard that is paid them by ye Crown in appropriating the favours to them in particular and securing them against the inroads of foreign competitors. In order to keep up the expectations it seems to be a good rule, not to promise any benefice before it comes actually vacant.

No Alteration of Rights of Crown.

This makes not ye least alteration in ye rights of patronage belonging to ye King or either of the chancellors, but only puts it in such a method as seems to be far more for ye service of ye Crown. The King, notwithstanding this, will have the dignities of all kinds that are in the gift of the Crown to dispose of to his own chaplains and other clergy of superior merit, in any part of ye nations, and ye Lord Chancellor will have ye prebends of ye four Churches, viz. Norwich, Rochester, Gloucester and Bristol to bestow in ye utmost latitude; besides ye provision for his own chaplains.

And if this proposal should be thought a restraint on ye King's ministers or the two chancellors, this will be no objection with them, if it appear manifestly that the method proposed will be an enlargement of the King's interest. As to ye Bishops and their patronage; it were to be wished that as they are naturally obliged to have a particular regard to ye clergy of their own dioceses, they would voluntarily come under ye forementioned limitations in ye disposal of their benefices at least; which is in itself reasonable, and would in consequence create a dependence among ye clergy, and by that means enable ye bishops to promote ye King's service to a far greater degree than is to be expected in the present promiscuous method of disposing of their favours.

[From N. Sykes, *Edmund Gibson* (Oxford, 1926).
Reprinted by permission of Oxford University Press]

3. Tithe collection, 1728, 1777 and 1802

Tithes, the clerical entitlement to a tenth of agricultural produce, were a source of both income and difficulty for eighteenth-century clergymen. The problems of calculation of payments, extracting payments and ministering to the people from whom a living was sought were inevitably causes of disagreement on occasion. The three accounts given here, from Benjamin Rogers, rector of Carlton, William Jones, vicar of Broxbourne, and Randle Darwell, rector of Haughton, paint a moderate picture. These three clergymen did not resort to tithe agents to collect their dues, or protracted legal suits to extract them or the horror of mass action by parishioners.

1. Carlton

May the 16th [1728] being Thursday, Mrs Mary, wife of Mr John Rey Junior, paid me for her father Mr Uriah's small tithes due for his cows, calves and pigeons for the year 1721 16s with the discount of 4d upon the balance of accounts betwixt him and me; and also for 18 sacks of chaff at 4d per sack being 6s, and for his small tithes for the year 1727, for which I gave him a receipt in full of all accounts. I also pay'd her for an hog £2 8s and for cheese £3 5s; the hog my son bought of him and the cheese my wife bought of his wife; and the said Mrs Mary promising me to bring a receipt in full of all accounts. . .

June the 22nd. Mr Uriah Rey and his son John abus'd me very much on Ryland Balk by No-man's-plat. His son Thomas was there, but was not so uncivil. The next day being Tuesday John Wallenger said that Mr Uriah Rey bid him tell John Hannah Senior that he had untith'd all the wheat he had tith'd in Carlton Churchfield.

2. Broxbourne 1802

Mr Jones has the pleasure of waiting on his worthy friends and parishioners, to solicit the offerings usual at this season of the year, which constitute the chief value of his vicarage, together with an equivalent for the tenths of gardens, etc. He hardly needs suggest to his friends that the liberality of many individuals, which cannot impoverish them, will (if it does not enrich), at least conduce to furnish him and his very numerous family with a cheerful competence, which is all that he desires, – not for his own sake only, but that, after twenty one years' residence here already, he may be able to attend to the solemn and very important duties of his ministerial office, for the remainder of his days, with as few worldly cares and distractions as possible.

3. Haughton 1777

The Rector has all tithes, great and small, due, and payable in their kind. Only, there's a parcel of ground in the liberty of Allston in the holding of Geo. Dickenson for which they claim a modus. And also in lieu of the tithe-hay of Booden Meadow, there's about half a dole in St Giles' Meadow allowed, which has gone under the name of a modus too, of late. But this I rather suspect to be an imposition; and a temporary agreement only of old Mr Royston's, the late Rector. As to the small tithes and customary dues of the parish there has been much confusion and irregularity of late years, in the gathering of them, that is next to an impossibility to ascertain the just rights. For I have not been able to get my predecessor's accounts, nor those of his son. And the terriers likewise that have been formerly given up, are vastly imperfect. Add to this that most of the old people of the parish are dead, and those that remain are either really, or pretendedly ignorant of the matter. But the best and truest information I've been able to get, is, as follows: calves, lambs, wool, pigs, are titheable one at seven (tho' nobody in the parish owns that they ever knew calves to be tithed in kind; but that 6d a piece has been paid for them more or less). Lambs and fleeces if under seven, one penny each. For every colt, three pence. For eggs: one for every cock and drake, for every milch cow, 1d; for every barren one three half-pence. 2d for every hen and duck. Easter dues for house, garden and offering 6 pence. Fish and fruit are titheable; but no regular way has been observed, that I can hear of. For a wedding by a licence 5s. By Banns 2s 6d. For churching a woman 10d. For a burial 10d.

[From A. T. Hart, *The Eighteenth Century Country Parson* (Shrewsbury: Wilding & Sons, 1955)]

4. A parson repairs his church, 1756

In December 1756 the Revd George Woodward of East Hendred wrote to his uncle of the efforts of Mr Wymondesold, a local parson, at repair and renovation of his church. The church-building resurgence of the eighteenth century was encouraged in London by the Act for building fifty city churches in 1711. In the provinces, besides the generosity of individuals like Wymondesold, there were opportunities to raise subscriptions for new churches and church rates, but also in loans from Queen Anne's Bounty. Although the Victorians erased many of the signs of the efforts of their Georgian predecessors, the century was one of remarkable church repair and building.

Our great and good neighbour, Mr Wymondesold, left the country yesterday morning; his parish will feel his absence, for he does a great deal of good amongst them, and employs a great many poor people: he has this and the last summer been about a very good piece of work; he has undertaken the repair and beautifying of his parish church, (the living is in the gift of All Souls College, Oxford) and he has made it from a little, dark, indecent place, one of the prettiest, neatest churches that we have anywhere at all; the pews have all been new built in a more commodious manner, the reading desk, clerk's seat, and pulpit, all enlarged and new painted, the chancel well-repaired, and the Commandments, Lord's Prayer, and belief, new done, and properly placed, the monuments cleaned, windows new glazed, with large crown glass, the pavement all new, with two handsome new porches at the north and south doors; the doors new painted, and the whole church both inside and out rough cast and white washed; and he is now employing people about making the ways about the village better, opening a little stream that runs through it, and sloping the banks, and planting trees upon the sides of it in regular rows, which will make it a sweet pretty place; and before it was as unsightly a thing as one could look upon: these and several other such things are his constant amusements whilst he is down here, besides clothing poor people, and doing several acts of charity amongst his neighbours. A man of his disposition cannot but be of great use where he lives, and as he is a very courteous, sensible man, we think our selves happy in such a neighbour.

[From D. Gibson (ed.), *A Parson in the Vale of the White Horse, 1753–1761* (Alan Sutton Publishing Ltd (an imprint of Sutton Publishing Ltd) 1982), with permission]

5. A squire records the demise of a parson, 1757

The brief eulogy below of Dr Richard Bulkeley, rector of Llanfechell on Anglesey from 1730 to 1757, is both affectionate and mildly critical of a parson by his squire and relative William Bulkeley. Dr Bulkeley was descended from a long line of parsons who held the living of Llanfechell since 1566. Although they were distant relatives, the parson and his squire did not always see eye to eye on religion, as the eulogy suggests. From time to time the squire would write notes to the parson on aspects of his sermons of which he disapproved, and carefully recorded occasions in his diary when the parson forgot his sermon (and had to send his maid back to the rectory for it) and when he announced the wrong psalm to his congregation. Nevertheless for nearly thirty years they accommodated one another's views with tolerance.

[March 13th 1757]
About 10 o'clock this night Mr Richard Bulkeley the Parson of this parish died after an illness of only five hours: he read both morning and evening service as usual and catechised the children at Evening Prayer: about five he came hither upon a little business of the charity bread, in his way hither he had something of faintness that attack'd him on the way, the faintness increased upon him more and more during a stay of a quarter of an hour when he resolved to go home. . . He was a man of as strict moral virtue, I believe as most in England, benevolent and charitable towards those he differed in principles, had a good share of learning, and led an exemplary life, but leaned much towards Popery and was a rigid observer of superstitious ceremonies and several that were not required by the rubric, and particularly in consecrating the bread and wine at the Sacrament he used to lift them

up and show them to the people and speak with an emphasis 'This is my Body', etc.

[From G. N. Evans, Religion and Politics in Mid-Eighteenth Century Anglesey (Cardiff, 1953), by permission of the University of Wales Press]

6. Henry Venn in Huddersfield, 1759

In 1759, Henry Venn was appointed vicar of Huddersfield by Sir John Ramsden who had heard of Venn's talents from the evangelical Lord Dartmouth. The move from Clapham to Huddersfield involved Venn in some loss of earnings, but the chance to save 5000 souls attracted him. The account below, written by John Venn, who was a youth during his father's time at Huddersfield, suggests both the qualities of Henry Venn, and the example that was laid out for the future of John Venn, himself a celebrated parson at Clapham. It also indicates the emphasis evangelical clergy placed on sermons.

As soon as he began to preach at Huddersfield, the Church became crowded to such an extent that any more were not able to obtain admission, numbers became deeply impressed with concern about their souls; persons flocked from the distant hamlets, inquiring what they must do to be saved. His bowels yearned over his flock; and he was never satisfied with his labours among them, though they were continued to a degree ruinous to his health. On the Sunday he would often address the congregation from the desk, briefly explaining and enforcing the Psalms and the lessons. He would frequently begin the service with a solemn and most impressive address, exhorting them to consider themselves as in the presence of the great God of Heaven, whose eye was in a particular manner upon them. His whole soul engaged in preaching; and as at this time he [had] only notes in the pulpit, ample room was left to indulge the compassion, tenderness, and love, with which he overflowed towards his people. In the week he statedly visited the different hamlets in his extensive parish; and collecting some of the inhabitants at a private house, he addressed them with a kindness and earnestness which moved every heart. . .

The deep impression made by his preaching upon all ranks of people was indeed very striking. The late Mr W. Hey of Leeds, who frequently went to Huddersfield to hear him preach, assured me that once, returning home with an intimate friend, they neither of them opened their lips to each other till they came within a mile of Leeds, a distance of about fifteen miles so deeply were they impressed by the truths they had heard from the pulpit and the manner in which these had been delivered.

He made a great point of the due observance of the Sabbath in the town and parish. He induced several of the most respectable and influential inhabitants to perambulate the town, and by persuasion, rather than by legal intimidation, to repress the open violation of the day. By such means a great and evident reformation was accomplished. He endeavoured to preserve the utmost reverence and devotion in public worship, constantly pressing this matter upon his people, he read the service with peculiar solemnity and effect. The Te Deum especially was recited with a triumphant air and tone, which often produced a perceptible sensation throughout the whole congregation. He succeeded in inducing the people to join in the responses and singing. Twice, in the course of his ministry at Huddersfield, he preached a course of sermons in explanation of the Liturgy. On one occasion, as he went up to church, he found a considerable number of persons in the church-yard waiting for the commencement of the service. He stopped to address them, saying he hoped they were preparing their hearts for the service of God, etc. He concluded by waving his hand for them to go into the Church before him, and waited till they had all entered. He took great pains in catechising the young persons in his congregation, chiefly those who were above fourteen years old. The number was often very considerable, and he wrote out for their use a very copious explanation of the Church catechism.

[From J. Venn, *Annals of a Clerical Family* (London, 1904)]

7. Irreligion and preaching, 1765

In his collected essays, Oliver Goldsmith gave an account of religion that ascribed the failure of religion among the poor and lower classes to the poverty of skill among English preachers. He charges sermons with dryness and an unemotional quality, which contrasted with the strengths of nonconformist preaching. Many Anglican clergy were brought up on Tillotson's sermons and their oratory was more carefully directed at logic and reason than emotional calls to religion. To Goldsmith, as perhaps to the Victorians, this was a fundamental flaw in the eighteenth-century Church.

The clergy are nowhere so little thought of, by the populace, as here; and though our divines are foremost with respect to abilities, yet they are found last in the effects of their ministry; the vulgar, in general, appearing no way impressed with a sense of religious duty. I am not for whining at the depravity of the times, or for endeavouring to paint a prospect more gloomy than in nature; but certain it is, no person who has travelled will contradict me, when I aver, that the lower orders of mankind, in other countries, testify, on every occasion, the profoundest awe of religion; while in England they are scarcely awakened into a sense of its duties, even in circumstances of the greatest distress.

This dissolute and fearless conduct foreigners are apt to attribute to climate and constitution; may not the vulgar being pretty much neglected in our exhortations from the pulpit, be a conspiring cause? Our divines seldom stoop to their mean capacities; and they who want instruction most, find least in our religious assemblies. . .

Men of real sense and understanding prefer a prudent mediocrity to a precarious popularity; and fearing to outdo their duty, leave it half done. Their discourses from the pulpit are generally dry, methodical, and unaffecting: delivered with the most insipid calmness; inasmuch that should the peaceful preacher lift his head over the cushion, which alone he seems to address, he might discover his audience, instead of being awakened to remorse, actually sleeping over this methodical and laboured composition. This method of preaching is, however, by some called an address to reason, and not to the passions; this is styled the making of converts from conviction; but such are indifferently acquainted with human nature, who are not sensible that men seldom reason about their debaucheries till they are committed. Reason is but a weak antagonist when headlong passion dictates: in all such cases we should arm one passion against another: it is with the human mind as in nature; from the mixture of two opposites, the result is most frequently neutral tranquillity. Those who attempt to reason us out of our follies, begin at the wrong end, since the attempt naturally presupposes us capable of reason; but to be made capable of this, is one great point of the cure.

There are but few talents requisite to become a popular preacher; for the people are easily pleased, if they perceive any endeavours in the orator to please them; the meanest qualifications will work this effect, if the preacher sincerely sets about it. Perhaps little, indeed very little more is required than sincerity and assurance; and a becoming sincerity is always certain of producing a becoming assurance.

[From O. Goldsmith, *Essays* (London, 1765)]

8. Archbishop Secker, 1768

This account of Archbishop Thomas Secker shows two features of his life. First, his assiduous attention to the written records of the dioceses he held. At Bristol, Oxford and Canterbury he took great pains to list the parishes and details of them in diocese books. Secondly, he was not a courtier. His banishment to the sees of Bristol and Oxford for many years was seen as punishment for his political waywardness, and at court too he did not carry great weight. The result was an even greater control of church matters in the hands of politicians than at the start of the century.

At the beginning of August 1768 died that great and excellent prelate Archbishop Secker. He was not only a most learned divine, as his useful writings abundantly testify, but was likewise a most indefatigable and exact man in all kinds of business; and everyone who hath succeeded him in any of his preferments has reaped the fruits of his labour and pains in the books and manuscripts which he left behind him. Bishop Newton found the benefit of them both in the see of Bristol and in the deanery of St Paul's, Bishop Secker sat in the See of Bristol not above three years, and yet in that time he drew up an account of all the leases and estates belonging to the bishopric; and also made a diocese-book with an account of the nature and value of every living, of the incumbents and curates, of the duty usually required and performed, and several other particulars. All the knowledge of the diocese was derived from his books and accounts: and it is surprising how little was added to them by the five intervening bishops. He was likewise very charitable, and besides the pensions and bounties which he distributed himself whenever application was made to him by others for a distressed object, he gave with a liberal hand, as Bishop Newton can attest upon his own experience as well as that of several others. At the same time he was too considerable a man to live in the world without enemies. Whether it was owing to their misrepresentations, or to a certain preciseness and formality in his own behaviour, he was never very acceptable and agreeable at Court, nor ever had the due weight and influence there. In former reigns the Archbishop or some of the bishops had usually the principal sway or direction in the disposition of ecclesiastical preferments; at least nothing of importance was concluded upon without first acquainting and consulting them upon it. But by degrees the ministers of state have engrossed all this power into their own hands, and bishops are regarded as little better than cyphers even in their own churches, unless the preferments happen to be in their own gift, and then perhaps the ministers are as troublesome by their solicitations. When his present Majesty first came to the throne, there were near twenty old chaplains discarded, and as many new ones appointed without the privity of the Archbishop, several whose names were scarcely known before, and some by no means worthy of the honour. . .

[From *The Lives of Dr Edward Pocock, Dr Zachary Pearce, Dr Thomas Newton*. . . (London, 1816)]

9. The incapacity of Bishop Thomas Newton of Bristol, 1776

Newton was a conscientious bishop, in spite of holding a see with an income of just three hundred pounds a year. The extract from his biography below shows how demanding diocesan duties could be in the eighteenth century. Newton, like most of his contemporaries, was scrupulous in the discharge of his duty of visiting his diocese. For the remaining six years of his life he was too ill to undertake the duty and relied on others to do it for him.

From the time that he was first made Bishop, he constantly went to Bristol every summer, and usually stayed there the three months intervening between his last residence at St Paul's and the next following; and when he was no longer able to go to St Paul's, he continued at Bristol four or five months, and went to church as often as his health and the weather would permit. In the summer of 1766 the Duke of York lodging at Clifton did him the honour of dining with him . . .

The Duke among other things asked the Bishop what might be the yearly value of his bishopric, and the Bishop answered that the fines were very uncertain, sometimes more, sometimes less, and sometimes none at all; the certain clear income was 300l. a year, and little more. How then, said he, can you afford to give me so good a dinner?. . .

The Bishop never failed going to Bristol every summer till the year 1776, when contrary to the advice of many friends he went upon his fifth visitation into Dorsetshire, and visited and confirmed at Blandford, and at Dorchester, and at Bridport; and by these exertions, it is supposed, he burst a vessel, and had a profuse spitting of blood, which lasted a week, and much alarmed his wife and all his friends. In this distress however it was some comfort, that he was at the house of his good old friend and Archdeacon, Mr Walker of Spetisbury, where he had good help from Dr Pulteney of Blandford, and was almost as well accommodated as he could have been at home. But he was not able to proceed any further in his visitation; the Archdeacon visited for him at Shaftesbury; and the visitation at Bristol he was forced to send and put off, and to order his servants who were there with his baggage to return to London, as he himself did by easy stages, as soon as he was in a condition to be moved. This was his first failure of going to Bristol; and by living and residing there so much, he was in hopes that his example would have induced the other members of the church to perform also their part, and to discharge at least their statutable duties . . .

[From *The Lives of Dr Edward Pocock, Dr Zachary Pearce, Dr Thomas Newton*. . . (London, 1816)]

10. Wiltshire visitation returns, 1783

The Wiltshire visitation of 1783 was the first conducted by Bishop Shute Barrington of Salisbury since his appointment to the diocese a year earlier. The visitation queries were sent to each parish by the Registrar and most returned in time for the bishop's tour of the diocese in May 1783. The parish returns selected here indicate some of the features of eighteenth-century parish life. The parishes of West Lavington and Market Lavington are good examples of how the effects of non-residence may be exaggerated. John Williams was curate of Bishop's Lavington, whose incumbent was Master of St Nicholas's Hospital, Salisbury; Williams also served Market Lavington a mile away. Technically therefore these two parishes were neglected by non-resident clergy, yet the curate was able to discharge many of the duties of the small parishes. The parishes of St Peter's, Marlborough and Preshute show how pluralism worked to the advantage of the Church. Mr Meyler was technically a pluralist, but the two parishes were only half a mile apart, Preshute was without a rectory and both were well served.

The Visitation Articles asked by the Bishop

Q.1. [a] How often and at what hours upon the Lord's day is divine service, both prayers and preaching, performed in your church or chapel? [b] If divine service be not performed twice every Lord's day, what is the reason?

Q.2. Is divine service performed in your church or chapel upon any weekdays, holidays, or festivals that happen on weekdays?

Q.3. Do you perform divine service as incumbent, or as curate, of your parish?

Q.4. [a] Do you serve any other cure? If so, what cure, and how many, and [b] at what distance are the cures you serve from one another? [c] Are you duly licensed to the cure which you serve?

Q.5. How often in the year is the holy sacrament of the Lord's Supper administered in your church or chapel? And at what times of the year?

Q.6. [a] What number of communicants have you, generally, in your parish? [b] In particular, what was the number which communicated at Easter last? [c] Was it greater or less than usual?

Q.7. [a] Are there any reputed papists in your parish, or chapelry, and how many and of what rank? [b] Have any persons been lately perverted to popery, and by whom and by what means? [c] Is there any place in your parish, or chapelry, in which they assemble for divine worship, and where is it? [d] Doth any popish priest reside in your parish, or resort to it? And by what name doth he go? [e] Is there any popish school kept in your parish?

Q.8. [a] Are there any Presbyterians, Independents, Anabaptists, or Quakers in your parish or chapelry? And how many of each sect? And of what rank? [b] Are there any other places made use of for divine worship, than such as are used by the above-mentioned sects? [c] What are the names of their teachers, and are they all licensed as the law directs? [d] Is their number greater or less of late years than formerly, according to your observation, and by what means? [e] Are there any persons in your parish who profess to disregard religion, or [f] who commonly absent themselves from public worship of God?

Q.9. [a] Do your parishioners duly send their children and servants, who have not learned their catechism, to be instructed by you? [b] And do you either expound to them yourself, or make use of some printed exposition, and what is it? [c] At what particular seasons of the year, and in what language, are the young persons of your parish, or chapelry, catechized?

Q.10. [a] Have you a register book of births and burials duly kept? [b] And do you regularly make your returns of births good preservation and burials into the registrar's office, as the canon requires? [c] How far back does your register of births and burials go?

Q.11. Is there a register book duly kept, according to the directions of the Act of Parliament against clandestine marriages?

Q.12 Are there any chapels of ease in your parish? What are the names of them? [b] How often are there prayers and sermons in them? [c] Have they any estates or funds particularly appropriated to their maintenance? [d] How far distant are they from the parish church?, [e] By whom are they served? [f] Have you any ruinated chapels in which there is no divine service performed?

Q.13. [a] Have you a true and perfect account or terrier of all houses, lands, tithes, pensions, and profits, which belong to you as minister of your parish? [b] Hath a duplicate thereof been laid up in the bishop's registry? [c] Hath there been, since that was done, any augmentation made of your living? [d] And hath an account of such augmentation been transmitted thither also?

Q.14. [a] Is there any free school, alms-house, hospital, or other charitable endowment in your parish? And for how many, and for what sort of persons? [b] Who was the founder? And who are the governors or trustees? [c] What are the revenues of it? Are they carefully preserved, and employed as they ought to be? Are the statutes and orders made concerning it well observed? [d] Have any lands or tenements been left for the repair of your church, or for any other pious use? [e] Who has the direction and management of such benefactions? And who takes an account of and conducts them?

Q.15. [a] Are the churchwardens in your parish chosen every year in the Easter week? [b] How are they chosen? By the minister and parishioners together, or one by the minister and the other by the parishioners?

Q.16. [a] Is there (or has there been founded) any public school in your parish? [b] Is there any charity school in your parish? How is it supported? by voluntary subscription, or by a settled endowment? Is it for boys or girls, and for how many? [c] What are the children taught? More particularly, [d] is care taken to instruct them in the principles of the Christian religion, and to bring them regularly to church?, [e] And are they also lodged, fed, and clothed?, [f] And how are they disposed of when they leave school? [g] Does your school flourish? And if not, for what reasons?

Q.17   [a] Do you constantly reside upon this cure, and in the house belonging to it? [b] If not, where, and at what distance from it, is your usual place of residence? [c] How long in each year are you absent? [d] And what is the reason for such absence?

Q.18.   By whom, and to what uses, is the money given at the offertory disposed of?

Q.19.   Is there any matter relating to your parish or chapelry of which it may be proper to give me information?

Q.20.   What is your place of residence, and the nearest post town?

Replies

WEST [Bishop's] LAVINGTON

1.   Divine service is performed in this church once every Lord's day at a quarter of an hour after two o'clock in the evening, excepting on Sundays when the holy sacrament of the Lord's Supper is administered; then it begins at a half of an hour after ten in the morning. The reason that divine service is not performed twice here each Lord's day is that the congregation who attend prayers in the afternoon [added in the margin 'I mean this when divine service did use to be twice, every Sunday, when prayers and sermon in the morning and prayers in the afternoon'] are but few in number, generally, go to hear a sermon and prayers across the field to Market Lavington.

2.   Yes, on Christmas day, Good Friday, and a few other holidays.

3.   As curate.

4.   I serve the curacy of Market Lavington with this, at the distance of one mile from hence; but am licensed to neither of my cures.

5.   Four times in the year (viz.) at Christmas, Easter, Whitsuntide and Michaelmas.

6.   About forty five. Rather more than the usual number, last Easter.

7.   [a] We have in this parish one professed Roman Catholic only and the same is an old woman in the workhouse, [b] No. [c] No. [d] No.[e] No.

8.   None of any sect except the Church of England, A few also who profess a disregard to religion, by absenting themselves from the public worship of the church, but none avowedly.

9.   Some do and some do not. I both expound to them myself and every Saturday at my school make use of a printed exposition the editor of which is Dr Stonhouse. The children of this parish are also publicly catechized at church in Lent; They all say it in English.

10.   [a. & b.] Yes. [c] As far as the year 1598.

11.   Yes.

12.   There are no chapels of ease belonging to this parish.

13.   I have an account of all the lands, tithes, and profits which at present belong to this living; but whether a duplicate thereof hath at any time been laid up in the bishop's registry is what I am totally ignorant of. This living also some years past has been augmented, an account of which augmentation shall be transmitted to the bishop's registrar at this visitation.

14.   There is a free school in this parish of which I am the deputy master. There is also in this parish an alms-house for 10 poor people, (viz;) 7 old widowers and 3 old widows. The founders, it is said, were some of the Danvers or Dantsey family. . .

17.   I constantly reside upon this cure and at the school-house, and am never absent from my cures.

18.   There is no collection made here.

19.   No other matter than what has already been related.

20.   My place of residence is West Lavington grammar school and the nearest post town is Market Lavington. I am an unbeneficed clergyman and no graduate. I was ord. D[eacon] on Sunday 4 Aug. 1776, by James, then bishop of St David's, now bishop of Ely, and ord. P[riest] on Trinity Sunday 14 June A.D. 1778. by Richard, then bishop of Lichfield and Coventry, now bishop of Worcester. Have been in this diocese ever since I was ordained a deacon A.D. 1776. And Market Lavington which I also serve at present was my first cure.

J. Williams, clerk. Bishop's Lavington, 28 July, 1783

MARKET LAVINGTON

1. Divine service is performed in this church twice every Lord's day. The morning service begins at half an hour after 10 o'clock. the evening service at half after three. There are also two sermons preached here during the summer half year, and one during the winter.
2. Yes every Friday and holiday throughout the year.
3. As curate.
4. I serve another cure, which is Bishop's Lavington at time distance of one mile from this; but am licensed to neither of my cures.
5. The holy sacrament of the Lord's Supper is administered in this church four times in the year, (viz.) at Christmas, Easter, Whitsuntide and Michaelmas.
6. Nearly about forty, and the usual number . . .

MARLBOROUGH, ST PETER

1. Twice on every Sunday, at half an hour past ten o'clock in the morning and at three in the afternoon, but the sermon is omitted on sacrament days in the morning, agreeable to the wishes of the most constant communicants, the aged and the infirm.
2. Morning prayers are read therein on Tuesdays, Thursdays, and Fridays weekly, and also on holidays.
3. As incumbent.
4. By the help of a constant assistant, I serve my other church of Preshute not half a mile distant from my church in Marlborough.
5. On the last Sunday in every month, and on Christmas day, Easter day, and Whitsunday.
6. At the monthly sacraments about 30 on an average. At the great festivals many more and at Easter last about 70, a number rather greater than less than usual.
7. There is a gentleman's family (of the name of Hyde) professing the popish religion. . .
8. There are five or six Presbyterian families, including their minister, resident in this parish, but their place of worship is not in it, one of them is a gentleman professing the law, but his wife and daughter constantly resort to our communion. Two other families are in trade. One of them comes to church when there is no meeting, but his wife and children

constantly, the children of the other and of the minister come to church when there is no meeting – which happens either morning or evening every Sunday, The other Presbyterians are elderly maidens. This sect is greatly reduced of late years, as by marrying wives of the Church of England, so by many of them turning Methodists, who assemble in a former Presbyterian meeting-house in this parish by the name of Independents, and licensed as such. This sect is supported, as I am informed, by Lady Huntingdon and an opulent tradesman of this parish. who is owner of the meeting-house. . .

9. The parishioners in general duly send their children and servants to say and be instructed in, their catechism according to my appointment, the junior part at prayer-time on Thursday mornings, and such as are of age to be confirmed, and servants, on Sunday evenings. . .

17. I constantly reside in the parsonage house.

18. By the minister at his discretion and on the recommendation of the communicants, to the sick, needy, and prisoners in Bridewell.

19. None.

20. At Marlborough, a post town, I, Thomas Meyler M.A., was ord. D. Ord, P, 13 June 1742, Collated to the rectory 21 Jan. 1774.

PRESHUTE

1. Divine service, both prayers and preaching, is performed once only every Lord's day, alternately in the morning at half an hour past ten o'clock and in the afternoon at three; and were prayers only to be read there the other part of the day, a congregation would seldom be muster'd here, as the church stands so near to Marlborough St Peter's, where they may hear a sermon also, together with the music of an organ erected there of late years.

2. On Christmas day and Good Friday there are performed herein both prayers and preaching.

3. As incumbent.

4. I serve also my church of Marlborough St Peter's, not half a mile distant here from.

5. Four times, on, or near, Christmas day, Easter day, Whitsunday, and Michaelmas day.

6.   The number of communicants continue about twelve,
sometimes more, sometimes fewer . . .

The house belonging to the vicar of Preshute having been destroyed
by fire in, or shortly before, the year 1607, and never since rebuilt, I
constantly reside at the parsonage house of Marlborough St Peter's, not
half a mile from Preshute church; and as the last and present incumbents
have enjoyed both benefices, it is to be wished that all future bishops
will confer them on one and the same person, as one will furnish him
with bread and cheese, and the other with a place to eat and sleep. . .

[From M. Ransome (ed.), *Wiltshire Visitation Returns to the Bishop's
Visitation Queries, 1783* (Wiltshire Record Society, vol. XXVII,
1972), by permission of the Wiltshire Record Society]

11. A plea for preferment, 1786

William Bickerstaffe, undermaster of the Grammar School, Leicester, wrote
the letter below to Lord Chancellor Thurlow in August 1786 in the hope of
soliciting preferment. This was a common feature of eighteenth-century church
life, indeed most lords chancellor kept records of their promises and
engagements for livings. The application came to nought. Thurlow was notorious for keeping livings vacant, and chose not to appoint Bickerstaffe on this
occasion. However, Bickerstaffe's plea may have melted Thurlow's icy heart
since, on Bickerstaffe's death, he was recorded as waiting on a promise from
the lord chancellor.

To the Rt Honourable Edward Lord Thurlow, Lord High Chancellor
of Great Britain. . .
Leicester, August 10, 1786.
My Lord,
By the advice of Mr Macnamara, a representative of Leicester, I am
instructed to appeal to your Lordship's humanity, to grant me a gracious
hearing, by a private address.
    At fifty-eight years of age, permit a poor curate, unsupported by
private property, to detain your attention a few moments. From 1750
I have been usher at the Free Grammar school here, with an
appointment of £19 16s. 0d. a year; seven years curate of St Mary's,
my native parish this borough; then six years curate at St Martin with
All Saints, lately bestowed by your Lordship on Mr Gregory of this
place and now an opportunity occurs to your Lordship, to give me an

occasion to pray for my benefactor, and those that are dear to him, during my life: 'tis this, a dispensation is expected every day, by the headmaster of the school where I serve, the Rev. Mr Pigot, vicar of Great Wigston, in this county, to connect a fresh acquisition in Lincolnshire with it; and he urges your Lordship's petitioner to try for the living of St Nicholas here, which he must relinquish. It is simply £35 a year; but as this corporation grants an annual aid to each living in Leicester of £10 a year, St Nicholas, joined to my school might render me comfortable for life, and prevent the uncertainty of a curacy and the hard necessity, at my time of life, of being harassed, in all weathers by a distant cure.

My Lord, if this freedom is disgusting, impute it to the sympathising heart of the generous Macnamara, who prompted me to it in these words, speaking of your Lordship: indeed I feel too forcibly my obligations to press further, or trespass more at present upon his Lordship; but, as you are a native of Leicester, and a freeman, I conceive it my duty to hint to you, that an application immediately from yourself, stating your situation exactly, as you have done to me, may have the desired effect, as his Lordship's great abilities can only be equalled by his humanity and benevolence.

May the almighty, all present and all-merciful God direct your Lordship, on this and on all occasions, to do His pleasure; and protect you from all dangers, which may threaten soul, body or estate; is the hearty prayer of your Lordship's humble suppliant,
Wm. Bickerstaffe.

[From A. T. Hart, *The Eighteenth Century Country Parson* (Shrewsbury: Wilding & Sons, 1955)]

12. A non-resident on non-residence, 1800

The letter below, from Bishop Richard Watson of Llandaff to William Pitt in 1800, may be regarded as a piece of remarkable effrontery. Watson, having graduated at Cambridge and obtained a professorship of Chemistry, impressed his contemporaries with his diligence and staunch whiggery. A canonry, an archdeaconry, a rectory followed and in 1782 he was made Bishop of Llandaff. Watson, finding that the diocese, valued at a few hundred pounds a year, had no residence for the bishop, lived in the Lakes, near Windermere, and retained his other church offices in plurality. He visited his diocese regularly. He has been seen, with Hoadly, as the apogee of episcopal neglect. In fact, as this letter shows, Watson was not without scruple. In spite of the modesty of the proposals, they attracted limited support, and faded from the public mind.

Great George Street, April 16th 1800.

Dear Sir, – On dining yesterday with the Archbishop of Canterbury, His Grace informed me that a bill for enforcing a better residence of the clergy was now in contemplation. Ignorant as I am of the provisions of the intended bill, I may be giving you unnecessary trouble in communicating such sentiments as at present occur to me on the subject. But I trust you will pardon this my presumption, proceeding from a sense of duty, especially as I shall be in the country when the business will be brought forward, and may have no other opportunity of suggesting any thing on a matter which has always been an object of my sincere and earnest wishes.

The safety of every civil government is fundamentally dependent on the hopes and fears of another world, which are entertained by its members; and the safety of every Christian civil government is brought into the most imminent danger, when infidelity is making a rapid progress in the minds of the people. This I apprehend is that state of danger in which Great Britain (to say nothing of Ireland) now stands. It may be difficult to find a full remedy for this evil; but the residence of a respectable clergyman in every parish and hamlet in which there is a place of established worship, appears to me to be more fitted than any other for that purpose.

I do not wish a bill respecting residence to have any violent retrospect as to the present pluralists: they perhaps ought to remain subject only to the existing laws; for it would bring ruin on many individuals, who are now married and happily settled, if they were compelled to change their situations. But I see no individual hardship and much public good which would attend a new law suffering, after it had passed, no man to hold two benefices of any kind.

As, however, there are many benefices utterly inadequate to the affording even a bare maintenance to an unmarried clergyman, a law abolishing in future all pluralities ought to be accompanied with another making a decent provision for every resident minister. An hundred pounds a year ought to be the very least stipend annexed to any benefice, and, such sum being annexed, service twice every Sunday should be required in all. Benefices above an hundred a year should remain, I think, as they are; unless it should be judged expedient, on a vacancy, to take the first fruits on a real valuation, constituting thereby a fund towards augmenting benefices under an hundred to that sum.

Houses of residence for the clergy should be bought or built at the public expense, or by the Governors of Queen Anne's bounty, for livings under an hundred pounds a year. The number of livings under an hundred a year, their respective values, and the state of their parsonage houses, should be accurately ascertained, and laid before parliament, in order that the additional public burden attending the giving a decent maintenance to the clergy might be known: it would, I am persuaded, whatever its magnitude might be, meet with no opposition from the judicious part of the community. The bishops would be able to make, if required, this return to parliament by means of their officers.

Livings held in commendam, or annexed without commendam to bishoprics, to headships and professorships in the Universities, to public schools, etc. should be exempted from the operation of this law, as the residence of their possessors cannot be expected. The greatest part of the benefices under an hundred pounds a year are in the patronage of lay impropriators. Many of these impropriators would, I doubt not, be moved by a sense of piety, and a regard for public safety, to contribute largely towards rendering the income of each place of worship in their patronage not less than the sum I have mentioned.

I cannot at present ascertain the number of livings in the patronage of the Universities and their respective colleges, in that of deans and chapters, of hospitals, corporations, etc; perhaps they may amount to above a thousand. But be the number what it may, would it be an unreasonable thing to expect, that these several bodies should make up from their own revenues every living in their patronage to a stipend of an hundred pounds? The property of these corporations has been greatly increased within the last forty years, whilst their poor vicarages, etc have remained nearly in statu quo.

In Denmark, and I believe in Scotland and other Protestant countries, (in Catholic countries non-residence is scarcely heard of) the stipends of their clergy are not paid in full, unless they reside the whole year. What defalcation of income might be proper to be exacted on a partial absence of a minister from his living is a question for the wisdom of the legislature to determine; but some deduction I think ought to be made, unless in cases of sickness or other emergencies to be allowed of by the bishop of the diocese.

If anything is attempted I wish the axe to be laid to the root of the evil. Sectaries are every where increasing, and some of them are thought to mingle political with religious opinions; and though all men ought to be allowed the liberty of worshipping God according to their conscience, yet serious persons would be glad to see a stop put to the miserable effusions of enthusiastic ignorance. The prudent zeal of a resident clergyman in watching over his flock would be more efficacious to this purpose than a whole code of penal laws.

I will not trespass on your time by entering into a longer detail, well knowing the facility with which your mind is able to fill up the outline of any plan which you may deem worthy of consideration.
I have the honour, etc.
R Llandaff

> [From R. Watson, *Anecdotes of the Life of Richard Watson, Bishop of Llandaff* (Philadelphia, 1818)]

13. The neglect of country parsons in the century

William Cowper's account of negligent country parsons, drawn largely from his experiences in Norfolk, was published in his letters in 1824, but was written towards the end of the eighteenth century – Cowper died in 1800. It paints a depressing picture of clerical disregard and laxity in care for the temporalities of their parishes, as well as for the decency of worship. Cowper was not an unbiased observer, however, having acted as a lay reader and district visitor for the evangelical John Newton of Olney. His pietistic zeal caused him to ostracize relatives who did not share it, and led to his eventual derangement. Nevertheless, Cowper's criticisms are those which other evangelicals would echo.

The ruinous condition of some of the churches gave me great offence; and I could not help wishing that the honest vicar, instead of indulging his genius for improvements, by enclosing his goose berry bushes within a Chinese rail, and converting half an acre of his glebe-land into a bowling-green, would have applied part of his income to the more laudable purpose of sheltering his parishioners from the weather, during their attendance on divine service. It is no uncommon thing to see the parsonage house well thatched, and in exceeding good repair, while the church perhaps has scarce any other roof than the ivy that grows over it. The noise of owls, bats, and magpies makes the principal part of the church music in many of these ancient edifices; and the walls, like a large map, seem to be portioned out into capes, seas, and promontories, by the various colours by which the damps have stained them. Sometimes, the foundation being too weak to support the steeple any longer, it has been expedient to pull down that part of the building, and to hang the bells under a wooden shed on the ground beside it. This is the case in a parish in Norfolk, through which I lately passed, and where the clerk and the sexton, like the two figures at St Dunstan's, serve the bells in capacity of clappers, by striking them alternately with a hammer.

In other churches I have observed, that nothing unseemly or ruinous is to be found, except in the clergyman, and the appendages of his person. The squire of the parish, or his ancestors, perhaps to testify their devotion, and leave a lasting monument of their magnificence, have adorned the altar-piece with the richest crimson velvet, embroidered with vine leaves and ears of wheat; and have dressed up the pulpit with the same splendour and expense; while the gentleman, who fills it, is exalted in the midst off all this finery, with a surplice as dirty as a farmer's frock, and a periwig that seems to have transferred its faculty of curling to the band which appears.

But if I was concerned to see several distressed pastors, as well as many of our country churches, in a tottering condition, I was more offended with the indecency of worship in others. I could wish that the clergy would inform their congregations, that the town-crier is not the only person qualified to pray with due devotion; and that he who bawls the loudest may nevertheless be the wickedest fellow in the parish. The old women too in the aisle might be told, that their time would be better employed in attending to the sermon, than in fumbling over their tattered testaments till they have found the text; by which time the discourse is near drawing to a conclusion: while a word or two of instruction might not be thrown away upon the younger part of the congregation, to teach them that making posies in summer time, and cracking nuts in autumn, is no part of the religious ceremony. . .

[From W. Cowper, *Letters* (London, 1824)]

SEVEN

CATHOLICISM

1. The finances of the Catholic church in England, 1731

In January 1731 Mr Royden, the 'Grand Vicar' for Lancashire, wrote to Bishop Williams, the Vicar Apostolic for the Northern District, replying to the bishop's appeal for funds, that he could find no Catholic grandee who would accommodate him. The effect was that Williams had to pay for his own accommodation, and sent out an appeal to his clergy which the canons of the Church said a bishop could do 'upon urgent occasions'. Royden held a meeting of clergy at Preston to raise money for him, but they were able to contribute only £20. The letter that he sent to the bishop is produced below.

We are all concerned, my Lord, to hear of your necessities, and most are willing to contribute some relief, as far as our narrow and unhappy circumstances will permit. But in good truth our funds at best were smaller than in other parts; and by the late misfortune of the times some are entirely lost, many are reduced, because the estates whereon they were settled have been forfeited, and the owners indebted and impoverished by their late purchases, and former incumbrances.

The consideration of their great hardships among the gentry, who have been generally sufferers, chiefly on the north of Ribble, and whose losses are very well known to us, and the world, have discouraged us from all application to them, whilst they are much straightened in paying their debts, and too many also more pinched by the necessary subscription of their growing families.

Notwithstanding these difficulties, your Lordship will receive some assistance from the laity. The necessities of some brethren can scarcely be imagined. These poor, but zealous labourers live on a mite, and have not a mite to spare. They lament the misfortune common to their prelate and to themselves; and are truly mortified that their Bishop is in want: that they cannot relieve him, nor be relieved by him: which was one comfort and resource they had from and under your predecessors.

The small number of those who are not absolutely able, but comparatively more able than the indigent, have at this our meeting resolved a collection, and sent it by the bearer. . . who is deputed to bring our little offering, and to report and explain the case of our clergy, and the condition of our circumstances in this district, where most of the families are possessed by the regulars, chiefly by the Society [of Jesus].

'Tis hoped their more plentiful contributions and gatherings will be a full supply to your Lordship's necessities.

Our mite is hastened to you for your more ready ease and present relief, though the method to raise it is not yet put in execution. Thus you have the result of our meeting, and we hope your Lordship's goodness will please to observe that we have exerted our poor ability towards your Lordship's assistance at this dead lift, as you were pleased to call it.

There is but one thing more to our power, viz a representation and petition to the propaganda for a yearly pension to supply your necessities; to support your character; and to ease our poor mission. This will cordially be subscribed to by all our brethren. . .

[From B. Hemphill, *The Early Vicars Apostolic of England 1685–1750* (London, 1954), by permission of Burns & Oates]

2. Edward Gibbon's path to Rome, 1752–53

In 1752 Edward Gibbon entered Magdalen College, Oxford, at the age of fifteen. He regarded his time at the University as wholly unprofitable and having been introduced to Middleton's *Free Enquiry* he quickly converted to Catholicism. It was a relatively short-lived conversion, as he was won back to Protestantism by his tutor at Lausanne, Pavillard. Gibbon's prejudice against Oxford, which he blamed for his youthful vacillations, was compounded by its ejection of John Locke, for which Gibbon could only hold the University in contempt.

. . .According to the statutes of the University, every student, before he is matriculated, must subscribe his assent to the thirty-nine articles of the Church of England, which are signed by more than read, and read by more than believe them. My insufficient age excused me, however, from the immediate performance of this legal ceremony; and the Vice-Chancellor directed me to return, as soon as I should have accomplished my fifteenth year, recommending me in the meanwhile to the instruction of my college. My college forgot to instruct: I forgot to return, and was myself forgotten by the first magistrate of the University. Without a single lecture, either public or private, either

Christian or Protestant, without any academical subscription, without any episcopal confirmation, I was left by the dim light of my catechism to grope my way to the chapel and communion table, where I was admitted, without a question, how far, or by what means, I might be qualified to receive the sacrament. Such almost incredible neglect was productive of the worst mischiefs. From my childhood I had been fond of religious disputation;. . . nor had the elastic spring been totally broken by the weight of the atmosphere of Oxford. The blind activity of idleness urged me to advance without armour into the dangerous mazes of controversy; and at the age of sixteen, I bewildered myself in the errors of the Church of Rome.

The progress of my conversion may tend to illustrate, at least, the history of my own mind. It was not long since Dr Middleton's *Free Inquiry* had sounded an alarm in the theological world: much ink and much gall had been spilt in the defence of the primitive miracles; and the two dullest of their champions were crowned with academic honours by the University of Oxford. . . The name of Middleton was unpopular; and his proscription very naturally led me to peruse his writings, and those of his antagonists. His bold criticism, which approaches the precipice of infidelity, produced on my mind a singular effect. . .

The elegance of style and freedom of argument were repelled by a shield of prejudice. I still revered the character, or rather the names, of the saints and fathers whom Dr Middleton exposes; nor could he destroy my implicit belief, that the gift of miraculous powers was continued in the Church, during the first four or five centuries of Christianity. But I was unable to resist the weight of historical evidence, that within the same period most of the leading doctrines of popery were already introduced in theory and practice. . .

In these dispositions, and already more than half a convert, I formed an unlucky intimacy with a young gentleman of our college, whose name I shall spare. With a character less resolute, Mr __ had imbibed the same religious opinions; and some Popish books, I know not through what channel, were conveyed into his possession. I read, I applauded, I believed. . .

No sooner had I settled my new religion than I resolved myself a Catholic. Youth is sincere and impetuous; and a momentary glow of enthusiasm had raised me above all temporal considerations.

By the keen Protestants, who would gladly retaliate the example of persecution, a clamour is raised of the increase of popery: and they are always loud to declaim against the toleration of priests and Jesuits, who pervert so many of His Majesty's subjects from their religion and allegiance. On the present occasion, the fall of one or more of her sons directed this clamour against the University; and it was confidently affirmed that popish missionaries were suffered, under various disguises, to introduce themselves into the colleges of Oxford. But justice obliges me to declare, that, as far as relates to myself, this assertion is false; and that I never conversed with a priest, or even with a papist, till my resolution from books was absolutely fixed . . .the gates of Magdalen College were for ever shut against my return.

[From *The Miscellaneous Work of Edward Gibbon* (London, 1796), vol. 1]

3. Bishop Newton's attitude to Catholicism, 1764

This account of a complaint made by Bristol Protestants to their bishop, Thomas Newton, about the activities of Catholics, is of greatest interest because of the light it sheds on the government's attitudes and Bishop Newton's response. The tolerance exhibited here was typical of the reaction of the establishment once the fear of Catholic support for Jacobites had been dispelled. However, Newton's sanguine response was not shared by the majority of the populace, who could be whipped into violent anti-Catholic fervour, as in the Gordon riots of 1780 in which about 800 people were killed.

During the time of Mr Grenville's administration, Mr Swymmer, the Mayor of Bristol and brother-in-law to the then Earl of Westmoreland, came to London, and made a complaint to the Bishop of some persons making preparations for opening a public mass-house at the Hot Wells under the protection of the Duke of Norfolk. Upon this information the Bishop went and consulted with Archbishop Secker what would be the best method of suppressing it, and they both agreed that nothing could be done effectually without the concurrence and assistance of the ministry; and ministers, whatever may be their reasons, seldom lend a favourable ear, or give a helping hand to such applications. But the Bishop met with a different reception from Mr Grenville, and represented the matter to him in such a light, that he desired the Bishop to take his measures with the Mayor for putting the laws in execution, but advised them first to try the gentler methods of argument and persuasion, and even of threatening; and if these should not avail, he would then be ready to support them with all the power and authority of government. As soon as the Bishop came to Bristol, a meeting by his desire was appointed at the Mayor's house of the Mayor, the Bishop, and Sir Abraham Elton the Town Clerk, and of the priest, the proprietor of the building, and their agent.

The Bishop argued with as much candour as he could upon the subject, that though he was no friend to their religion as it stood distinguished from our common Christianity, yet he was no enemy to their persons; that they could not but be sensible that they were acting directly contrary to the laws; that the Duke of Norfolk had no more authority to break the laws than any private man; that their offence was the more provoking, as the building stood upon Church land, and was held by lease from the Dean and Chapter; that they had already a private mass house at Bristol, where this same priest had officiated many years, and having behaved decently and given no great offence, they were suffered to go on without molestation; but to presume upon opening a public mass-house in such a public place was so daring an affront, so contemptuous a defiance of all law and authority, that no government would or could endure it; he hoped therefore that they would desist from their design; as they were unmolested themselves, they ought not to molest others. . .

[From *The Lives of Dr Edward Pocock, Dr Zachary Pearce, Dr Thomas Newton.* . . (London, 1816)]

4. The Catholic Relief Act, 1778

Relief for Catholics had to surmount the prejudices engendered by Jacobite attempts to restore the Stuarts in 1715 and 1745. The Catholic Relief Act of 1778 was the result of bi-partisan sympathy for Catholics from Lords North and Rockingham. The Act was eased through parliament by the Thatched House Petition, a loyalist statement by the leading Catholic laity of the nation, and by the willingness of Catholics to agree to subscribe to an oath of loyalty and allegiance to George III if they held any posts of responsibility.

Catholic Relief Act, 1778

An Act for relieving His Majesty's subjects professing the popish religion from certain penalties and disabilities imposed on them by an Act, made in the eleventh and twelfth years of the reign of King William the Third, intituled, An Act for the further preventing the growth of popery.

Whereas it is expedient to repeal certain provisions in an Act of the eleventh and twelfth years of the reign of King William the Third, intituled an Act for the further preventing the growth of popery, whereby certain penalties and disabilities are imposed on persons professing the popish religion;. . . be it enacted; that so much of the said Act as relates to the apprehending, taking, or prosecuting, of popish bishops; priests, or Jesuits; and also so much of the said Acts as subjects popish bishops, priests, or Jesuits, and papists, or persons professing the popish religion, and keeping school, or taking upon themselves the education or government or boarding of youth, within this realm, or the dominions thereto belonging, to perpetual imprisonment; and also so much of the said Act as disables persons educated in the popish religion, or professing the same, under the circumstances therein mentioned, to inherit or take by descent, devise, or limitation in possession, reversion, or remainder, any lands, tenements, or hereditaments, within the Kingdom of England dominion of Wales, and town of Berwick upon Tweed, and gives to the next of kin, being a Protestant, a right to have and enjoy such lands [etc.]; and also so much of the said Act as disables papists, or persons professing the popish religion, to purchase any manors, lands, profits out of lands, tenements, rents, terms, or hereditaments, within the Kingdom of England [etc.] and makes void all and singular estates, terms, and other interests or profits whatsoever out of lands, to be made, suffered, or done, from and after the day therein mentioned, to or for the use or behoof of any such person or persons, or upon any trust or confidence, mediately or immediately, for the relief of any such person or persons; shall be, and the same, and every clause and matter and thing herein-before mentioned, is and are hereby repealed.

. . .Provided also, that nothing herein contained shall extend, or be construed to extend, to any person or persons, but such who shall, within the space of six calendar months after the passing of this Act, or of accruing of his, her, or their title, being of the age of twenty-one years, or who, being under the age of twenty-one years, shall, within six months after he or she shall attain the age of twenty-one years, or being of unsound mind, or in prison, or beyond the seas, then within six months after such disability removed, take and subscribe an oath in the words following:

I, A. B. do sincerely promise and swear, that I will be faithful and bear true allegiance to His Majesty King George the Third, and him will defend, to the utmost of my power, against all conspiracies and attempts whatever that shall be made against his person, crown, or dignity and I will do my utmost endeavour to disclose and make known to His Majesty, his heirs and successors, all treasons and traitorous conspiracies which may be formed against him or them; and I do faithfully promise to maintain, support, and defend, to the utmost of my power, the succession of the crown in His Majesty's family, against any person or persons whatsoever; hereby utterly renouncing and abjuring any obedience or allegiance unto the person taking upon himself the stile and title of Prince of Wales, in the life time of his father, and who, since his death, is said to have assumed the stile and title of King of Britain, by the name of Charles the Third, and to any other person claiming or pretending a right to the crown of these realms; and I do swear, that I do reject and detest, as an unchristian and impious position. That it is lawful to murder or destroy any person or persons whatsoever, for or under pretence of their being heretics; and also that unchristian and impious principle, that no faith is to be kept with heretics: I further declare, that it is no article of my faith, and that I do renounce, reject, and abjure, the opinion, that princes excommunicated by the pope and council, or by any authority of the see of Rome or by any authority whatsoever, may be deposed or murdered by their subjects, or any person whatsoever, and I do declare, that I do not believe that the pope of Rome, or any other foreign prince, prelate, state, or potentate, hath, or ought to have, any temporal or civil jurisdiction, power, superiority, or pre-eminence, directly or indirectly, within this realm. And I do solemnly, in the presence of God, profess, testify, and declare, that I do make this declaration, and every part thereof, in the plain and ordinary sense of the words of this oath; without any evasion, equivocation, or mental reservation whatever, and without any dispensation already granted by the pope, or any authority of the see of Rome, or any person whatever and, without thinking that I am or can be acquitted before God or man, or absolved of this declaration, or any part thereof although the pope, or any other persons or authority whatsoever, shall dispense with or annul the same, or declare that it was null or void. . .

Provided always, that nothing in this Act contained shall extend, or be construed to extend, to any popish bishop, priest, Jesuit, or schoolmaster, who shall not have taken and subscribed the above oath in the above words before he shall have been apprehended or any prosecution commenced against him.

[18 George III, c. 60]

5. Berington describes Catholics in England, 1780

In 1780, Joseph Berington, a Catholic priest in Staffordshire, gave a gloomy picture of Catholic numbers in England. He estimated the numbers at 56,000 in total, of which 25,000 were in London and 20,000 in the north. This gave a Catholic community below 1 per cent of the population of the country. Perhaps it should be admitted that this was the nadir of Catholicism and that from time to time Catholicism flourished in the century. Indeed by 1812 one estimate put the total number of Catholics in London at 400,000.

The few Catholics I have mentioned are also dispersed in the different counties. In many, particularly in the west, in south Wales, and in some of the Midland counties, there is scarcely a Catholic to be found. After London, by far the greatest number is in Lancashire. In Staffordshire are a good many, as also in the northern counties of York, Durham and Northumberland. Some of the manufacturing and trading towns, such as Norwich, Manchester, Liverpool, Wolverhampton and Newcastle-on-Tyne have chapels which are rather crowded. . . Excepting in the towns and out of Lancashire, the chief situation of Catholics is in the neighbourhood of the old families of that persuasion. They are the servants, or the children of servants who have married from those families. . . The truth is, within the past century we have most rapidly decreased. Many congregations have entirely disappeared. . . In the nature of things it could not possibly be otherwise. Where one cause can be discovered tending to their increase, there will be twenty found to work [to] their diminution. Among the principal are the loss of families by death, or by conforming to the Established church; the marrying with Protestants, and that general indifference about religion which gains so perceptibly among all ranks of Christians. . .

[From B. Hemphill, *The Early Vicars Apostolic of England 1685–1750* (London, 1954), by permission of Burns & Oates]

EIGHT

RELIGIOUS CONTINUITY AND CHANGE

1. Domestic chaplains and worship, 1689

In 1689, Sir George Wheler described the practice, then still widespread, of keeping chaplains in noble and gentry houses to lead worship. He also indicated the preparations needed to prepare the domestic chapel or place of worship in the noble house for services.

. . .1. Persons of the first magnitude usually do, and all should, like Micah, keep a divine to be a spiritual father and priest to the family: who as he is obliged to say daily morning and evening prayers privately or publicly according to the rule of the Common Prayer Book; so should there be a decent chapel in the house, set apart to perform this office in. . . If this were fixt to, or near to six in the morning, at midday and after six at night, it would affect this most conveniently.
2. It is very decent to adorn the place we worship God in, with such decent and proper ornaments, as are useful for the service we are about, or any way tend to the edification of those present. . . which consists not in the great pomp and splendour, but neatness; in convenient and edifying ornaments, with cleanliness. . . A decent desk or table to read the word of God, and pray on, set in the most convenient and respectable place; then to have convenient seats set in comely order for all present. If the room be necessarily used about domestic occasions, to have the furniture put in due order, and not lying in unseemly confusion, is no more than a good housewife would do to receive her ordinary neighbours. If it be adorned with any picture, I would have them as represent some profitable history out of the Old or New Testament . . .

[From Sir George Wheler, *The Protestant Monastery*
(London, 1689)]

2. Women's piety

The following extracts give an insight into the piety of noble women during the period. The first is a funeral eulogy of Lady Maynard by Bishop Thomas Ken, who directed her devotions. The second, from John Evelyn's life of Mrs Godolphin, suggests that sabbatarianism was not only a feature of Victorian religious life and that women were in the forefront of support for a movement from quarterly to weekly communions. The third extract, from William Law's *Serious Call*, shows Flavia, a hypocrite, who pays only modest service to the idea of keeping Sunday sacred.

1. Lady Maynard

Her oratory was the place, where she principally resided, and where she was most at home, and her chief employment, was prayer, and praise. Out of several authors, she for her own use transcribed many excellent forms, the very choice of which does argue a most experienced piety, she had devotions suited to all the primitive hours of prayer, which she used, as far as her bodily infirmities, and necessary avocations would permit, and with David, praised God seven times a day, or supplied the want of those solemn hours by a kind of perpetuity of ejaculations. . .

2. Mrs Godolphin

How would this Lady rejoice at the approach of the Lord's day. She has often told me she felt another soul in her; and that there was nothing more afflicted her than those impertinent visits on Sunday evenings, which she avoided with all imaginable industry; whilst yet seldom did she pass one without going to visit, pray by, or instruct some poor religious creature or other, tho' it were to the remotest part of the town; and sometimes, if the season were inviting, walk into the fields or gardens to contemplate the works of God. In a word, she was always so solemnly cheerful upon that day, and so devout, that without looking into the calendar, one might have read it in her countenance. Thus was the Sunday taken up in prayers, hearing, receiving, meditating on the word and works of God, acts of charity, and other holy exercises, without the least formality or confusion; because she had cast all her affairs into such a method, as rendered it delightful as well as holy. . . . .

For some of the laity (particularly the Duchess of Monmouth) do receive weekly, when they can have the opportunity already. Mrs Godolphin also rarely missed a Sunday throughout the whole year, wherein she did not receive the holy Sacrament, if she were in town and tolerable health . . . not seldom on the week days assisting at one pore creature's or other; and when sometimes, being in the country, or on a journey, she had not these opportunities, she made use of a devout meditation upon that sacred mystery, byway of mental communion, so as she was in a continual state of preparation. And O, with what unspeakable care and niceness did she use to dress and trim her soul against this heavenly banquet; with what flagrant devotion at the altar. . .

3. Flavia

If you visit Flavia on the Sunday, you will always meet good company, you will know what is doing in the world, you will hear the last lampoon, be told who wrote it, and who is meant by every name that is in it. . . Flavia thinks they are atheists that play at cards on the Sunday, but she will tell you the nicety of all the games, what cards she held, how she play'd them, and the history of all that happened at play as soon as she comes from Church . . . But still she has so great a regard for the holiness of the Sunday, that she has turned a poor old widow out of her house, as a profane wretch, for having been found once mending her clothes on the Sunday night . . .

[From J. T. Round, *The Prose Work of Bishop Ken* (London, 1838); J. Evelyn, *The Life of Mrs Godolphin* (London, 1888); W. Law, *A Serious Call to a Devout and Holy Life* (London, 1753)]

3. Chester visitation records, 1778

The appointment of Beilby Porteus to the diocese of Chester in 1777 ushered in a refreshing approach to the problems of the Church in the north-west. Porteus was an energetic bishop determined to do his best for the huge and populous diocese. His visitation of 1778 was perhaps the most detailed since Bishop Gastrell's in 1722. The state of the Church revealed by his enquiries is a fascinating indication of the effects, and perceived effects, of the industrial revolution. The evidence below is from Bolton, Middleton, Congleton, Blackburn and Easby.

The Parish of Bolton, is from its southern to its northern extremity twenty miles in extent, from east to west its breadth is considerable but frequently intermixed on the SW side with the parishes of Middleton, Dean and Standish – it contains. . . sixteen townships. . . Bolton being the centre of the cotton manufacture is extremely populous, but too near Manchester, which is the great mart, to have many opulent tradesmen resident in it – the number of houses in Bolton are about 1,500 and in the rest of the parish not less than 9,000 three-fourths of which are cottages inhabited by weavers and other labouring poor. In different parts of the parish are many old deserted mansions formerly the residences of families of some note. At present James Bradshaw Esq of Darcy Lever and Robert Andrews Esq of Rivington two gentlemen in the commission of the peace are its principal inhabitants. . .

Many of the common sort who disregard religion as in all countries where large manufactures are established which, however they may profit the State, never fail to corrupt the morals of people. What adds much to the evil. . . and encouragement of vice is the great and increasing number of alehouses. . . truly shocking are the scenes on the evening of the Lord's Day and continued thro' out the night and succeeding day. . .

I assign no other reason for their disorderly conduct than the flourishing state of manufacturers which have enabled them to earn a sufficiency for people in their situation by employing themselves three days a week and the remainder they frequently spend in the alehouses which are open also on the Lord's Day and ever ready to receive them. . .

The wardens and sidesmen are so far from admonishing such persons as those who wholly absent themselves from church and are guilty of incontinence, drunkenness, swearing that they encourage them in their wickedness by their own evil example. . .

The town and neighbourhood of Blackburn is very populous and hath of late years increased so much that the parish church is not able by any means to contain them. Several meeting houses lately erected, to which our people have resorted when they could not be received into the church. . .

Many of the labouring class absent themselves on Sundays, I believe from no determined motive. The great distance of the villages from the church may be one reason, and a more prevalent one, the long impolitic practice of making pews in churches private property, which grievance has nearly banished the lower orders from the church for want of seats, and has driven many more persons to the meeting houses than seems to have been ever considered by either churchmen or statesmen.

[From Chester Diocesan Record Office, EDV7/1, with the permission of Cheshire County Council]

4. Lancashire dissent, 1786

The following extract from a letter of Benjamin La Trobe to Evan Roberts mentions the state of dissent in Lancashire, where new chapels were built in large numbers during the late eighteenth century. The huge seatings possible in these large edifices suggest one of the reasons why nonconformity gained support: thousands of seats were freely available in these chapels, compared with the poorest benches at the rear of the churches.

In July 1785 I was a considerable time in Lancashire where we have erected a new place [for the] congregation, I opened the chapel which was and continues to be well fitted. I send an ode which was performed upon the occasion. My son Christian set it to music, all our brethren who are musicians come from Yorkshire, and there were thirty one performers. The best was, our Lord's presence was felt in a particular manner throughout the whole. There are at present beside the Brn & Srs [brethren and sisters'] houses and the chapel and houses of the labourers thirteen new family houses built, and we trust the Lord will not only bless them together, but make it light and salt to the country round about. I spent some time also in Fulneck, where a large house has been built and was opened for a boys school and the Lord blesses that place. Before I took that journey I preached by Mr J Wesley's invitation in his chapel at West Street to a great auditory. I was in the north invited to preach in several of his chapels, and preached in Pudsey to a great number; in his chapel at Leeds to above 2000 and in his chapel at Sheffield to about 3000 and our Saviour owned the word. May our Lord break down all partition walls.

[From G. M. Roberts (ed.), *Selected Trevecca Letters 1747–1794* (Caernarvon, 1962), by permission of the Presbyterian Church of Wales Historical Society]

5. Sale of pews in Sheffield, 1792 and 1806

Sheffield was one of the towns dramatically affected by the population growth of the eighteenth century. Though most industrial cities saw considerable church building, few could keep up with the urban population booms of the period. An effect of the growth was a shortage of seats and pews in churches. There were some solutions to this problem: galleries were erected in the aisles and nave. In 1800 Sheffield parish church was renovated and 1500 pews were installed in the renewed church. However, one effect of the growth of population was greater demand for pews which were owned or rented. The two advertisements below represent some of the sales of pews in Sheffield.

1.

TO BE SOLD BY AUCTION, by Mr Bardwell, on Tuesday, June 12th. . . at Mr Peech's, Angel Inn a seat (No. 6) in St Paul's Chapel, containing five sittings, belonging to Mr Gregory, a Bankrupt.

Likewise the third seat under the North Singing Loft in the Old Church, containing five sittings.

2.

AUCTION BY MR BARDWELL, at his Auction Room, Sheffield . . .

Lot 13 a pew in the north gallery of the Parish Church of Sheffield No. 20.

Lot 14 two Sittings lettered F, G in the Pew No. 23 in the same gallery.

Lot 15 four Sittings lettered A, B, C, D, in the Pew on the north side of the middle aisle in the same Church No. 49.

NB The above premises are of the nature of Freehold.

Lot 18 a Pew in the north gallery of St James Chapel, Sheffield, No. 36

Lot 19 a pew in the same gallery No. 59.

Lot 20 a Pew in the South gallery of the same chapel No. 16.

Lot 21 a Pew in the West gallery of the same chapel No. 29.

Lot 22 a Pew on the ground floor of the same chapel No. 34.

Lot 23 a Pew on the same floor No. 39.

NB The above premises are of the nature of personality. For a view of the land and houses apply to the respective tenants, and of the Pews and Sittings, to the clerks of the Church and chapel.

[From *The Sheffield Register* (8 June 1792); and Handbill advertising sale on 28 April 1806 in Sheffield City Library, Special Collection no. 5194]

6. An enclosure at Blunham, 1792

Enclosure in the eighteenth century changed the face of many villages. In the process of enclosing land some accommodation had to be reached with the parson. Sometimes this involved an exchange of tithes for land yielded by the enclosure, sometimes by converting the tithe to a cash sum or *modus*. Those clergy who feared inflation opted instead for a 'corn rent', a cash sum tied to the price of corn; the corn rent sought to secure the income of the incumbent for the future. The accounts given below are those of the enclosure by Marchioness Grey of land at Blunham in Bedfordshire. The first letter, from Lady Grey's steward, advises her of the preference for corn rents; the second, from the incumbent of the parish, Samuel Lawry, suggests some of the reasons why corn rents were more attractive than tithes or farming the glebe.

1.

If your Ladyship takes the Rector's allotment of land at Blunham, and pay them a corn rent; I beg leave to inform your Ladyship that it is customary in all these cases that to make a corn rent secure for time to come and that the church may at all times be secure in its income that whoever takes the land, suppose 250 acres, must add to it 250 acres more of their own private property, that the church may have a very, and over and above, good security, in case of any default in paying the corn rent for time to come: this is as it were locking up a part of your own property to make the church secure. . . This is what Mr Edwards does at Henlow; and what Mr Thornton agrees to do for the Muggerhanger district of Blunham; and what your ladyship had better do, (as the Bishop & Rector seem bent on a corn rent in money) for the Blunham districts, the rectors share of land will be allotted to your Ladyship and will let with your other estates at Blunham; I should wish the rectory barn to be kept standing as it would be always convenient for your Ladyships tenant of the tithe allotment to lay the corn in arising from it. But if the tithe allotment should happen to be at too great a distance from the village, a new barn etc. must be built – Mrs Campbell will not take any share of the tithe allotment, and as the living is your Ladyship's, it had better be taken by your Ladyship; but I am sorry to discover such avidity in the Bishop and Rector, that they wish to lay all the trouble hazard and expense on the shoulders of the laity; if this living was a 'small one' and the Rector had a large family to support I should think it an act of charity to be generous to him; he has now had the living thirteen years, and made very little residence in the parish, nor visited the sick, nor done much alms to the poor; I fear these are the reasons that so many go to hear Revd Mr Male, the Dissenting Minister . . .

2.

I cannot but accord with the Bishop of Lincoln in his opinion the same arrangement (i.e. a corn rent) would be most advantageous for the preferment throughout the parish should it meet with your Ladyship's opinion, to whom I submit the matter with the utmost deference. The glebe at Blunham is more than adequate to the purposes of the resident rector, and land has in almost every instance been found very troublesome and detrimental to the clergy. The Bishop's permission to pull down a part of the buildings which are very ruinous and a great burden to the preferment if it meets likewise with your consent will render me a most essential benefit. If land was taken in lieu of tithes the barns must be removed, an expense I could very ill support after having expended a considerable sum from my private property on the house and premises; and it would not be possible for a tenant to live under the same roof with myself and family when resident . . .

[From the Wrest Park Mss, L30/9/73/21 and L30/9/66, by permission of Bedfordshire County Records Office]

7. John Venn in Clapham, 1793

John Venn followed his father, Henry, into the Church and was as strong an evangelical as his father. His appointment to Clapham in 1792 by John Thornton was a tribute to his father, whose friend Thornton was. In the time since his father had been curate there, Clapham had become a more fashionable suburb than the poor village it had been. For John Venn, therefore, the challenges of evangelizing in a more sophisticated community were different from those of his father in Huddersfield. The proposal Venn made on his entry to the living of an evening lecture was addressed to the middle classes of the parish, and anticipates some of the reactions to such an innovation.

GENTLEMEN – Your attendance has been requested to-day, for the purpose of considering the propriety of my establishing a Sunday evening lecture in the parish church. It will not, I hope, be censured as pertinacious in me, if I maintain the right of the rector of the church to establish such a lecture by his own authority, since I am supported in it by the best legal information I could obtain on that subject; but the expediency of exercising that right at the present time is a different question, and it is this which I now willingly submit to your decision, being well assured that an entire harmony between a minister and his parishioners is the best foundation of that general good which it is the object of his labours to produce. I am aware that objections have frequently been made to evening lectures, and I am ready to acknowledge that some particular bad effects have sometimes taken place in consequence of them; but I still think, after mature consideration, that those effects may be prevented by prudent precautions on the part of heads of families and of the minister; and that, allowing them still to exist in some degree, they are more than over-balanced by the general good which a greater degree of religious instruction, and the formation of habits of piety, are likely to produce. The morning and afternoon services may perhaps be thought sufficient, but when it is considered how many are prevented by necessary avocations from attendance upon these, and how much among the lower classes, especially the misspending of the evening, more than balances the advantages of the day, I think the establishment of an additional evening service will not appear to be precluded. One objection which may be made in the present case would, I own, have considerable weight with me if I thought it justly founded, namely, that it may injure the income of the afternoon preacher. On this head I wish to declare in the fullest terms, that I propose it in the persuasion that it will not have this effect. The expenses attending it will be defrayed by a few persons, of whom I have every reason to expect that they will not on that account diminish their subscription to the lecturer, and I do not think that any others would, on account of their having more duty, desire to pay less. I have only further to observe, that as it is entirely voluntary on my part, I do not wish to have it considered as a necessary duty attached to the living, but that it may be dropped at the option of myself or my successors whenever it is thought expedient.

[From J. Venn, *Annals of a Clerical Family* (London, 1904)]

NINE

POLITICS AND RELIGION

1. Bishop Compton asks clergy to support a candidate for parliament, 1701

In this letter, Bishop Henry Compton of London asks the rural deans of his diocese to recommend Sir Charles Barrington and Mr Bullock to his clergy as the candidates for election to parliament who would best defend the interests of the Church.

Fulham, Nov. 20, 1701
Sir,
I entreat you to let the clergy of your deanery know, that it is my opinion, that the peace, honour, and safety of this Church and nation depend in a great measure upon the good success of this next election, and that I doe therefore think it our common duty, especially for us of the clergy, to contribute all we can to get in good men. Now, I confess, from these considerations, and as matters stand in Essex, in my judgement, we shall be greatly wanting to ourselves and our common good, if we do not take the best interest we can, and be vigorous ourselves for the choice of Sir Charles Barrington and Mr Bullock. It will be for the reputation of the Church, and for its service, if we be unanimous.
Your most assured
Friend and Brother
H. London
[From H. Ellis (ed.), *The Original Letters of Eminent Literary Men* (Camden Society, 1843), 191]

2. Clergy appointed for electoral advantage, 1733

Clergy accepted a role in politics in the eighteenth century. They were often freeholders and men of standing, who expected to have a voice in politics.

Inevitably therefore the appointments to livings were important when from the pulpit the clergy had a means of influencing votes. In this letter Dean Lynch of Canterbury discusses with the Whig power broker, the Duke of Newcastle, the political nature of the appointment to the parish of Ringmer. The parson who obtained the living of Ringmer was a staunch Whig, who even attended cricket matches to obtain political intelligence from the clergy and gentry of the county of Sussex.

Lambeth Oct. 17th 1733
May it Please Your Grace
I was myself this morning (when the letter Your Grace was pleas'd to honour me with was brought here) with the gentleman for whom My Lord Archbishop intends the living of Ringmer, who very readily promis'd me to serve Mr Pelham and Mr Butler with his vote and interest at the next election, and I make no question he will be very punctual in the performance of his promise, this I beg leave to assure Your Grace (tho' I do not at all distrust him) his future friendship with me shall certainly stand or fall according to his behaviour at the next election in Sussex; I shall likewise recommend to him, when he goes down, to take his measures in these affairs from the gentleman Your Grace is pleas'd to direct him to; and I beg leave to return my thanks for him (as I doubt not when he comes to know it he will do for himself) for yr Grace's goodness in promising him your countenance and regard, I hope, and make no question but he will always so behave himself as that Your Grace shall think fit to continue it to him. . .
I have the honour to assure Your Grace that I am with all possible respect and regard.
May it Please Your Grace
Your Grace's
Most dutiful
& Most obedient Humble Servant
J. Lynch
                    [From British Library, Add. Mss. 32,688, by permission]

3. Dissenters seek access to political power, 1735

The Whig governments ushered in by the Hanoverian succession of 1714 were, in part, dependent on the votes of dissenters, and sought to relieve dissenters' desire for access to political power as much as possible. By early in 1730 the Protestant Dissenting Deputies realized that they needed to organize a political body to lobby the Whigs. The first extract below recounts the decision to form the body at Salter's Hall. The second extract recounts Walpole's response: an attempt to balance dissenters with parliamentary managment.

1. The Protestant Dissenting Deputies

On the 9th of November 1732, a general meeting of Protestant Dissenters was held, at the meeting-house in Silver Street, London, to consider of an application to the legislature for the repeal of the Corporation and Test Acts. At this meeting a committee of twenty-one persons was appointed, to consider, and report to a subsequent meeting, when, and in what manner, it would be proper to make the application. Another general meeting being held on the 29th of the same month, the committee reported that they had consulted many persons of consequence in the state; that they found every reason to believe such an application would not then be successful; and therefore could not think it advisable to make the attempt. This report was not very cordially received. The committee was enlarged by the addition of four other gentlemen, and instructed to reconsider the subject. It was at the same time resolved, that every congregation of the three denominations of Protestant Dissenters, Presbyterians, Independents, and Baptists, in and within ten miles of London, should be recommended to appoint two Deputies; and to a general assembly of these Deputies, the Committee were instructed to make their report . . .

It soon became evident that whatever might be the fate of their attempts to procure a repeal of the Corporation and Test Acts, the Dissenters would derive considerable advantage, in other respects, from establishing a permanent body to superintend their civil concerns. It was accordingly resolved, at a general meeting of the Deputies, held at Salter's Hall meeting-house, on the 14th of January, 1735–6, 'That there should be an annual choice of Deputies to take care of the Civil Affairs of the Dissenters'. In order to carry this resolution into effect, it was further resolved, 'That the chairman do write to the ministers of the several congregations, some convenient time before the second Wednesday in January next, to return the names of their Deputies to him fourteen days before. . .'

2. Walpole's response

From the multiplicity of business at the beginning of a new Parliament and the nature of affairs before them together with what had already passed as well as the crisis which foreign affairs seemed coming to abroad His Majesty's servants with whom he (Walpole) had consulted did not judge this a proper time and thought that the Dissenters themselves must be of this way of thinking. But as the Dissenters had in deference to the administration and at their desire deferred the application to Parliament from year to year and had at the late elections behaved so exceeding well they would not desire the Dissenters to put off the intended application any longer but leave it to them if they saw fitting to make the attempt the next Sessions.

> [From *The Sketch of the Protestant Dissenting Deputies. . .* (London, 1813), and, by permission, the Guildhall Library, Corporation of London, Ms 3083, Minute books of the committee and general meetings of the Dissenting Deputies, vol. 1, 6 March 1735 (n.s.)]

4. Bishop Gibson's public opposition to Quaker tithe relief, 1736

The decision of Walpole's government to support Quaker tithe relief in 1736 caused great anger among the bishops, especially those who felt that their alliance with the Whig governments had secured a measure of protection against anti-clericalism. When Walpole was forced by electoral considerations to propose some relief for Quakers, Bishop Gibson of London, in an open letter to his clergy, risked his relationship with the government to declare himself against the measure.

Good Sir,

I think it proper to acquaint you, that leave is given for a bill to be brought into the House of Commons, by which if it pass into a law, the clergy will be deprived of their present remedies in the Exchequer and Ecclesiastical courts, for the recovery of all tithes due from Quakers, which do not exceed ten pounds; and so are to have no remedy left, but before two justices of the peace, with an appeal to the Quarter Sessions.

It is apprehended, that this may, in many cases prove a great handicap upon the parochial clergy; and if you and your neighbouring incumbents be of the same opinion, it will be convenient that you take the first opportunity to signify your sense of it by letters to such members as you are acquainted with, and particularly your own representatives.

I am Sir,

Your assured friend and brother,

E(mund) L(ondo)n.

[From *Weekly Miscellany*, no. 187 (24 July 1736)]

5. Thomas Ball declines preferment, 1741

This letter is one of the most extraordinary political acts of the century. Archdeacon Thomas Ball, a Sussex clergyman and a staunch supporter of the Duke of Newcastle and the Whig interest in the county, declined the offer of the deanery of Chichester. His grounds, expounded in this letter, were that he could do more good for the Whig cause in the lesser position of archdeacon. Doubtless the fact that the deanery carried no greater income that his archdeaconry was a consideration, but for an ambitious clergyman a deanery was a useful stepping stone.

Chichester, 13 October 1741

My Lord Duke,

I am infinitely obliged to your Grace and my other great friends for the high honour and favour first designed me in case of a vacancy here and in return beg leave to assure you all that I would not decline any station in which I could be further serviceable to your interest, however unworthy I might think myself of it in other respects and however inconsiderable it might appear to me in point of personal advantage. But I can't see, my Lord Duke, how it could possibly answer your ends or my own unless I could keep my archdeaconry and some other little things I now enjoy along with the deanery, which either the law or at least my superiors might perhaps disallow of. As Archdeacon and Judge of the Ecclesiastical Court I have a pretty considerable intercourse with and influence over members of the clergy, churchwardens, and other freeholders in this half of the county, whereas the authority and interest of a Dean of Chichester, as such, is infinitely less extensive and chiefly confined to this city and suburbs and even there I cannot conceive he has any greater capacity of doing good offices or engaging more persons to his interest than an active and hospitable residentiary in the disposal of all the offices, places, and perhaps ferments belonging to the Church and I have often observed that one is apter to make enemies than friends by having the power of punishing delinquents and exercising even the necessary points of choir discipline over the respective inferior officers. This I apprehend is a true state of the case with respect to my present and future proposed capacity of serving my friends on the supposition of my not holding both and I shall only add with respect to myself that the exchange would not in all probability advance my income above ten pounds a year certain for which I must be 250 or 300£ out of pocket presently. . .

I shall ever retain a grateful sense of the honour as well as the high trust and confidence reposed in me by this intended overture not doubting the future assistance of such good friends in any other reasonable addition I might hereafter desire to the great happiness I already enjoy through their good offices and intercession. . .
I am, my Lord Duke, with the utmost esteem and gratitude
Your Grace's most obedient and obliged humble servant
Tho. Ball

> [From L. P. Curtis, *Chichester Towers* (New Haven, 1966), by permission of Yale University Press]

6. Archbishop Herring defends the regime, 1745

The following letters between Lord Hardwicke, the Lord Chancellor, and Archbishop Thomas Herring of York were written during the alarms of the 1745 rebellion raised by Prince Charles Edward Stuart. Herring was resident at Bishopthorpe in Yorkshire during the rebellion and was able to rouse popular support, report intelligence to the government and act as the government's agent in the north. He was the last bishop to raise arms in the defence of the government, a feature of life in the seventeenth century which was fairly common.

Hardwicke to Herring, 31 August 1745

We are threatened with having the disposition of the Kingdom wrested out of our hands, and in the north the storm is gathered. Archbishops of York have before now drawn the secular, as well as the spiritual sword, and I hope your Grace will stand between us and danger. That the Pretender's son is actually in the north west Highlands of Scotland, and that he is joined by some of the clans of Macdonald and the Camerons, mostly papists, I take to be very certain. Infidelity has much prevailed here concerning this fact, though I think it is something altered; but I cannot help agreeing with your elder brother of Cant: that in this case, want of faith proceeds partly from want of zeal, which in political faith is the worst source. There seems to be a certain indifference and deadness among many, and the spirit of the nation wants to be roused and animated to a right tone. Any degree of danger at home ought to be vastly the more attended to from the state of things abroad. That I lament from my heart. . .

Herring to Hardwicke, 7 September 1745

So far as my example or monitions can go, I shall not be wanting in my duty, but your Lordship will give me leave to observe, that preaching will be of little avail, where the countenance of the magistrate is wanting. To say the truth, I think his immediate help is necessary in a place where the numbers and spirit and boldness of the papists is such, that their public mass house joins in a manner to the Cathedral; their service is performed daily there, and their congregation formed by the same public notice, and their congregation as large or larger than that of the Protestant Church. In this respect I doubt the lenity of our government has almost proceeded to establishment, and the check that gentlemen received last year in their prosecution of the papists agreeably to the King's Proclamation has cooled their spirit. As to their present actings, I believe the wolf must be actually at the door, before they will rise off their seats to guard against him. This I think I see as plain matter of fact. I beg of your Lordship to forgive the length and impertinence of this letter, but the wisest men know sometimes how to profit by the suggestions of weak ones. I own, I am frighted at our present situation, and it looks like a demonstration to me, that we are now, as to the health of the body politic, in the condition of a man who does not ask his doctor whether he may recover, but how long he thinks he can hold out. I am sure your Lordship will not imagine by these observations that I am going to list myself among the factious. I scorn it. I will ever be dutiful to the King, and faithfully grateful to my friends, who will not be displeased with me for speaking like an honest man, though a weak one. I will answer for my heart, though I cannot for my head. It is always my heart that dictates, when I subscribe myself,
My Lord, your ever obliged and most faithful Friend & Servt.
Tho: Ebor:

Herring to Hardwicke, 13 September 1745

My Lord, – The history of the enclosed paper, which I trouble your Lordship with, in a few words is this. As I had received repeated and clear and concurrent evidence of the distress of Cope in Scotland, and the increase and strength and progress of the rebels there, I thought it my duty to communicate it to the Lord Lieutenant and other gentlemen of distinction in the West Riding. Their intelligence as to Scotland, though not quite so particular as mine, agreed in the main with it, and was sufficient to give them a very strong alarm. A meeting was agreed upon at Birom, Sir J Ramsden's seat, for Wednesday morning, where were present; Lords Lonsdale, Malton, Irwin, Galway; Sir Rowland Winn, Sir William Lowther, Sir John Ramsden and myself. The evidences were produced and compared together, and at the same time the information which his Grace the Duke of Newcastle thought proper to communicate to Lord Lonsdale concerning the preparations from abroad; and Lord Malton produced His Majesty's Commission to put the country into the best posture of defence. All these things being laid together, it was the unanimous opinion of all present that something should be done to animate the King's friends, and, if possible, to repel the enemy, if it should please God they advanced upon us. The first step, in the common opinion, was for the Lords Lieutenant to advertise a general meeting at York, and there it is their intention, I believe, to enter into an association agreeably to His Majesty's direction on the Commission, and to engage in some measure of defence, to be adjusted previously to the meeting, and these to be prepared. As the application is to the clergy, as well as gentlemen, I thought it became me to sign, with the Lords. The 24th was the soonest and most commodious day. The advertisement will be worked off today and distributed as fast as possible. When I returned from Birom, I communicated the business to Lord Burlington, and Lord Falconbridge, and went myself yesterday to Lord Carlisle, who approved the step extremely, and I have no reason to doubt but the meeting will be such as will give a Life to the King's friends. If there has been any error committed, it was not through want of zeal, but judgement. If the thing be right, I leave it to your Lordship's judgement whether it wont be proper to approve it, to the noblemen concerned in it, and to give any orders from London that may be thought proper, before the meeting. Your Lordship is quite right in your notion of the public lethargy, and I must take the liberty to say, that the gentlemen of this country, who are His Majesty's staunch friends, apprehend too little attention is paid to this affair above, and too little care taken to communicate right information. The rebels are certainly bold, and the Kings troops in the command of a man who (as the soldiers say who have served in Scotland) has shown most unsoldierlike conduct. The accounts here, of the 7th inst. from Edinburgh, are that the rebels are 7000 strong; that perhaps is the number of fear, but it is certain, that transports were that day getting ready at Edinburgh to bring Cope and his men by sea from Inverness.

I am, my Lord,

Your Lordship's most obliged and faithful servant,

Tho. Ebor:

Hardwicke to Herring, 28 September 1745

I informed His Majesty of the substance of your letter, the sermon your Grace had preached last Sunday, and with such prodigious expedition printed and dispersed; and when I came to your speech, he desired me to show it to him. His Majesty read it from beginning to end, and gave it the just praise it so highly deserves, and said it must be printed. I said I believed it was printed at York, but it is determined to print it in the *Gazette*. If in this my commission be exceeded, I plead my Master's commands, but I hope your Grace will not disapprove it, since my sincere opinion is that it deserves to be so published, and that the topics and animated spirit of your composition are calculated to do much good. When I had gone through this part, I said: 'Your Majesty will give me leave to acquaint my Lord Archbishop that you approve his zeal and activity in your service.' To this the King answered quick: 'My Lord, that is not enough; you must also tell the Archbishop that I heartily thank him for it. . .'

Hardwicke to Herring, 5 October 1745

Everybody here is so highly sensible your Grace's eminent usefulness in those parts, that we are all of opinion that your Grace should postpone your journey for a short time at least, and that your presence in Yorkshire will be of infinitely greater service than it can be at Westminster, where no opposition is expected to any measures for the security of the King and Kingdom. You may be sure nobody pretends to prescribe to your Grace. I only lay before you our thoughts, leaving it entirely to your own judgement, which will be best formed upon the spot, where all circumstances must appear in the proper light. And in truth I don't know but this may be a better way than speaking directly to the King, for I am so fully apprised of the high opinion of the part your Grace has acted, and of the utility of your being there, that I know beforehand what his answer would be, and that might possibly put you under a difficulty. . .

I entirely approve of what your Grace has done in order to suppress the distribution of that treasonable paper the *Caledonian Mercury*. The like orders have been given here, and will undoubtedly be justified and supported.

[From British Library, Add. Mss. 35,598, by permission]

TEN

FOREIGN VIEWS OF
ENGLISH RELIGION

1. César de Saussure's account, 1729

César de Saussure was a French Protestant whose family had sought relief from persecution in Switzerland. In 1725 he began to travel across Europe and for a time acted as secretary to Lord Kinnoull, British ambassador in Constantinople. It was to be the first of a series of short-term posts he held, culminating in the post of secretary to Lord Cathcart. His account of England was written to his family in Switzerland, and, though not always technically accurate, shows much of the interest of a foreign Protestant in another Protestant land.

LONDON, April 29, 1729

The Anglican, also called High Church, is the established religion, and is still on the same footing as it was placed by Queen Elizabeth. This wise sovereign, in reforming religion, preserved certain innocent customs and rites of the Roman Catholic Church; and in my humble opinion she was wise, for very probably, had the English reformers endeavoured to destroy every vestige of that religion, they might not have been so successful; and I also believe that if the French reformers had followed the example of their English brethren, France might have been Protestant at the present day. The Divine Providence that directs everything has not willed it so.

I have told you that several Roman Catholic ceremonies have been preserved, and are in use, in the Anglican services at the present time. The Book of Common Prayer, which is the liturgy, is almost a missal, if you cut off the prayers addressed to the Holy Virgin and to the saints, and those for the dead. The priests and choristers all wear white surplices when they celebrate divine service, but the preachers take them off before stepping into the pulpit. In the royal chapels, the cathedrals, and collegiate churches the services are chanted in a tone resembling that used by the Roman Catholics in their services.

In all the churches the altars are covered with a velvet or damask silk cloth; candlesticks are placed upon them, and pictures are frequently hung above as ornaments. Communion is taken kneeling, because this attitude is that of humility. The sign of the cross is made only on a child's forehead at baptism. Several saints' days are celebrated – not to invoke the saints, but only as an opportunity for reading those portions of the Bible in which their noble acts and lives are described. One custom, however, that has continued from Roman Catholic times, and which no doubt gives satisfaction to the clergy, and even might, if it had not been permitted, have prevented the Reformation, is the collection of tithes, which custom has been continued with great exactitude.

Only persons professing the Anglican religion may fill civil and military posts. King George I abandoned the Lutheran religion and embraced the Anglican before ascending the throne, and the present reigning King followed his father's example. A member of Parliament must, before sitting, take the Communion according to the Anglican rite in his parish church, and then swear fealty before a magistrate.

In England the Low Church is composed of Presbyterians, in Scotland it becomes the High Church. The churches of this sect are chapels and have no bells; neither have those of the Non-conformists, as all Protestants who do not conform to the ceremonials of the Anglican Church are termed. . .

I think that it is principally owing to [Presbyterians] that Sunday is solemnised as it is in England. During the Commonwealth Cromwell, who was a Presbyterian, severely forbade shows or amusements of any kind, as well as concerts and games. All these are still forbidden, and on Sundays you never hear the sound of music. There is no opera, no comedy, no sounds in the streets. Card playing on this day is also strictly forbidden, at least for the citizens and common people, for persons of rank, I believe, do not scruple to play. Unfortunately a great number of the people divert themselves in the taverns, and there indulge in debauch.

The curious sect of Quakers, or Shakers, arose in the troubled times when England was torn by revolutions, anarchy, and fanaticism, that is to say in the time of Cromwell. A rather crazy shoemaker's apprentice, George Fox, was of this sect. It can almost be said that the Quakers form a particular nation of people, quite different from ordinary English citizens, by their language, manner of dressing, and religion.

Amongst their other customs, one of which is the use of the pronoun 'thou', is that of never giving any man his titles, whatever his position or worth may be, for everyone to them is but a vile earthworm inhabiting this planet for a few years. Quakers make use of a sort of Bible talk, which strikes you more particularly, as it appears to date two hundred years back, no Bible having been printed in England in the fine modern language, the earliest edition of the Holy Book being still in use.

The Quakers' mode of dressing is as curious as is their language; the men wear large, unlooped, flapping hats, without buttons or loops; their coats are as plain as possible, with no pleatings or trimmings, and no buttons or button-holes on the sleeves, pockets, or waists. If any brother were to wear ruffles to his shirts or powder on his hair, he be considered impious. The most austere and zealous do not even wear shoe-buckles, but tie their shoes with cords. The women wear no ribbons, no lace, their gowns being of one modest colour, without hoops, and their caps have no frills or pleatings, and are of a peculiar shape, made of silk, and worn pleated on the forehead in a certain fashion particular to them. It must be owned, in truth, that this simple and modest attire suits many of these women admirably. Quakers' clothes, though of the simplest and plainest cut, are of excellent quality; their hats, clothes, and linen are of the finest, and so are the silken tissues the women wear. These people call each other 'brother' and 'sister,' and to persons who are not of their sect they give the name of 'friend'; they never make any compliments, and do not salute by taking off their hats or by making a curtsey. . .

There are many other sects in England, but I cannot dwell on this subject, for I should like to tell you something of the Roman Catholics, who are very numerous in England, where they live in perfect peace and security, with every facility for celebrating their religion publicly. On every Sunday and Saints' day services are held in the chapels belonging to the ministers of Germany, France, Spain, Portugal, and Sardinia. These chapels are always crowded. Many peers, such as the Duke of Norfolk, the Earl of Dumbarton, Lord Petre, and others, have their own chapels and chaplain. This, to tell the truth, is contrary to the law, but the present minister is tolerant, and wisely pretends to ignore these facts, Jesuits, however, are looked upon as disturbers of the peace and of public welfare.

No Roman Catholic may occupy a post of any sort whatever. When soldiers are enrolled – and this is the case more especially with the Guards – they are made to take the oath that they are Protestants. If after enrolment any one of them should be discovered to be a Roman

Catholic attending mass he would be condemned to death. Commerce is considered to be England's strength, and care has been taken not to drive away anyone who contributes to build it up. Jews therefore are protected by laws, and are even granted certain privileges. They are not forced to bear a distinctive mark, as is the case in many countries; if you see Jews wearing beards you will know that they are Rabbis, or new-comers to this country. All Jews are merchants, and many of them are extraordinarily wealthy. They possess two synagogues in the City, one of them for German and Dutch Jews, the other for Spanish and Portuguese; that is to say, for Jews who have had to fly from these countries. I was curious enough to visit the former of these synagogues, and remarked that the women did not mix with the men, but that they stood in a sort of shut-off gallery, The men covered their heads with a piece of white silken stuff or veil, the Rabbis' veils being black, as also their cloaks and garments. On that same day a child was circumcised. Some of the Rabbis stood up on a sort of wooden stand, together with the father and the infant's sponsor, whilst sentences were read out of the Bible in Hebrew. The sponsor then sat down on a chair in the centre of the stand, the priests chanting alone, I was by chance seated next to a young Englishwoman, who had evidently also come out of curiosity. Seeing no infant (for it had not yet been brought in) she imagined that the sponsor, the young, good-looking man who was seated on the chair, was the intended victim.

I could not resist confirming her in this view, and she then made as if she would retire, and even rose to leave the synagogue, but I cannot tell whether her curiosity got the better of her modesty. Anyhow, she pretended that the crowd around prevented her from leaving, but by this time the infant had been brought in, and she understood her mistake. . .

[From M. Van Muyden (ed.), *A Foreign View of England in the Reigns of George I and George II* (London, 1902)]

2. Carl Moritz's account of Nettlebed, 1782

In 1782 Carl Moritz visited England. He was a Pietist, educated at a German grammar school and a theatrical academy, and he studied theology at Wittenberg University. Moritz was an Anglophile whose visit to England in 1782 was an attempt to see Dr Johnson, Oxford and the glories of the English countryside. His visit to Nettlebed, which he saw as a kind of model village, is recounted here.

It was Sunday and everyone in the house had put on his best clothes. I found myself extraordinarily drawn to this pleasant village and resolved to stay and attend divine service that morning. To this end I borrowed a prayer-book from my host, Mr Illing. (This was his name! It struck me the more because it is such a common name in Germany.) I turned over the leaves during breakfast and read several parts of the English liturgy. My attention was taken by the fact that every word was set down for the priest for his conformity. If he were visiting a sick man, for example, he had to say 'Peace dwell in this house,' etc. That such a book is called a prayer-book and not a hymn-book is because the English service is usually not sung but prayed. Nevertheless the Psalms translated into English verse are included in this prayer-book.

That which my host lent me was truly a family possession containing the date of his wedding and the birthdays and baptismal days of all his children. It had all the more value consequently in my eyes. Divine service was due to begin at half-past nine. Right opposite our house the boys of the village were lined up all bright and beautiful, very nice and clean, and their hair (cut round in a fringe after the English fashion) combed. The white collars of their shirts were turned back at both sides and their breasts were open to the air. It seemed they were gathered here at the entrance of the village to await the parson.

I went out of the village for a short walk towards where I saw some men coming from another village to attend divine service in ours. At last the parson arrived on horseback. The boys took off their hats and bowed low to him. He had a somewhat elderly appearance, with his own hair dressed very much as if in natural curls. The bell rang and I went into the church with the general public, my prayer-book under my arm. The clerk or verger showed me into a seat in front of the pulpit very politely.

The furnishing of the church was quite simple. Right above the altar were displayed the Ten Commandments in large letters on two tablets. And indeed there can be no better way of impressing the essential qualities of the faith on a waiting congregation than this. Under the pulpit was a reading-desk where the preacher stood before the sermon and read out a very long liturgy to which the parish clerk responded each time, the congregation joining in softly. When, for example, the preacher said: 'God have mercy upon us,' the clerk and congregation answered: 'and forgive us our sins'. Or the preacher read a prayer and the whole congregation said 'Amen' to it. This is very difficult for the preacher, since he must not only address the people while preaching his sermon but continually do so during the service. The responding of the people, however, has something about it very restful and ceremonially appropriate. Two soldiers sitting by me, who had recently come from London and considered themselves to be keen wits, did not pray aloud.

After the ritual had gone on for some time I noticed some shuffling in the choir. The clerk was very busy and they all seemed to be getting ready for some special ceremony. I noticed also several musical instruments of various sorts as the preacher stopped his reading and the clerk announced from the choir: 'Let us praise God by singing the forty-seventh Psalm: Awake, our hearts, awake with joy'.

How peaceful and heart-uplifting it was to hear vocal and instrumental music in this little country church, not made by hired musicians but joyfully offered by the happy dwellers in the place in praise of their God. This kin of music now began to alternate several times with the ritual prayers, and the tunes of the metrical psalms were so lively and joyful – and yet so wholly sincere – that I gave my heart unrestrainedly to devotion and was often touched to tears.

The preacher now stood up and gave a short address on the text: 'Not all who say "Lord! Lord!" shall enter into the Kingdom of Heaven.' He dealt with the subject in common terms and his presentation was sturdy. He spoke of the need to do God's will, but there was nothing out of the usual run in his matter. The sermon lasted less than half-an-hour.

Apart from all this the preacher was unsociable; he seemed haughty when he acknowledged the greetings of the country people, doing so with a superior nod. I stayed until the service was all over and then went out of the church with the congregation. I then examined the gravestones in the churchyard and their inscriptions, which, because of their restraint, were simpler and in better taste than ours. . .

All the farmers I saw here were dressed in good cloth and good taste. (Not as ours are, in coarse smocks.) In appearance they are to be distinguished from townsmen less by their dress than by their natural dignity. A few soldiers trying to show off joined me as I was looking at the church. They seemed thoroughly ashamed – saying it was a most contemptible church. At this I took the liberty to tell them that no church was contemptible if it held well-behaved and sensible people.

I remained in Nettlebed over midday. In the afternoon there was no divine service but the villagers again made music together. They sang several psalms while others listened to them. All this was done in so seemly a manner that it might have been a kind of service too. I stayed until it was over, as one enchanted by this village. Three times I started to leave it to continue my walk, and each time I was drawn back to it, on the verge of resolving to stay there a week or longer.

[From R. Nettel (ed.), *Journeys of a German in England in 1782* (London: Jonathan Cape, 1965), by permission of Random House UK Ltd]

3. François de la Rochefoucauld's account of an English Sunday, 1784

François de la Rochefoucauld was the son of the Master of the Wardrobe to Louis XVI. He became a gentleman cadet officer. His leisure time as an army officer was spent travelling and writing. His visit to England was in part to help him learn English. His account of a typical English Sunday is an entertaining caricature of English religion.

Is there in the world anything so wearisome as the English Sunday? If working days are gloomy, they are festal days by comparison with Sunday. I cannot precisely ascertain whether it is to some article of religion or to the observance of an Act of Parliament that the gloom of this day, which in every other country is characterised by gaiety, is due. I am inclined to think that it is connected with both; for, inasmuch as religion is bound up with politics, anything that relates to the one must also relate to the other. The fact remains that you are forbidden, on this day, to do anything enjoyable. You may neither sing, nor play upon an instrument, much less dance; every form of card game is forbidden, the lower classes may not play ball games, or skittles, or any game whatsoever. The strictest of those who observe this fantastic regulation do not even join with any congregation of people, but religiously, or rather absurdly, stay in their homes to read the Bible, which all of them have in their houses.

They avoid even getting on a horse, since every form of recreation is unseemly. Lest you should think that all this is not the result of observation, I see evidence of it before me once a week and I dread Sunday more than anything. The Act of Parliament which governs this practice imposes quite heavy fines upon offenders and, what is more, offers a reward to informers, Justices of the Peace, magistrates who are distributed in large numbers in every district, both in town and country, rigidly exact the fines from Sabbath-breakers, and the amount is too considerable for a man of the lower classes to forget it. The smallest fine payable is five shillings; if you prefer to go to prison for a day or two, the choice is open to you. . .

But what, you ask, do people do on Sunday? All the men collect together for the whole day in taverns, where they spend their week's earnings, perhaps, in drink. The women meet after dinner and take tea together, and then go for a walk along the main roads and forget the labours of the week in the pleasures of conversation. In the evening the family reassembles in time for supper and afterwards for bed. Either the father or mother reads aloud from the Bible as fashioned according to Henry VIII, and, more often than not, at the end of half an hour everyone is asleep in his chair. All this is strictly true, I have seen it happen many times with my own eyes in the family with whom we spent the whole winter of 1784. A gentleman of this county made an admirable drawing, of which an engraving has been made, and you see prints of it everywhere. The subject is Sunday evening: the father is seen at a table, lighted by a candle, and is reading the Bible; he has a pair of spectacles on his nose; the mother is listening with half-closed eyes and the children are asleep with their heads on each other's shoulders. The whole forms a delightful group. . .

In the matter of belief they differ very little from us. They do not believe either in the transubstantiation of the Body and Blood of Jesus Christ in the Sacrament of the Eucharist or in the authority which God has given to the Pope as the visible head of the Church, or in the Intercession of Saints, or in the power of the priest to remit sins. Such are the main points in our religion which they do not accept. The rest is common to both. Their religion enjoins upon them the practice of the virtues, as ours does; and so a virtuous man anywhere will be a man of good and sound religion.

As to the way in which the English practise their religion, it is much more easy-going than ours. They do not go to confession, they go to the holy table very rarely. When they do so, they go in a different spirit: they do not believe (as I have already said) that they receive the body of Jesus Christ, but they approach the holy table as an act of commemoration.

They are not under an obligation to go to church every Sunday through rain or fog or heat – a very slight excuse will keep them away; but they are under an obligation to read the Bible as often as they can. It is in this book that children learn and grown-up people perfect their reading.

I went to a service on two occasions. It lasts an hour and a half and consists of a prayer in which the people make their responses to the minister, followed by a reading from the Bible and a sermon. There are always two ministers, one in a pulpit and the other below him, who read alternately. The sermon is based on a text, which is either some point of morals, or a passage from Scripture, or something calculated to enjoin observance of the laws, The evening service is shorter. Everything that is read, or spoken, or preached is in English so that it may be within the reach of everybody. There are certain days appointed for the administration of the Eucharist, on which the minister conducts the service at an altar which is always placed at the end of the chancel and is entirely without ornament. I imagine that this service is very similar to that which I have seen myself. The whole of this religion is founded upon the principle of political equality. The only superior authority is Parliament. Everyone else is on an equal footing.

To pass to another point, for I must make some reference to every point which is of general interest, I should like to say something of the Sacraments, English baptism is like ours and is performed with the same intention, save that the child is not committed to the protection of the saints, in whose power of intercession they do not believe; a baptismal name is given to the child as an addition to his surname to distinguish him from the others who share his family name.

No confession of any kind is necessary. An Anglican may, if he likes, make a confession; the priest will absolve him, but it will be simply the absolution of a man in his own eyes; it will count for nothing towards his salvation. Of what use can it be? Nevertheless a certain number of people make their confession to expiate, by this form of humiliation, the sins which they have committed. But this is very rare. Not more than one English man in ten thousand will make his confession.

Confirmation is regarded as much more necessary – in fact, according to the Protestant religion it is practically indispensable. The view is that a baptised child of himself cannot participate in anything and therefore, as soon as he has reached an age when he can think for himself, he must take on the part of a good Christian and by Confirmation fulfil within himself the benefits received at Baptism. Such is the account given or to me by all those with whom I have discussed the subject. They do not feel that this Sacrament necessarily stamps an indelible character, for there are some who are confirmed more than once, I was told yesterday that at Bury there are three or four old women who are confirmed every time the Bishop comes into the town. Their plea is that you cannot have too much of a good thing. . .

Marriage is something quite distinctive. In fact it is so different from our way of administering the Sacrament that the account of it which was kindly given to me had to be repeated two or three times before I could properly grasp it.

Parish churches and certain chapels are the two places in which you may be married; but with the permission (for which you pay a fee) of the Archbishop of Canterbury, you may be married in a private house or some ordinary hall and need not trouble about a chapel. It consists of both parties being asked whether they freely give their consent and whether the parents give theirs; then the priest puts a ring on the bride's and the whole thing is done. A deed is prepared and, after being duly signed by all the interested parties, is deposited with the vicar of the parish.

Thirty years ago, not only was it unnecessary a priest to perform this ceremony, but no mention even was made of the consent of the parents. The first man who came in sight could marry the pair, the deed was deposited with the vicar and often had no more than the three indispensable signatures. . .

According to the Protestant faith, Extreme Unction has no validity and is in fact so regarded. Protestants will put no trust in anything done by man and simply commend themselves to God. They are alone when they die, whether their feelings are of confident hope or of sorrowful remorse. This is the principal reason why I should not like this religion. When a Catholic is dying, he at least has a priest at his side who comforts him if he is afraid and sets before him a pleasant picture of the future; if the dying man feels guilty in God's sight, he makes his confession, receives absolution, and, I am persuaded, dies in the conviction that he is about to enter Paradise. That hope for the best, which is always with us, combined with the dying man's physical weakness, serves, if I mistake not, to banish his fears and to enable him to close his eyes without any feeling of terror. This is the great advantage of our religion. But the English die just like dogs. They die and often one doesn't hear of it for some time afterwards, for they commonly shut themselves in solitude all the time that they are ill. All this time they are left free to their own meditations on the future state. What consolations has a suffering man who is bound to see things in a gloomy light, who has perhaps some grave sins with which to reproach himself, and is borne down by the weight of reflections which another might dispel? It is my belief that one of the main advantages of a religion, whatever it be, is that it should bring the believer comfort and I cannot see that this Protestant religion conduces much to that end.

I have just said something of the administration of the Sacraments in comparing the religion of England with our own, but I must not omit to say that they recognise only two sacraments: Baptism and the

Eucharist – of the others three are treated simply as ceremonies, and two do not exist at all.

From this short review it may be clearly seen how easy it is for the English to fulfil the obligations of their religion. Nothing could be simpler – they have no fasts, no fish-days, no Lent; even their Sunday service is not obligatory. What is there that they must do? To this it may be replied that it is not church-going or eating fish instead of meat or anything of the kind that makes a man truly pious; that it is faith only that ranges him under the standard of religion; and that when it is a pure religion, it is the observance of its precepts which makes a man a good Christian; after which I shall be treated to a sermon in which all the good points of religion will be displayed. But it will be on our religion that the panegyric will be pronounced; I cannot believe that the same convincing reasons can be given in regard to the religion of the English, for, so far as my rather slight knowledge goes, I find in it neither comfort nor edification. . .

The ministers of this religion are not occupied in the same way as ours, whose most laborious tasks are hearing confessions, carrying the Blessed Sacrament into the country by day or night, and so on. The parishes, too, are much larger than in France and the duties are performed by a rector, who corresponds to the French cure. He is paid by means of tithe and has a house, a garden, and several acres of land. These places are conferred in accordance with immemorial custom, or by virtue of certain charters, or by the squire of the parish, or by the bishop, or by the King. Generally speaking, the position of a rector is well worth having and the rectors themselves are men of some merit.

Besides the rectors, a large number of clergy live partly in the country and partly in the parishes. Most of them derive a considerable stipend from some ecclesiastical source, such as a canonry carved off from the ancient endowments of the Catholic Church. They help the parishioners not only by their alms, but also by their sermons, for each of them usually preaches in his turn. These ecclesiastical benefices are generally in the gift of either the King or of the bishop, or of the Lord Chancellor.

I must say something of English burials, which are sometimes the occasion of a greater measure of pomp being introduced into the Anglican religion. It is the custom to keep the dead in their houses as long as possible, provided there is no danger of infection to the living. The reason for this is that apoplexy and long drawn-out lethargy are common in England, and it is alleged that in early days a large number of people were buried alive. Accordingly, to guard against the horror of such a mistake, they choose rather to keep their dead for a longer period – sometimes for as much as a week before burial. . .

All religions are tolerated in England – not by law, but in fact. In my section on London I have already referred to the chapels of the various sects and to the number of them. They are similarly tolerated in other parts of the kingdom. At Bury, for example, there are six different sects, all of which have their tabernacles or chapels and each one of them practises its religion in peace. It is, however, forbidden to practise them in public or to summon the worshippers by church bells. It is only the established Protestant religion which has the right to make itself heard. All the sects, except the Catholics, have the right to maintain tabernacles, which may belong to the religious community and not to an individual member of it. But for the Catholics to have a chapel, it is necessary that it should be the property of one of their body. It is thus that civil liberty, which is so widely respected in England and makes every citizen absolute master of his own actions in his own house, secures his worship against interference. At the same time an Act of Parliament, which forbids the practice of the Catholic religion in England, also forbids the assembly of more than eleven persons – it is an Act passed in Cromwell's time. Consequently, if any man whatsoever should seek out a Justice of the Peace and report to him that he had been inside a Catholic chapel, that he saw such and such a priest saying mass, describing the actions and naming some of those present and their number, the Justice of the Peace would have no choice but to order the penalties laid down by the Act, namely, life imprisonment for the priest, and fines and a year's imprisonment for those attending the service. But, in fact, the Justice of the Peace always evades the rigour of the law. It is never actually put into force, since the Justice of the Peace seeks for some ground on which to confute the informer. He may ask him, for instance, whether he is quite sure that the prayers he heard were Catholic prayers; he may suggest that he was only saying them by way of imitating them; he may ask whether the priest was drinking the wine and eating the bread and so on. In fact he puts so many questions, demanding so much detail of explanation, that the informer is barely able to answer them and is dismissed without having made good his case. As all the Justices of the Peace are in agreement as to the policy to be adopted in all such cases, the Catholics are wholly undisturbed, in spite of the severity of the laws against them. They practise their religion without even concealing it and everybody knows it and accepts it.

The chapel at Bury belongs to the priest himself and all Catholics go there on Sundays and Saints' days without ever being disturbed. There is a Catholic bishop at Norwich who has jurisdiction over the individual priests, sends them instructions, visits them from time to time and so on. The government, which tolerates Catholic worship, excludes those who practise it from all posts either in the state or in the army or navy; magistracies are similarly forbidden to them, and the result is that they are absolutely cut off from the English body politic. They have no power to vote at elections for members of Parliament, even though they may otherwise have all the necessary qualifications. In order to be admitted to office, they must take an oath that they do not believe in transubstantiation, an oath which no Catholic can take. They must also swear that they renounce the Pope and recognise Parliament as the head of the Church. I find the Catholics in England much more zealous than those in France; they are much stricter in the performance of their religious duties for the simple reason that they are persecuted. All men in all countries are the same – they delight in doing what is forbidden them. . .

[From S. C. Roberts, *A Frenchman in England 1784* (Cambridge, 1933), by permission of Cambridge University Press]

BIBLIOGRAPHY

J. Addy, *Sin and Society in the Seventeenth Century* (London, 1989).

L. W. Barnard, *John Potter, An Eighteenth Century Archbishop* (Ilfracombe, 1989).

V. Barrie-Curien, *Clergé et Pastorale en Angleterre au XVIIIe siècle. Le diocèse de Londres* (Paris, 1992).

G. V. Bennett, *White Kennett, 1660–1728* (London, 1957).

— *The Tory Crisis in Church and State, 1688–1739* (Oxford, 1975).

R. Browning, *The Political and Constitutional Ideas of the Court Whigs* (Baton Rouge, 1982).

E. Carpenter, *Thomas Sherlock* (London, 1936).

— *Thomas Tenison* (London, 1948).

— *The Protestant Bishop* (London, 1956).

O. F. Christie (ed.), *The Diary of The Revd William Jones 1777–1821* (London, 1929).

J. C. D. Clark, *English Society 1688–1832* (Cambridge, 1991).

David Cressy and Lori Anne Ferrell (eds), *Religion and Society in Early Modern England: A Sourcebook* (London, 1996).

L. P. Curtis, *Chichester Towers* (New Haven, 1966).

G. C. B. Davies, *The Early Cornish Evangelicals 1735–1760* (London, 1951).

D. C. Douglas, *English Scholars 1660–1730* (London, 1951).

G. N. Evans, *Religion and Politics in Mid-Eighteenth Century Anglesey* (Cardiff, 1953).

G. Every, *The High Church Party, 1688–1718* (London, 1956).

D. Gibson, *A Parson in the Vale of the White Horse, 1753–1761* (Gloucester, 1982).

W. T. Gibson, *Church, State and Society, 1760–1850* (London, 1994).

— *The Achievement of the Anglican Church, 1689–1800* (Evanston, IL, 1995).

A. D. Gilbert, *Religion and Society in Industrial England, 1740–1914* (London, 1976).

J. R. Guy, *The Diocese of Llandaff in 1763* (South Wales Record Society, 1991).

P. Hair, *Before the Bawdy Court* (London, 1971).

A. T. Hart, *Some Clerical Oddities in the Church of England from Medieval to Modern Times* (Bognor, 1980).

— *The Life and Times of John Sharp, Archbishop of York* (London, 1949).

— *William Lloyd 1627–1717* (London, 1952).

— *The Eighteenth Century Country Parson* (Shrewsbury, 1955).

— *The Country Priest in English History* (London, 1960).

— *Clergy and Society 1600–1800* (London, 1968).

— *The Curate's Lot* (Newton Abbot, 1971).

— *Ebor* (York, 1986).

F. J. C. Hearnshaw, *The Social and Political Ideas of Some English Thinkers of the Augustan Age 1650–1750* (London, 1928).

B. Hemphill, *The Early Vicars Apostolic of England 1685–1750* (London, 1954).

D. Hempton, *Methodism and Politics in British Society 1750–1850* (London, 1987).

R. Hodgson, *The Works of the Rt Revd Beilby Porteus DD. . . With His Life* (London, 1811).

G. Holmes, *The Trial of Dr Sacheverell* (London, 1973).

— *Augustan England* (London, 1982).

E. Hughes (ed.), *The Letters of Spencer Cowper Dean of Durham 1746–1774* (Surtees Society, 1956).

N. C. Hunt, *Sir Robert Walpole, Samuel Holden and the Dissenting Deputies* (Dr Williams Trust, 1957).

W. M. Jacob, *Lay People and Religion in the Early Eighteenth Century* (Cambridge, 1996).

D. E. Jenkins (ed.), *Religious Societies, Dr Woodward's Account* (Liverpool, 1935).

J. Wickham Legg, *English Church Life from the Restoration to the Tractarian Movement* (London, 1914).

M. D. R. Leys, *Catholics in England 1559–1829* (London, 1961).

C. L. S. Linnell, *The Diary of Benjamin Rogers, Rector of Carlton, 1720–1771* (Bedfordshire Historical Records Society, vol. XXX, 1950).

— *Some East Anglian Clergy* (London, 1961).

— *The Diaries of Thomas Wilson DD, 1731–1737 & 1750* (London, 1964).

W. K. Lowther Clarke, *Eighteenth Century Piety* (London, 1945).

J. Marchand (ed.), *A Frenchman in England, 1784* (Cambridge, 1933).

F. Mather, *High Church Prophet: Bp Samuel Horsley* (Oxford, 1992).

B. Mitchell and H. Penrose (eds), *Letters from Bath, 1766–1767 by the Revd John Penrose* (Stroud, 1990).

J. R. H. Moorman (ed.), *The Curate of Souls 1660–1760* (London, 1958).

R. Nelson, *The Life of Dr George Bull. . .* (London, 1714).

— *A Companion for the Festivals and Fasts of the Church of England* (London, 1837).

R. Nettel (ed.), *Journeys of a German in England in 1782* (London, 1965).

P. Nockles, *The Oxford Movement in Context* (Cambridge, 1995).

S. L. Ollard, *The Six Students of St Edmund Hall, Expelled from Oxford in 1768* (London, 1911).

E. Paley, *The Works of William Paley DD. . .* (London, 1825).

G. W. Pilcher, *The Revd Samuel Davies Abroad, 1753–55* (Urbana, IL, 1967).

The Lives of Dr Edward Pocock, Dr Zachary Pearce, Dr Thomas Newton. . . (London, 1816).

G. Portus, *Caritas Anglicana* (London, 1912).

M. Ransome (ed.), *The State of the Bishopric of Worcester 1782–1808* (Worcestershire Historical Society, vol. 6, 1968).

— (ed.), *Wiltshire Returns to the Bishop's Visitation Queries, 1783* (Wiltshire Record Society, vol. XXVII, 1972).

N. Ravitch, *Sword and Mitre* (The Hague, 1966).

S. C. Roberts, *A Frenchman in England 1784* (Cambridge, 1933).

A. W. Rowden, *The Primates of the Four Georges* (London, 1916).

E. Saunders, *A View of the State of Religion in the Diocese of St David's about the beginning of the Eighteenth Century* (Cardiff, 1949).

C. de Saussure, ed. M. van Muyden, *Foreign Views of England in the Reigns of George I and George II* (London, 1902).

A. Smith, *The Established Church and Popular Religion, 1750–1850* (London, 1971).

H. Stowell, *The Life of Thomas Wilson* (London, 1819).

N. Sykes, *Edmund Gibson* (Oxford, 1926).

— *Church and State in England in the Eighteenth Century* (Cambridge, 1934).

— *William Wake* (2 vols, Cambridge, 1957).

— *From Sheldon to Secker* (Cambridge, 1959).

The Life of Silas Told written by himself (London, 1954).

J. Walsh, C. Haydon and S. Taylor (eds), *The Church of England c. 1689–1833* (Cambridge, 1994).

R. Watson, *Anecdotes of the Life of Richard Watson, Bishop of Llandaff* (Philadelphia, 1818).

D. H. Woodforde, *Woodforde Papers and Diaries* (London, 1932).

INDEX